DISCOGRAPHIES

'This is a lucid, informative, engagingly written and stimulating work. It admirably covers a variety of different theoretical issues and takes off from dance to raise all sorts of questions about the treatment of music in cultural studies.'

Simon Frith, University of Stirling

'*Discographies* is contemporary, committed and compelling. The strengths of the book lie in its ability to combine academic expertise with an obvious immersion in dance music culture.'

Will Straw, McGill University

Experiencing disco, hip hop, house, techno, drum 'n' bass and garage, *Discographies* plots a course through the transatlantic dance scene of the last twenty-five years. Tracing the history of ideas about music and dance in western culture and the ways in which dance music is produced and received, the authors assess the importance and relevance of dance culture in the 1990s and beyond.

Discographies considers the formal, aesthetic and political characteristics of dance music. It discusses the problems posed by contemporary dance culture of both academic and cultural study and finds these origins in the history of opposition to music as a source of sensory pleasure.

Discussing such issues as technology, club space, drugs, the musical body, gender, sexuality and pleasure, *Discographies* explores the ecstatic experiences at the heart of contemporary dance culture. It suggests why politicians and agencies as diverse as the independent music press and public broadcasting should be so hostile to this cultural phenomenon.

Jeremy Gilbert teaches Media and Cultural Studies at the University of East London. He is a contributor to *Living Through Pop* and *The Moderniser's Dilemma*. **Ewan Pearson** has been a visiting lecturer in Cultural Studies at the University of East London. He is now a full-time musician and has recorded for several UK dance labels, including Glasgow's Soma Recordings.

14-99

DISCOGRAPHIES

Dance music, culture and the
politics of sound

Jeremy Gilbert and Ewan Pearson

London and New York

THIS BOOK IS FOR OUR MUMS

First published 1999
by Routledge
11 New Fetter Lane, London EC4P 4EE

Simultaneously published in the USA and Canada
by Routledge
29 West 35th Street, New York, NY 10001

Routledge is an imprint of the Taylor & Francis group.

© 1999 Jeremy Gilbert and Ewan Pearson

Typeset in Bembo by Routledge
Printed and bound in Great Britain by TJ International Ltd, Padstow, Cornwall

British Library Cataloguing in Publication Data
A catalogue record for this book is available from the British Library

Library of Congress Cataloguing in Publication Data
Gilbert, Jeremy
Discographies: dance music, culture and the politics of sound / Jeremy Gilbert and
Ewan Pearson
Includes bibliographical references and index
1. Dance music–20th century–History and criticism. 2. Dance music–Social aspects. 3.
Music and society. I. Pearson, Ewan. II. Title. III. Title: Dance music, culture and the
politics of sound.
ML3406.G55   1999
784.18'8–dc21   99-10971

ISBN 0–415–17032–X (hbk)
ISBN 0–415–17033–8 (pbk)

CONTENTS

PREFACE

Why this book is rubbish

This a specific project with a specific agenda, and it can never hope to be all things to all people. There are many things which this book does not do. This is not because we think those things are not either interesting or important.

First, *Discographies* does not attempt to be a coherent account of dance music cultures, either historical or sociological. It does not tell the story of dance culture. Those who are looking for a clear and concise narrative history of British dance culture, from its pre-history in disco to its possible future, should refer to Matthew Collin's excellent *Altered State* (1997), a tremendously thorough and insightful work. They should also read Simon Reynolds' *Energy Flash* (1998), not only for the wealth of information on the historical events and happenings of dance culture both in the UK and in the United States, but for its brilliant and exhaustive account of dance music forms. *Discographies* does not attempt to offer any such musicological depth of approach.

For an insightful collection of reflections – historical, political and theoretical – on the milieu in which much of the more politically radical developments in UK dance culture have taken place, we refer readers to George McKay (ed.), DiY Culture (1998), a book that engages with many important issues, from Ecstasy to free parties to road protests to the legacy of anarchism.

Neither does this book offer a sociology or an anthropology of dance or dance music culture. As we explain in Chapter 1, we are sceptical as to the possibility of producing such a study. 'Dance cultures' are fluid, multifarious formations which will always exceed any attempt to map them. Excellent work is produced in the course of trying to do so, however, and we would recommend to anyone looking for such work Sarah Thornton's *Club Cultures* (1995), Helen Thomas' (ed.) *Dance in the City* (1997) and Mary Anna Wright's (ed.) *Dance Culture, Party Politics and Beyond* (Verso, forthcoming).

This book does not concern itself greatly with the processes of economic, social or cultural production according to which dance culture is generated and reproduced. Excellent research is being carried out in this area by other people (see, for instance, David Hesmondhalgh's essay in *Soundings* 5, Spring 1997) and we look forward to its wider dissemination. We are entirely sympathetic to those who wish to see the study of culture turn its attention to the empirical realities of such processes, but we do not think that such an approach is sufficient in and of itself, and it is not what we have tried to do here.

This book is not directly concerned with the politics of identity. Brilliant work is forthcoming from others on the politics of dance music, conceived primarily as black/diasporic musics, and on the specific experiences of women in rave and post-rave cultures (see, for instance, the work of Maria Pini as referred to in this book). We hope that our work will prove complementary to theirs.

Finally, while this book deploys theoretical and political insights drawn from areas of continental philosophy, its approach (following Foucault) is to treat such bodies of idea as tool kits, to be used as we find useful rather than with an eye to unimpeachable rigour (not that we have not tried always to use the right tool for the job in hand...). The world can undoubtedly look forward to work which will engage with these issues from similar perspectives but with a wider philosophical sweep and with a sharper theoretical edge. The work of Drew Hemment, who has contributed to George McKay's DiY Culture (1998) and is the organizer of the FUTUREsonic symposium (www.futuresonic.com), may well prove such.

Why this book is brilliant

What we do try to do in Discographies is respond, from the point of view of 'cultural studies' and 'critical theory', to some of the effects which dance culture has generated over the last twenty years. These ask a number of essential questions of cultural studies, which needs to respond by developing tools that can begin to address them; we hope to offer some pointers towards such tools and how they might be used.

In the process we address a number of themes which we see as indispensable to a proper engagement with the musics and cultures of social dance: the difficulties inherent in mapping and narrating popular culture; the problematic status of sound in general and instrumental music in particular in western culture; the complex significance of technology in post-modern society; the complex relationships between music, meaning, and the body in that culture; issues of individual and communal pleasure and the historical legacy of puritan modernity; and the ambivalent nature of contemporary popular cultural politics. In the process of engaging with these issues, we hope to have provoked at least as many questions as we have answered, suggesting further avenues for research and analysis in the future. At the same time, we hope to have provided a framework within which to consider a range of important and often neglected issues: the theorization of music as *sound* being one example.

Finally, Discographies is written from the point of view of a politics which, while abjuring the grand narratives of earlier moments, remains committed to the ongoing project of democratization in all spheres of life – social, economic, cultural, personal. Like Ernesto Laclau and Chantal Mouffe (1985), we regard anti-essentialism as the philosophical *sine qua non* of such a politics. As such, the agenda of this book is not to concern itself so much with a politics of *identity* (although we recognize that there can ultimately be no politics without identity), as with a politics of *experience*, addressing those forms of culture which contain within themselves the potential not just to tell us who we are, but to challenge us with a sense of who we might be.

Jeremy Gilbert and Ewan Pearson
April 1999

ACKNOWLEDGEMENTS

Material written by Jeremy Gilbert, and contained in this volume in Chapters 6 and 7, has previously been published as part of two essays: 'Soundtrack to an Uncivil Society: Rave Culture, the Criminal Justice Act and the Politics of Modernity', New Formations, Summer 1997 (London: Lawrence and Wishart, 1997) and 'Blurred Vision: Pop, Populism and Politics', in Anne Coddington and Mark Perryman (eds) The Moderniser's Dilemma (London: Lawrence and Wishart; published in association with Signs of the Times, London, 1998).

Chapter 1 contains a quote from Pulp's 'Sorted For E's and Wizz'. Written by Nick Banks, Jarvis Cocker, Candida Doyle, Steve Mackey, Russell Senior and Mark Webber. © Copyright 1995 Island Music Ltd. Lyrics reproduced by kind permission of the publisher and Music Sales Ltd. All Rights in the USA and Canada Administered by Songs of PolyGram International, Inc. International Copyright Secured. All Rights Reserved.

The authors met at a conference held by Signs of the Times, an independent, London-based group who organize seminars, publications and conferences on a range of topics, from Blairism to Britpop. Signs of the Times can be contacted at PO Box 10684, London N15 6XA, telephone: 0181 809–7336.

Much of the work presented here resulted from research for both authors' MA dissertations and Jeremy Gilbert's D.Phil thesis, all undertaken between 1995 and 1999 at the University of Sussex (Jeremy Gilbert), and Royal Holloway, University of London (Ewan Pearson), and funded by the British Academy, whose support the authors' acknowledge with grateful thanks. Jeremy would also like to acknowledge the invaluable support of the University of Sussex Graduate Research Centre in Culture and Communications during this period. We would both like to thank the students and faculty at the Department of Cultural Studies, University of East London, where we had a great time teaching together in 1996.

We would like to say a particular thank you to our editors at Routledge, Rebecca Barden and Christopher Cudmore, for their encouragement and considerable patience during this project.

Jeremy would also like to thank a number of individuals who are owed particular debts of gratitude:

Without Andrew Blake's support, encouragement and advice at every conceivable stage, this book would certainly not have come into existence. Without Eoin O'Broin's inspired nagging, we would never have got it together. Mandy Merck and Couze Venn provided support and advice in the writing of the earliest material here: thanks to them for that. As my D.Phil supervisors, James Donald and William Outhwaite have provided, as they continue to do, indispensable support and encouragement as well, importantly, as space. The journal *New Formations* and the *Signs of the Times* group have also provided me with unique spaces within which to try out ideas and to be inspired by those of others. Drew Hemment made some very useful comments on a late draft of the book. Graham Kendall was helpful as ever, and never far away. Thanks to Jos for the printing.

Love and thanks to my mum, Suzanne Stephenson, for everything. This is for you. I hope you like it. Love to Emma. Love to Jo. Love to my sisters, Mary and Lucy – I hope you're as proud of me as I am of you. Love to Dad and Joan.

Love to all the Club Fillebrook crew (always different, always the same). Love to everyone who's been there with me when it mattered, to every stranger who's been a momentary friend, to every friend who's never been a stranger; it's not over yet.... Finally, thanks to Ewan Pearson!

Ewan would also like to thank:

Jem for ensuring that I produced written evidence of at least part of a somewhat itinerant academic career, and for helping me confirm my suspicions about a future in teaching ... I did enjoy it, honest!

All my former teachers and supervisors, but especially Kev Madden, Anne Fernihough, Andrew Gibson and Adam Roberts: I will always be grateful for your inspiration and friendship. Everyone on the 1994–5 Postmodernism and Popular Culture MA at Royal Holloway who heard and helped shape a lot of the material found in this book, especially Lorraine Morley – the best DJ I never heard in a club.

Mike Deeley, who frequently dragged me out of Cambridgeshire and into the likes of the Soho Theatre Club, the Haçienda, Venus et al., between 1990–3, and everyone else who came too: we might have missed Shoom but I wouldn't have missed all that for the world. Steve Bates for driving up the western seaboard of the US in three weeks and still finding the time to locate a copy of Albert Goldman's *Disco en route* – and you always said you weren't any good at buying presents. All the other many friends who have tolerated the complaining and frankly anti-social behaviour that I might have dished out in the course of writing this book.

Nathan Gregory and Jeb Loy Nichols, obsessive discophiles both, for sharing stories, records and ideas. James Endeacott at Rough Trade for helping with copyright clearance and Tracey Cox at Polygram Music for coming through with it in the nick of time. Dave and Rick at Soma (and all my buddies in Glasgow), everyone at Ideal, Ian Clifford and Tom Bainton at Mumbo Jumbo: sorry for the lack of musical productivity during 1997–8 – I hope to have begun to remedy it by the time you read this.

Yvonne, for being the sweetest thing....

My immediate family: my dad Andrew, my sister Anna, and particularly my mum, Jane, for not worrying that I preferred books over fresh air as a child, and for not laughing too loud when I discovered discos some ten years later. You did all of this long before me – and I'm glad. This one's for you, with love.

1

THE TRIBAL RITES OF
SATURDAY NIGHT

Discos and intellectuals

Sometimes I get the feeling that they were intellectuals from the high
bourgeoisie who wanted to discover another world. They have always
been fascinated by discotheques and girls, and coming from the sort of
social background and education they did, music was the only way.

Paul Allesandrini, on Kraftwerk[1]

They came to dance, but ended up getting an education.

Advertisement for the film *Thank God it's Friday* (1978)[2]

Sorted? Writing dance music culture after acid house

June 1995. Ten years after the release of Jamie Principal's 'Waiting on Your Angel'
and J.M. Silk's 'Music is the Key' – the prototypical records of Chicago house –
Pulp, a pop band from Sheffield on the cusp of success after an eighteen-year
career, are playing their most prestigious gig thus far, headlining at the
Glastonbury Festival. They premiere a new song, a forthcoming single about the
rave scene called 'Sorted for E's and Wizz' which reflects wryly on the comedowns
of the second 'summer of love'. In the opening lines, frontman Jarvis Cocker asks
the crowd of several thousands of people gathered within the grounds of organiser Michael Eavis's farm in Wiltshire 'Oh is this the way they say the future's
meant to feel? Or just 20,000 people standing in a field?'[3] When released some
weeks later, amid much tabloid invective concerning its title (exacerbated by the
fact that the sleeve bore a step-by-step illustration of how to construct a wrap, the
paper container used to house doses of powdered drugs such as speed and
cocaine), it was a hit, entering the UK Top Forty at number two.

Though several newspapers predictably frothed with rage at the drug references
– 'E's' and 'Wizz' being slang for ecstasy and amphetamines – the song itself was
hardly guilty of glamourization or even celebration. Although not a cautionary
tale in the mould of the tragic teen pop of the late 1950s and early 1960s, it
pointedly evoked the bewilderment and sense of disorientation that accompanied
the ecstasy comedown: 'You want to phone your mother and say "Mother, I can
never come home again 'cause I seem to have left an important part of my brain

1

somewhere, somewhere in a field in Hampshire." ' The press was not of course interested in the content of the lyric but in reviving the hysteria that dogged acid house and its attendent drug cultures during their heyday in the late 1980s. In such an atmosphere, as Gavin Hills pointed out, 'every aspect of dance culture, even its satire, is considered controversial.'[4] The controversy did not end there, however. For those who were listening, the song's ambivalence towards its subject invited feelings both of identification – the shared acknowledgement that when chemically piloted, emotions could go down as well as up – and unease: here was a new pop icon making dark comedy out of what many considered one of youth culture's great positives, a cross-cultural movement that had made a difference.

However one chooses to gloss its evocation of rave, the release of 'Sorted For E's and Wizz' coincided with the beginning of a period of historicization and reflection, a process of mediation within which one would see the term 'sorted' gaining new meanings beyond its limited scope as a euphemism for being on 'E'. The more widespread slang usage, from which the drug term was derived, abbreviated the phrase 'sorted out', connoting that something had been satisfactorily effected or organized to a state of completion or finality. The expression 'sorted' only resided within the drug lexicon for a short period during 1988–92: by 1995 it was already dated. Like 'loved-up', 'on one' and other such euphemisms it had become a rave archaism, utilized lyrically to give a sense of ironic specificity to the song's subject. Yet the term refused to be consigned to the realm of historical linguistics. Later that same year it was resurrected once more for both the subcultural edification of parents and the moral education of the youths who were considered to be at risk from the drug cultures associated with dance. Printed this time on black hoardings in bold white capitals, next to a smiling picture of an eighteen-year-old girl, this fleeting piece of drug argot was transformed into a terrible pun for the nation at large. 'Sorted' became the slogan in the anti-drug poster campaign which followed the death by dilutional hyponatrema (water intoxication) of teenager Leah Betts in November 1995.[5]

Since, if not because of, Leah Betts' death (one teenager dying as a result of taking Ecstasy was never going to trigger this kind of major reassessment: by 1995 up to sixty deaths had been attributed to Ecstasy use in the United Kingdom[6]) the sense of an ending, or at the very least, a reckoning of what has preceded, has characterized much coverage of British dance culture. The term 'sorted' has taken on further resonance: since 1995, a great deal of 'sorting' has been going on, as journalists, writers and cultural commentators labour to gather, arrange and anthologize their various accounts of the baptisms and oblivions, the scams and the epiphanies which unfolded on dancefloors and in fields across the UK. The various mediators of British youth culture have been dealing with a historicizing impulse accompanying the passing of a decade since 1986, the year Chicago house first arrived on British shores and entered both the clubs and the charts. But the celebrations and reconsiderations have not ended there. Each subsequent year after 1995 marks the passing of a decade in which some key moment took place in the history of dance culture; and with each anniversary, music and style magazines have mounted detailed retrospectives, celebrating, glossing and generally picking over the cultural debris. From the mid-1990s onwards, numerous books on the subject have been published: collections on graphic design and visual culture; rave fiction; short story collections and novels; biographies; taxonomies; and cultural histories. At the time of writing, the ever accelerating quantity of historical and critical texts concerned with dance (to which this book is a further contribution) seems unlikely to peter out.

Inherent in both these senses of the term 'sorted', suspended between the sense of conclusion, and the sense of ordering and arranging which characterizes the anthologies, re-issues and greatest hit collections, the histories and the narratives, there is a feeling of anxiety over the attribution of meaning to the acid house and rave movements which were credited with having such an influence. The inlay to Pulp's single, 'Sorted…', carried the following text:

> The summer of '89: Centreforce FM, Santa Pod, Sunrise 5000, 'Ecstasy Airport', ride the white horse, the strings of life, dancing at motorway service stations, falling asleep at the wheel on the way home. There's so many people – it's got to mean something, it needs to mean something, surely it must mean something.
> IT DIDN'T MEAN NOTHING.

The ambiguity found here in the double negative – 'It didn't mean nothing' – encapsulates the kernel of doubt at the centre of many responses to instrumental dance and music cultures; where a culturally-inherited insistence that *value* inheres in attributable *meaning* collides desperately with a sense that dance and dance music have traditionally resisted or negated familiar modes of communicating either value or meaning.

Simon Reynolds, in his article 'Rave Culture: Living Dream or Living Death?',[7] alludes both to the sense of an ending and a rising scepticism as to the meanings that have been attributed to musical moments like rave. He takes his titular image of the inspirational music culture turned zombie from Greil Marcus' 'Note on the Life & Death and Incandescent Banality of Rock 'n' Roll'.[8] Marcus excavates repeated diagnoses of the death of rock, made 'because rock 'n' roll – as a cultural force rather than as a catchphrase – no longer seems to mean anything. It no longer seems to speak in unknown tongues that turn into new and common languages, to say anything that is not instantly translated back into the dominant discourse of our day'.[9] This is transposed by Reynolds on to a British dance culture drained of cultural meaning. As a formalist music critic, Reynolds is positive: he sees dance music changing, profligating, renewing itself – creatively in no danger of stagnating or ossifying. The caveat is that as rave fissures into many musical sub-genres, its political promise of new collectivity, of a unifying cultural movement ebbs too: 'Talk of the death of rock or the death of rave refers not to the exhaustion of the music's formal possibilities, then, but to the seeping away of meaning, the loss of a collective sense of going somewhere.'[10] For certain commentators the all-too fleeting glimpse of a new social formation, which quickly passed, was a bitter disappointment. Hence Reynolds' quoting of John Lydon's words at the Sex Pistols' final gig in Rosewood, in the States: 'Ever get the feeling you've been cheated?'

So why the anxiety? Over ten years on from the advent of house, it is tempting to suggest that this is an inevitable period of comedown, the downswing of a pharmaceutical arc experienced by a generation now learning that 'pleasure is not without its consequences'.[11] Matthew Collin has stated that 'the typical cycle of Ecstasy use can be mapped culturally'[12]: coming up, followed by the high which cannot be sustained without continual increases in dosage (which must inevitably be relinquished), and a difficult period of comedown, eased by the promise of greater maturity and self-knowledge for those who have not fallen by the wayside. Such a 'pharmacological narrative' does often seem to shape the stories and histories of acid house (and other dance cultures). But this is just one narrative, and not a new one at that: it echoes a familiar mythic structure, the rise and fall which marks the tales of the Great Men of History, or the *Bildungsroman*, the novel form which charts the journey of a youthful hero from innocence to experience. Indeed the sheer familiarity of this model should give us pause before invoking it once more; it is too easy to map such a loaded (in several senses) chemical micro-narrative of euphoria and comedown on to the complexities of cultural history. Just as pharmacological usage and experience varies among the constituencies of youth, and its various club cultures, so too the models that code and are coded by those experiences need to be recognized and considered in all their complexity.

It might be suggested that the ten-year delay in producing the histories of acid house marked an awareness that too many rash promises had been made and too many hopes invested in the sweat-soaked, serotonin-washed moments of 1988–92. There are no doubt many commentators who have reconsidered some of the predictions and analyses which they made at the time: from the end of football hooliganism (inspired by the temporary collision of football terrace and 'E' cultures[13]), to the suggestion by the NME dance journalist, Jack Barron, that MDMA (Ecstasy) could end the war in Northern Ireland.[14] Yet however naive both suggestions might seem with the benefit of hindsight, they were inspired by concrete manifestations of rave culture. Nicholas Saunders cites statistics that suggest a statistical drop in football violence did coincide with the spread of E-use on the terraces.[15] Similarly, the late blooming of house clubs in Belfast and Derry in Northern Ireland opened up non-segregated leisure spaces within which historical and cultural divisions were displaced, if not healed: where identity came second to the temporary pleasures of dance.[16]

In this sense, the mid- to late 1990s should represent not a moment of comedown, but rather the final stage in the pharmacological narrative: a calmer and wiser space from within which one can reassess the preceding rollercoaster ride. The problem with this notion of 'perspective' is that it privileges an epistemology which places the reliable narrator *outside* that which he or she describes. This is a familiar characteristic of the western *episteme*; the notion that the telescopic power of discourse to inscribe and describe inheres in a vantage point some distance away from the object of scrutiny. The only narratives that can be trusted are the ones that position themselves at a safe distance from the objects and activities which they are describing.

The problems of location for those attempting to describe, evaluate or analyse dance cultures are several. Ironically many accounts provided by those with significant cultural capital invested in the era, with some of the best credentials, are characterized by the considerable care taken not to label their stories as definitive. Perhaps aware of some of the inadequacies and discursive priorities of those accounts which have traded on the metaphysics of presence, commentators like Matthew Collin, a former editor of i-D and the most accomplished historian on the UK's Ecstasy culture, are sure to preface their histories with disclaimers:

> The story of Ecstasy culture is itself a remix – a collage of facts, opinions and experiences. Differing outlooks and vested interests combine to deny the possibility of a history that everyone can agree as truth; some things are forgotten, others are exaggerated; stories are embellished, even invented, and the past is polished to suit the necessities of the present. Behind one narrative are hundreds of thousands of unwritten ones and who is to say any one of them is not equally important?[17]

Journalist, DJ and record producer John Macready also expresses a seemingly representative sense of doubt or angst with regard to the intellectualization or historicization of popular music culture, an activity in which, as a journalist, he has participated:

> Dance music is a really transient thing, and he [Kevin Saunderson, Detroit record producer] really appreciates it for what it is; whereas I'm always trying to see some meaning in it, and that's the problem with English people who like dance music ... We're like historians, the way we approach the whole package, doing interviews and placing it in a context. They throw records out in twelve inch bags you know, they're not bothered.[18]

Similarly, in a book on the free party movement, the journalist C.J. Stone[19] describes his initial intention and subsequent failure to write even a brief definitive history of the 'new dance culture':

> This is the third time I've tried to write this chapter. This was the worst chapter in the book. In the earliest version, when you reached this point, there was a section about the history of counter-culture ... But somehow it didn't work. It was clumsy and uncomfortable, schematic and vague,

and bore as much resemblance to real history as the Gold Blend ads do to real love.

So I've changed my tack. I thought, 'What do I really know? Only what I remember.' So what follows is personal testament. Maybe that's all any of us can offer in the end: personal testimony.[20]

Instead Stone offers a personal narrative of his experiences and frustrations on the counter-cultural fringes. The pertinence of his book stems, in part, from his refusal to make generalizations about music cultures; instead Stone shows how they intersect with local and specific experiences of people he has encountered, within the free party movement and elsewhere.

This specific cultural reluctance – not to mention their shared penchant for considered narrative reflexivity – echoes a wider sense of self-doubt which has characterized a great deal of intellectual activity in an age which has seen many intellectuals address the validity of their repeated acts of evaluation. These are writers who acknowledge that, to quote Sadie Plant, 'there is no single perspective that can hold the world still enough to understand it'.[21] Deleuze and Foucault ascribe the dynamic of this realization to the radical student uprisings of 1968, the moment at which the 'intellectual discovered that the masses no longer need him to gain knowledge':

They know perfectly well, without illusion; they know far better than he and they are certainly capable of expressing themselves. But there exists a system of power which blocks, prohibits and invalidates this discourse … Intellectuals are themselves the agents of this system of power.[22]

These anxieties are exacerbated by academic acknowledgements that both music and dance are problematic territories. Speaking at a conference in 1995,[23] Paul Gilroy advised wariness when attempting the articulation of an experience which itself refuses to articulate experience: drawing attention to the danger that we may overburden what is an expressly non-representational form. Similarly the difficulties of writing about dance, which offers up no texts or scores to study after its happening, are realized by those who have attempted to create definitive histories and studies. Dance seems to resist discourse; and some discourses have resisted writing about dance – failing to deal with the *dance* at the heart of *dance culture* whatsoever. Andrew Ward[24] suggests that at the heart of the refusal to write about dance, even in books supposedly concerned with its culture, is a deprecation of the 'non-rational' that renders the activity of dance itself invisible, incommensurable with the ' "verbal forms" … "prioritised" in "logocentric western societies" '.[25] Dance seems to occupy a critical space 'beyond the grasp of reason'.

As the anxieties expressed above indicate, some writers (ourselves included) are now beginning to acknowledge the failings and limit points of both former and current accounts and methodologies. We are confronting the problems which inhere in intellectual pretensions to map and to explain cultural 'phenomena' such as disco or acid house, rather than to experience or open themselves up to the dance itself. To this end, taking Andrew Ross' broad definition of the intellectual,[26] in this first chapter we examine a number of different treatments of the leisure activities and behavioural displays of youth – from academic discourses informed by sociology and cultural studies, to examples of journalism, fiction and film – some of which share a number of themes: the repeated political critique of youth culture as escapism, a fascination with the anthropological gaze and the privileging of visual aspects of culture at the expense of the aural or bodily. We compare the intellectual treatments of disco with those of acid house, to see if the latter has provoked any theoretical or discursive divergence from the familiar tropes by which dance and youth music cultures have been evoked – so long informed by the tenacious appeal of subculture theory.

The intention is not to try and be an inclusive survey of the approaches taken in the mediation and representation of dance culture, but rather to be a mixture of intellectual history and cautionary tale, a recognition of the difficulties and also the potential rewards offered by the study of the dancefloor. If such writers as Collin, Macready and Stone are to be believed, then the rise of dance musics like disco, house and techno, and the contemporary popularity of dancing and clubbing among young people, challenge both the discursive methods and usual conclusions of cultural critics, theorists, journalists and historians of pop. This is a challenge worth taking up, if we're careful where we put our feet.

Night fever

> He was eighteen years old, almost eighteen and a half. Soon he'd be nineteen, twenty. What did he have besides Saturday night? Besides dancing? What in his whole life ever equalled that rush? That high?
>
> H.B. Gilmour, Saturday Night Fever[27]

In 1975, after finding that his interest in British pop and youth culture was waning, writer and journalist Nik Cohn crossed the Atlantic looking for new inspiration. Since the age of seventeen, Cohn had been producing both fiction and journalism, and was one of a number of influential writers who sought to mediate the new adolescent fashions created by the birth of pop to a wider public eager to thrill to their excesses. Cohn made his name with a host of articles and books accounting for the patterns of the emerging pop cultures and associated behaviours and style cultures of the young, based on his experiences of the cultural 'front line'.[28] After tiring of the UK, in the course of a series of articles for New York magazine he transposed his subcultural prototype on to New York disco space. 'Another Saturday Night' was the New York's cover story for the 7 June 1976, suggestively headlined 'The tribal rites of the new Saturday night'.[29]

Cohn's disco narrative was not especially concerned with a new musical phenomenon.[30] As Albert Goldman has noted, he was 'deaf' to disco music, producing in the article an unpleasant caricature of a PA (personal appearance) by Crown Heights Affair, seemingly ignorant that they were one of the foremost black disco bands of the time.[31] Nor did he make any attempt to ground its context or history; disco's origins in gay New York's illicit cultures of the night, such as David Mancuso's Loft parties, would later be explored in the novel by Andrew Holleran, *Dancer from the Dance*.[32] Instead, Cohn chose to relate the activities and mores of a particular gang of working-class Italian-American youths from Bay Ridge, and describe their peculiar social patterns and rituals. His article focused primarily on 'Vincent', an eighteen year old who worked as a delivery boy for a paint store and was an accomplished disco dancer and 'Face' at the local discotheque, the 2001 Odyssey. As the term 'Face' indicates, the article was partly a study of mod culture, of the self-styled most stylish, the 'top boys' (as Cohn points out, it is only boys who can be Faces[33]).

As the article title suggested, this was in many ways a familiar anthropological tale of American youth, fiercely tribal, perennially warring. Cohn's fascination with cultural identity and its symbolic display is shared by his subjects. Ethnicity is the absolute which striates New York's cultural landscape, keeping each group distinct, yet rendering them also alike.

> There was no overlapping. Italians were Italian, Latins were greaseballs, Jews were different, and Blacks were born to lose. Each group had its own ideal, its own style of Face. But they never touched. If one member erred, ventured beyond his own allotted territory, he was beaten up. That was the law. There was no alternative.[34]

Cohn's archaeology of this particular youth group is quasi-academic in its attention to ethnographic detail. The homogeneity of his subjects – the white Catholic heterosexuals who attend the Odyssey 2001 in Brooklyn – would be undermined had Cohn instead chosen the diverse constituents of Manhattan's decadent and infamous nightclubs. There is no inkling of disco space as being heterogeneous, as a site of commixture, or neutrality beyond the territorialities of the streets around it.

Instead, the discotheque is both the Faces' parade ground and their place of worship. Cohn likens it to a cathedral: for these Italian-American Catholics dancing is 'sacrament', a seeking after the immaculate within which devotion negates pleasure. Dance is an arcane rite enacted to code self-identity: their ascetic adherence to its regimen is a means to the performance of subjective security. The Faces are not only high priests but military police, ensuring that the correct steps for each month are executed with strict discipline: 'there were certain rules, watertight. Only obey them, and nothing could go wrong'.[35] As guardians of taste they author a bodily narrative that others may emulate but will never equal.[36] This grim precision is a far cry from the terms by which contemporary discourse has characterized social dance from disco onward: ecstatic release, diffusion of self, and encounter with otherness.

Cohn's account of suburban nightlife and its subcultural mores articulates a classic Marxist account of leisure in which disco space operates to invert the social position of the Faces while preserving the strictly hierarchical system which oppresses them outside.

> It was a true sanctuary. Once inside, the Faces were unreachable. Nothing could molest them. They were no longer the oppressed, wretched teen menials who must take orders, toe the line. Here they took command, they reigned.[37]

They are the ruling classes of the 2001 Odyssey discotheque, with Vincent enthroned as sovereign, ruling by means of a divine right 'beyond words, deep down in the blood'.[38] Their contempt for their subjects is considerable: 'Across America there were millions and millions of kids who were nothing special. Just kids. Zombies. Professional dummies going through the motions, following like sheep. School, jobs, routines. A vast faceless blob. And then there were the Faces.'[39] From within the 'secret underground, a Saturday-night cabal, known only to initiates'[40] the Faces express a disdain for those in thrall to the dissemination of cultural forms, content merely to follow and absorb, which is strongly resonant of the hostile terms with which various critical and intellectual orthodoxies, from the Leavises and modernists through to the Frankfurt School, had treated the recipients and audience for popular cultural forms. These same orthodoxies had long since rejected social dancing and dance music as both distractions from and symptoms of a wider malaise.

Cohn's article, optioned by Australian impresario Robert Stigwood, formed the basis of John Badham's extraordinarily successful film *Saturday Night Fever*.[41] Released in 1977, some four years into the life span of disco, the movie marked a significant point of transition: during 1977–8, disco went from being the occupation of a significant few to a nationwide craze, forever linked in the popular imagination to a paradigmatic iconography of mirror-balls and underfloor lighting. Disco was no longer the sole property of the clubgoer: it had become a broader entertainment commodity, an industry in its own right.[42] *Saturday Night Fever: the Soundtrack* became the highest selling long-playing album of all time, until it was deposed by Michael Jackson's *Thriller* six years later.

From Cohn's material, director John Badham and scriptwriter Norman Wexler made a film that mixed domestic-drama, rites of passage melodrama and exuberant musical romance. Vincent is renamed Tony Manero, and the film opens out his imagined social and familial background as an Italian-American Catholic, envied and bullied by his redundant father, and considered inferior to his absent and idealized brother, Frank Jnr, a priest. Tony, as the hero, is not idealized: he is arrogant, narcissistic and selfish, and compliant in the routine racism, homophobia and misogyny of his peers. After the dance contest he comes close to raping his dancing partner in the back of a car when she resists his advances. Badham is not afraid to show the unpleasant aspects of Tony's world, and the early part of the movie especially bears the patina of the 1970s urban expressionism beloved of film-makers like Martin Scorsese. Yet at the film's core is a familiar bourgeois narrative: the passage into adulthood. It is clear that Tony is in the process of relinquishing a life of drugs, gang-banging, and fumbling attempts at sexual assault. In contrast, such characters as Annette and Bobby C are injured and killed in their attempt to make the transition between childhood pleasures and adult morality.

At the movie's conclusion, tragedy (the pathetic Bobby C falls accidentally to his death from Brooklyn Bridge, his recklessness fuelled by despair at his girl-friend's pregnancy and community pressure to 'do the right thing') is succeeded by a degree of optimism. Whereas Vincent leaves Cohn's text to pursue one of the Latino gangs the young Italian-Americans perennially vie with, using violence as a placebo to dull their various grievances, Tony Manero is shown as growing up. He ends the film having realized that the spaces provided by gang membership and dancefloor escapism are no longer viable. They will, one presumes, have to be replaced by monogamy and a career – perhaps fulfilling his dream of profession-ally exploiting his dancing talent. This bourgeois impetus is sugared by a rhetoric of emancipation, of resisting the paths society has ordained (following his brother Frank who has left the priesthood in personal crisis). In Cohn's article Vincent has only the inevitability of his departure from the disco hierarchy to look forward to, prefiguring his ultimate death. By the end of the movie Tony is all too happy to be given a chance to relinquish his youthful pursuits, although we are none the wiser as to what his next move might be.

If Badham's film is about escape, it is escape from the strictures and values of blue-collar Catholic life rather than the ecstatic freedoms offered by dance. In a community in which a surfeit of aspiration is outweighed by the absence of real opportunity, Tony is delineated from those around him by the possession of genuine talent, which could give him a chance to do what his partner Stephanie has done and escape over the river. Initially the dance contest seems to offer such a route. But when Tony and Stephanie win the top prize, despite being out-danced by the Puerto Rican couple who follow them, the disco too is confirmed as a site from which Tony must escape. Now fully espousing a bourgeois meritocratic value system, Tony is disgusted with the judges' local favouritism, and gives the runners up the trophy and the prize money before fleeing the disco.

Thus *Saturday Night Fever* is about the escape from subculture – but whereas it appeared initially that dance would offer this release, it is soon confirmed that bourgeois romance and adult responsibility are the actual paths on offer. In this sense the film's relationship with dance is an ambiguous one: the vibrant excite-ment of the early disco sequences gives way to a different dynamic as the film progresses. In the first night at the Odyssey, the dancefloor is bustling and the dance sequences are communal: first Tony dances with Annette, and then he leads the line dance. These early scenes in the disco are intoxicating, and are characterized by the constantly moving camerawork that takes the audience around the dancefloor. The film exhibits a sense of exhilaration and *jouissance* at the dance, something which is absent from Cohn's article, with its image of Vincent as a general who grimly marshals his troops in 'strict ranks' for the Odyssey Hustle.

The second sequence, in which Tony performs his freestyle dance, attests to the virtuosity of both Manero as hero and John Travolta (who plays him) as star. At the time, Travolta admitted that this sequence was added at his insistence: 'I had to enforce that scene. They were basing this movie on his being the best dancer, and he didn't have a solo. I had to prove to the audience that he was the best.'[43] The act of confirming him as the star centre of the movie means that the sequence takes place on a cleared dancefloor with other dancers becoming our representatives, the whooping audience. The camera does not follow too closely, but stays back, as Tony/John is framed by a pulsing grid of underfloor lighting. The dance – still thrilling – is now to be wondered at from a position of removal. With the shift from inclusive social dance towards the observation of spectacle the dancefloor is transformed into a zone of competition, aspiration and wonder, the dancers are there to be watched and worshipped, their glamour proximate but remote.

This is compounded by the introduction of Stephanie as Tony's dance partner and love interest: the subsequent dancing competition sub-plot positions *Saturday Night Fever* as a down-at-heel cousin to a succession of earlier Hollywood musicals, with their dreams of hoofers escaping from small-town America to Broadway. With Stephanie's arrival on the scene the disco is no longer the sole locus – the dance studio becomes as important. Tony's initial attempts to woo Stephanie as she practises ballet echo the comic romance between Gene Kelly and Vera-Ellen in *On the Town*.[44] Just as Ellen's Ivy Smith allows Kelly's honest but simple dancing sailor Gabey to believe that she is a society girl (when in fact she comes from the same small Midwest town as he does), so Stephanie takes advantage of Tony's ignorance with her *arriviste* boasting about lunches with musicians and actors (she works in a Manhattan entertainment agency) and only drinking tea with lemon.

The disco contest in many ways subsumes the dance itself, becoming instead the medium for the development of the romantic sub-plot; with dramatic emphasis resting on whether Tony and Stephanie become a couple rather than on whether they succeed in the competition. Indeed their dance in the competition is the least somatic out of all the dance sequences. It functions as the final stage in their courtship; slower and more balletic than that of the other contestants, it exists solely to culminate in their kiss – the expression of romantic love. This is 'touch dancing' at its most ballroom, and is the palest dance sequence in the movie. The two earlier disco scenes are more memorable and more exciting. Travolta's skilful freestyle exposition as the king of the dancefloor,[45] and the earlier Bus Stop line dance sequence to the strains of 'Night Fever' are the sequences we take with us as we leave the cinema, both of which forget for a few blissful minutes the film's bourgeois grain.

As we have seen, the several texts that comprise *Saturday Night Fever* play across interdependent zones of fictional 'realism', anthropologically motivated journalistic reportage and the inexorable rise of sociology and cultural studies, all purporting in some way to map the patterns of leisure and behavioural displays of young people. In different ways both Cohn's article and Badham's film are paradigmatic of 'intellectual' (in Ross' broad sense) treatments of youth dance cultures. Their major concern is the articulation of issues of identity and style, as well as a political critique on the notion of escape. Their approaches are characterized by the anthropological fascination with the gaze, with the visual and the specular, at the expense of the bodily and aural. Badham's film can be considered the more complex of the two texts in that it also seeks to convey the intoxicating power of the dancefloor, by means of its soundtrack and dance sequences. Its evocation – rather than explanation – of disco, contributed to the film's enormous success, at a time when disco had proved itself well able to escape from the strict realm of subculture.

Floorplans

[The Hustle] started in the Barrio, then worked its way outwards, to Brooklyn, Queens, the Bronx. Along the way it got simplified, cheapened, and soon it was turned into hit records, great fortunes.

Nik Cohn, 'Tu Sweet, No Sweat'[46]

The popularity of *Saturday Night Fever* crowned disco's crossover into pop culture, and set in motion its commodification. For a short time, those disco records which became hits achieved massive sales, and ever larger volumes of new disco records were produced in the hope that they too would reach the charts. Just as Tony Manero's story tracked disco's passage to the suburbs, 1977–8 saw disco leave New York and the other urban centres which had been its home, and spread out over the States, beyond the strict realm of the young, the ethnic, or the hip. The process of mediating disco to a new constituency that was not *au fait* with nightclubbing, necessarily moved it out of the environs of the club dancefloor and into movie theatres, the domicile (through soundtrack albums, pop radio stations, popular novels) and the dance studios that had begun to teach disco dance styles and techniques.

One of the means by which disco was articulated to a wider public was through verbal description and documentation; a profusion of books were published on the subject, including many which outlined the various dance steps in diagrammatic form for the benefit of those who had not yet been able to learn them by observation or participation.[47] Popular disco dances were transcribed; their fluidities and variations transformed into two-dimensional geometric representations, a series of footmarks traced on a page. These books combined apparently democratic motives with a ruthlessly commercial agenda: on the one hand they effected the inclusion of a broader demographic of dancer who might not be party to the cultural capital held by those who attended discos; on the other hand they seemed to want to *refine* disco, to transform it into something akin to swing dancing, so that it might easily be mapped and sold to Middle America. These handbooks downplayed the multiple forms of disco dancing, focusing instead on one partnered manifestation – the Hustle – rather than the freestyle, solo forms, which by definition could not be reduced to a strictly ordered set of moves, magically effected by the correct placement of the soles of the feet.

Any attempt to inscribe, to verbalize or to diagrammatize an alogogenic culture such as dance is fraught with difficulty.[48] Attempts by academics to describe and explain dance practices – and in so doing give them meanings – are no exception.[49] In many ways the academic accounts of social dance practices resemble the floorplans found in disco handbooks – they are exercises in *ichnography* (the art of drawing of ground plans, *ichnos* being the imprint of the foot[50]) which fail to capture the transient and fluid complexities of the dancer, and through abstraction achieve only reduction. Ted Polhemus, for example, describes how disco's apparently ' "alternative" popular connotations (i.e. one's parents saw it as completely opposed to the dance styles of their day) actually heralded the return of Western society's traditional assumptions of gender'.[51] His evaluation assumes that disco dance styles consisted solely of the partnered, so-called 'touch' dances, like the Hustle, which he contrasts with the solo or freestyle dancing that conquered popular dance among the young during the 1960s with the likes of the Twist:

> Here we saw a complete return at least in terms of gender differentiation
> to the norms of dance, behaviour and culture which existed prior to the
> unisex experiments of the late 1960's. The male asks the girl to be his
> partner. The male physically supports the female. The male sets the pace
> and style of the dance; the male is the centre of attention.[52]

The validity of his political reading is based on a narrow characterization of disco dance solely in terms of the Hustle – apparently its most 'conservative' manifestation. As noted above, the Hustle, which had its origins in Latin American dance styles, formed one of the primary means by which disco crossed the various social demarcations reserved for youth cultures. As a dance for couples, holding hands, it appealed to an older generation familiar with the partnered swing styles which dominated youth dance cultures before the 1960s, and through handbooks and instruction records formed the means by which disco was articulated to a wider public than just the denizens of certain urban nightclubs.

But the Hustle was not confined to partnered dance; as contemporary accounts of disco indicate there were a range of variants.[53] One of the most popular of these was the California Hustle, or the Bus Stop, which was a form of line dance, with participants dancing singly but facing in the same direction, performing the same set of moves. Social dances, for example line dancing, have very different potential readings to potentially heterosexist partnered dances. Indeed one could say that the recent popularity of country and western line dancing in America, Europe and Australia is due to its creation of an inclusive social space; no partner is required and its rapid rise in popularity is largely due to its appeal to older and single women. (For similar reasons, line dancing has been popular with gays and lesbians for whom same-sex partnered dance might be frowned upon.) Most importantly, Polhemus seems unaware that, despite the cultural rapacity of the Hustle and its representations, freestyle dance remained the beating heart of disco,[54] powering its rhetorics of social, romantic, sexual and somatic emancipation. Freestyle required neither a partner or training, nor did one need inherent grace or skill. Freed from the technical and social demands of previous generations of ballroom or dancehall, anyone, regardless of gender, sexuality, age or ability could participate.

Polhemus' implication that rather than being a part of marginal culture, disco was in fact mainstream, is in one important sense correct. By the end of the 1970s disco had become a full-scale dance 'craze' across America, vaulting the demographic barriers (age, sexuality, race and class) which underwrote the specific scientific credentials of much socio-ethnographic research. But his account fails to provide any contextual information about this transformation: he passes up the opportunity to identify what might be considered the 'authentic' origins of disco in American gay night-time culture, or antecedent dance forms; and no attempt is made to provide an account of disco's mediation, and its concomitant adoption of apparently retrogressive 'mainstream' gender politics. Disco's dance styles were various, making the attribution of a single political reading – whether through formal analysis of dance or the contexts in which dance occurred – unsatisfactory. In Polhemus' account the disco becomes a younger and shinier version of the ballroom: *Come Dancing* with neon underfloor lighting. As noted above, a film like *Saturday Night Fever* would appear to concur with this reading, although the vivacity of the non-partnered dance sequences in comparison to the final contest suggests differently: neither one neatly confirms the analyses of those who would chastise disco's conservatism.

Polhemus is unwilling, or unable to provide a *diachronic* reading which might attempt to evoke some of the complexities and variants of dance and its attendant culture. Instead he chooses to freeze the cultural continuum, utilizing the subcultural schematic of youth culture as comprising a number of distinct and discrete tribal groupings, 'each with its own values, beliefs, lifestyle assumptions, adornment styles and dance styles'[55], each of which, in turn, can diligently be catalogued and classified. In many ways the texts produced by popular journalists, writers of disco handbooks and subcultural sociologists like Polhemus become interchangeable. In a dance manual from 1979, the author describes dancefloor fashion for the unenlightened reader:

> Young women wear colourful leotards with matching or co-ordinated wraparound skirts. Their shoes are feminine-looking and danceable. Male youths look clean and well-groomed wearing fancy shirts with matching

14

or co-ordinated vests, no neckties but well-tailored pants. Comfort is the keynote. True, some people dress in bizarre fashion to attract attention on the dancefloor, but these form a small minority.[56]

Calmly and confidently this passage evokes the world of disco in its most asinine and fully commodified state, comforting the reader whose participation might depend on it with a description of unthreatening sartorial uniformity. Even though this is a dancing manual rather than a sociological text, its guiding principles are very similar to anthropologically informed accounts of youth subcultures connected with dance. In similar ways, both work to enlighten the reader with regard to homologies of style (clothes, hair and other presentational and aesthetic choices), either in order to recuperate the value of popular/youth cultures as a space of resistance, or to document how they remain in thrall to hegemonic social structures. Whether positive or disparaging the judgement always occurs within this spatial framework of centre and periphery.

The anthropological accounts of social dance practices and styles which have so strongly influenced the discursive practices of sociology and contemporary cultural studies are various, although they share the same aim of attempting to read the semiotics of dance as if it were some systematic and coherent language system in order to make it signify. Any suggestion that we might consider dance to be what Paul Spencer has called 'an end in itself that transcends utility'[57] is strongly resisted. All such accounts agree that there must be a function, or a telos, in the activity of dance and various candidates have been forwarded. To this end, social dance is evoked in terms of the symbolic reinforcement of community structures, and the regulation of social behaviour (for example, the historical function of such dances as the minuet in the educative development of sensibility). As Spencer has pointed out, dance is seen to function as a safety-valve, to relieve participants from such anxieties as feudalism, epidemics, war, industrial capitalism, social marginalization, millennial angst.[58] This is contrasted by writers like Suzanne Langer with high-art dance perceived as being an artistic representation of emotion, detached and performative, whereas social dance in comparison is considered to lack any 'spiritually strenuous achievement'.[59] Dancing also releases the pressure of mounting libidinal impulses, as an expression of emotional hunger: this reading helps to explain the continual 'explanation' of dance as courtship ritual. David Walsh, in his essay 'Saturday Night Fever: An ethnography of disco dancing', echoes Polhemus' assessment of the retrograde sexual politics of disco, and describes the various practices of masculine 'display' and mating ritual now permitted by the popularity of dancing as if he were describing peacocks or monkeys.[60] Such accounts ignore the work done on asexual dance cultures such as northern soul and rave, both sites of amphetamine-based drug intake and non-spectacular dancing practice which question the received view of the dancefloor as little more than a place to meet a prospective partner.

Perhaps part of the problem, as Andrew Ward has pointed out,[61] is that the functionalist interpretation of dance culture is in thrall to a 'rationalist' imperative, which requires the postulation of a function or purpose beyond the zone of immediate bodily pleasure. Pleasure must relieve a social burden, sublimate a libidinal desire, facilitate a communal or ritual function, and either subvert or reinforce a social structure – it cannot (and the implication is, must not) merely be sought in and for itself. Ward observes that newspaper journalists during 1988–9 found it impossible to believe 'that people would want to travel many miles in secret to dance in fields or warehouses'; such acts are 'beyond the grasp of reason'.[62] The refusal of disco or acid house to sublimate pleasure to any other function – the solipsism of those 'lost in music' – inspires confusion and/or outrage in those who are unable to fit the activity into any moral function. Social dance practices can quickly become misunderstood and feared modes of popular cultural activity, considered a kind of pathology or 'craze'. Certain intellectual attempts at the functional location of 'ritual' activity are informed by the same fear of the irrational, of ecstasy and delirium, as was exhibited in the headlines of the tabloid press during the popularity of acid house.

There are also implications for consideration of the dancing subjects. Non-verbal and non-rational structures of dance are considered more important within pre-literate social structures. The groups for whom dancing plays a prominent role in literate societies are either marginal or in some way suspect, which helps to explain some of the precepts of subcultural theory, in which youth cultures are tribal groupings identifiable by particular style markers, be they sartorial or musical. There is an equation of the primitive and the infantile (which has also been applied to musical forms) with the body and its zones of pleasure, whereas adults reside in the realm of language and the mental faculties. As Ward comments, at least youth is only transitionally marginal: like Tony Manero, the young will soon grow out of dancing and pursue more serious cultural activities.

For such writers as Ward and ourselves, 'it is no longer appropriate to approach this or that dance as if it had a message to reveal, or as if it was a discrete narrative moment, or as if it was a mirror of, or cipher for, some more real or fundamental (social, economic, or psychological) phenomena'.[63] It is necessary to re-evaluate the model of dance as 'mere' escapism, and simultaneously to recognize the inadequacy of seeing dance as but a means of telling important stories, with the implication that consequent verbal extrapolations occupy a higher ontological space than the more trivial dance itself.

You should be dancing

Sociologists see the current dance mania as part of modern man's revolt against being a perpetual spectator.

Over the years they say, the majority of us have done less and less participating and more and more watching…. Unlike the customers of nightclubs or cabarets who pay their money and then sit back to be entertained, the customers at discotheques are paying their money to entertain themselves. It's the people who are the real show at the discos – and they haven't come to find fault. They've come to play.

Kitty Hanson, *Disco Fever*[64]

When they reached the car, they found Vincent already waiting, combing his hair. 'Where were you?' asked Gus. 'Watching,' said Vincent.

Nik Cohn, 'Another Saturday Night'[65]

Any intellectual attempt to describe, analyse or account for shared experience would, we might suggest, stand to benefit from sharing in that experience. But the issue of engagement is not a simple one. First, there is the danger that evidence of engagement can easily turn into arguments over authority and authenticity: who is or is not in possession of the appropriate cultural capital. As we have noted, those with significant portions of experience often seem most anxious that their accounts do not appear 'over-authoritative'. On the other hand, some of the histories and accounts that have been constructed around the ten-year anniversary of acid house have attempted to assert their superior claims to authenticity in an ever-more crowded marketplace. Wayne Anthony, sometime acid house promoter, published his memoir *Class of '88* in 1997, subtitling it 'The True Acid House Experience'.[66] In such cases the value of the experience in question potentially overrides the importance of the discourse by which it is evoked. What is important for intellectual accounts of dance is not merely the fact of being or having been there (the ultimate claim of both the eyewitness and the fan), textually signalling presence or participation, but a recognition of the responsibilities that 'being there', and writing about it afterward, entail.

There is a significant split between accounts which privilege the metaphysics of presence and those that prize their distance from the topic in question. Writing about social dance further widens this fissure, in the sense that the act of writing could be said to represent as absolute a withdrawal or contrast from the act of dancing as it is possible to achieve. As we suggested in the introduction, while for some writers (and we include ourselves in this category) this separation is a source of anxiety, some academic discourses may consider it a mark of virtue – believing that the text becomes stronger when the eye is free to observe, and the intellect to compose, without being seduced or tempted away from reason by the pleasures of the dance.

The ability to demonstrate experiential capital and thereby claim authority for one's account is still an important quantity for many academics. This seems especially true of those writing within a discourse which prides itself on its basis in demonstrable proof, on empirical data, such as social science. The statistically-driven, positivist school of sociology and the tradition of 'participant observation'[67] tend to converge on an obsession with the scientifically authoritative veracity of their accounts of social 'reality'. For example, in the introduction to what is certainly the most useful sociological account of dance cultures to date,

17

Sarah Thornton's *Club Cultures*, the writer states her research credentials: 'I acted as a participant-observer at over two hundred discos, clubs and raves.' This acts to grant the text which follows it authority, to affirm that its insights are gleaned from data rather than from pontification, and that this data does not merely constitute 'raw' experience, but experience filtered through a respected ethnographic methodology.

Yet as admirable and thorough as it is, Thornton's book is at its least convincing in the short section within which she provides a first-person account of her experiences in the field. In 'A night of research',[68] Thornton describes a visit to several clubs with one of the people she has met in the course of her investigations. In the name of research she and her guide share an MDMA capsule (a rather daring admission for an academic).

> We go to the toilets, cram into a cubicle where Kate opens the capsule and divides the contents. I put my share in my glass and drink. I'm not a personal fan of drugs – I worry about my brain cells. But they're a fact of this youth culture, so I submit myself to the experiment in the name of thorough research (thereby confirming every stereotype of the subcultural sociologist).[69]

The apparent purpose of this interlude within the structure of the book is to provide affirmation of Thornton's commitment to a 'reflexive methodological approach' to her subject – the remainder of the chapter is a comparison between the discourses of clubland itself and the 'social worlds [Thornton] observed as an ethnographer'.[70] However, its effect is rather to highlight the inherent contradiction within the phrase 'participant-observer' and the shortcomings of the discourses which employ it. When the author is out researching, she claims to be both participating and observing, but can only account for the latter activity.

Thornton's intention here is to demonstrate salient experience – to prove that she has done the work – yet her attempt to make light of the epistemological imperatives of sociologist discourse seem awkward. At the point when she attempts to demonstrate her commitment to experiencing club culture on its own terms, in this instance in a specifically chemical form, she divides herself from the constituency she is present to study. Thornton's references to having taken Ecstasy become an anomaly. After stating that she is only taking the drug in the name of research, she makes no further reference to her chemical experience. She makes no comment on whether her taking the MDMA has affected any alteration of her mood or observational trajectory, and there is no mention of her *dancing*. The reader is entitled to ask why she has taken a 'dance drug' if she is not going to repair to the dancefloor. Instead she moves through three clubs with a known club face, seemingly spending most of her time in VIP rooms talking to promoters, or describing the fashions of the stage dancers and the constituency of the crowd. The agenda of such research is still that the eye is all – observation, interview and encounter seemingly give all the necessary information to make worthwhile academic judgement. On those few occasions when Thornton is present within the narrative in the first person, her I/eye is actively observing.[71]

In the book's introduction, Thornton simultaneously attempts to demonstrate her credentials *and* to distance herself from the clubbers who form the constituents of the book:

> Despite once having been an avid clubber, I was an outsider to the cultures in which I conducted research for several reasons. First and foremost, I was *working* in a cultural space in which everyone else (except the DJs, door and bar staff, and perhaps the odd journalist) was at their *leisure*. Not only did I have intents and purposes that were alien to the rest of the crowd, but for the most part I tried to maintain an analytical frame of mind that is truly anathema to the 'lose yourself' and 'let the rhythm take control' ethos of clubs and raves.[72]

Thornton's attempt to be doubly located, both inside and outside the topic, conflicts with an epistemological impetus which maintains that objectivity is still paramount, and suspects those who are too close to the objects of their study. Once again, despite her several protestations, observation is the privileged term in the participation–observation dualism. This, we might suggest, is an impossible duality for social science to maintain, the result being that the author, no doubt well-intentioned, appears to balk at participation while claiming her right to derive firm and authoritative conclusions from a limited portion of 'experience'. In the final sentence, Thornton demonstrates her ultimate dilemma: the academic discourse within which she is schooled, and within which her work will be assessed and legitimated, still considers that to understand the irrational, the loss of self, one must cling tightly to the rational. Dance, 'beyond the grasp of reason', remains 'anathema' to the social scientist.

Faced with such difficulties, the temptation for many writer-intellectuals is simultaneously to bemoan and to romanticize their uncertain location. Dick Hebdige, in his conclusion to his book *Subculture: The Meaning of Style*,[73] as Steven Connor points out, 'mourns the excluded condition of the cultural analyst,' who is 'in society but not inside it, producing analyses of popular culture which are themselves anything but popular'[74] (a comment which failed to anticipate the success and influence his book subsequently enjoyed). Connor notes the 'reverse hubris' at work in such a statement: it only further amplifies the romantic valorization of the outsider, the lonely existential figure condemned to chronicle, not to participate. A similar example appears in Cohn's 'Another Saturday Night'. Cohn (who forms a character within the narrative, 'the man in the tweed suit' who sits in the bleachers at the Odyssey listening to the stories told to him by the Faces) makes his self-pity at watching and not participating the note which lingers after his account has ceased:

>The man in the suit wanted to go along, wanted to watch, but they
>wouldn't let him. They said that he didn't belong, that this was no night
>for tourists, spectators.[75]

Here, though, the pathos of this moment of exclusion – at which the writer sees
his licence to observe terminated – actually implies more than an epistemological
quandary. What appeared to be merely a symptom of subcultural romanticism –
the intimation that his subjects are more real, more authentic than he – was more
than mere writerly hubris: it was as much a rueful admission of fraudulent
activity. After having written himself into the narrative, and attesting to having
been present, watching, listening and recording, Cohn was hinting at just how
much more of an outsider he was than either his editor or his audience realized.

For Cohn admitted to New York magazine, twenty years after he wrote the article
that inspired Saturday Night Fever, that he had made up his 'true story'.[76] Its central
character, Vincent, the basis for John Travolta's Tony, was a 'complete fabrication',
inspired by a figure Cohn had seen loitering in a doorway at the 2001 Odyssey
(which Cohn did visit in December 1975 with his acquaintance Tu Sweet) but had
failed to talk to. He allowed his editors to believe that what they were getting was
reportage, when what they were really reading contained a great deal more fiction
than he would or could admit to at the time. For all its supposed anthropological
rigour, the empirical foundations on which Cohn constructed his article were
shallow – consisting of but two visits to the Bay Ridge discotheque. 'Another
Saturday Night' was imagined ethnography.

This 'revelation', though widely reported,[77] would not have been particularly
shocking to anyone who had read Gordon Burn's introduction to Cohn's collected
writings published some eight years previously.[78] Burn suggests that the writer
could never maintain an impermeable barrier between his journalism and his
fiction, and Cohn admits that, 'not having been to a place never stopped me from
describing it … Any more than not meeting someone stopped me talking about my
interview with them'.[79]

A hint of this blurring of fiction and non-fiction can perhaps be seen in
another Cohn New York magazine article from the 1970s, '24 on 42'.[80] Here Cohn
presents another account of participant-observation, another Saturday night in
New York, this time a twenty-four hour endurance test spent with the denizens of
Forty-Second street. Ripped on coke, speed and alcohol, he manages to spend a
day and a night in Times Square. While exhibiting considerable sympathy towards
this underworld and its inhabitants, the article once again turns inward to
describe Cohn's own feelings of urban alienation and homesickness, and to rumi-
nate on his mortality and the writer-as-voyeur (which, within the red-light
district, becomes literal – Cohn attends porn films, peep shows and spends part of
the morning with a prostitute in his attempt to make it through the twenty-four
hours). The article closes with a similar pay-off to its predecessor too. Having
allowed him to spend some time within it, the street ultimately spits Cohn out,
albeit more violently than the disco. Having survived twenty-four hours on the

streets, at the moment of victory he meets his nemesis, a drunken woman who punches him out.

> As we passed, she seemed to be staring into space, oblivious. Then somehow her eye caught mine, and she jumped to her feet, incensed.
> Red faced with fury, hands shaking in wildest outrage, the woman pointed at my face, and then at my paper bag. 'Impostor! Fraud!' she cried. 'You've got nothing in that bag. And, may God be my witness, you never will.'[81]

Cohn's style of writing himself, the observing author, into his articles seemed at the time perhaps to confirm their basis in empirical fact; re-examined it marks a guilty reflexivity. Certainly the closing paragraph of '24 on 42' (which comprise the last words of the volume *Ball the Wall*) seem as close to shouting 'I'm making it up!' as a professional journalist could get without losing his job.

Nik Cohn is a fascinating figure; a brilliant writer who for twenty years was a passionate and powerful advocate for the cultural importance of the activities of youth, who built a career fictionalizing and reporting on their music cultures, their fashions and their values, from policing what was vital or authentic and what was flimsy, mannered or bogus. Yet Cohn seemed cognisant of his and others' role in the applying the narrative cement which bound these subcultures – aware that authenticities are authored, and seemingly loath to continue to take advantage of the fact without a tacit marker of this awareness. Where the texts themselves subtly hinted at the fictions they contained, their origins in empirical research – the author's 'presence' at the scene – suggested no such thing. Ethnography – the power of observation – was a Trojan horse: although Cohn neglected to tell his editors that articles like 'Another Saturday Night' were not quite truths from the front, he certainly believed in the potency and the importance of their content. Cohn appropriated the perceived truth value of journalism as a cover for his belief in the greater resonance of myth. In so doing he both illustrated and wholeheartedly contributed to the romanticism at the heart of subcultural discourse. 'Another Saturday Night' – retracing a 1950s paradigm of pop culture and alienated youth, Brando and Dean[82] – mused on the fictional inspirations for modes of youth cultural identity: Vincent's Mitty-like fantasies utilize such contemporary movie heroes as Al Pacino and Lee Van Cleef (it was no wonder Robert Stigwood saw its big-screen potential). Cohn demonstrated that the 'reality' of the streets was a fabulous one indeed.

A way of life

The first year contained the thrill of newness, and the thrill of exclusivity – that all these people who might not even know each other, but who knew who each other were, had been brought together in the winter, in this little room, without having done a single thing to bring it about. They all knew each other without having to be introduced. They found a group of people who had danced with each other over the years, gone to the same parties, the same beaches on the same trains, yet, in some cases, never even nodded at each other. They were bound together by a common love of a certain kind of music, physical beauty, and style – all the things one shouldn't throw away an ounce of energy pursuing, and sometimes throw away a life pursuing.[83]

The subcultural theory that writers like Cohn did so much to inspire has enjoyed a vigorous career, and a shelf-life beyond, perhaps, its due. The instruments which initially appeared so incisive in accounting for the activities and practices of youth, like Cohn's tale of the 2001 Odyssey disco, have tarnished somewhat in the twenty years since they were first wielded. The academic language of stylistic identification, resistance and re-enforcement was codified by Birmingham University's Centre for Contemporary Cultural Studies (for example, such texts as Hall *et al.* (eds), *Resistance Through Rituals* and Dick Hebdige, *Subculture*) and proved highly influential: the term 'subculture' entered the wider non-academic lexicon. What became known as subcultural theory continued to ground the epistemology of a large part of the media with regard to its treatments of youth and music cultures, not least the style press who made it their credo during the 1980s. Subcultural constructions still constitute seductive rhetorical fictions by which contemporary youth cultures are pressed into service as re-enactments of familiar myths of identity. Indeed, the tenacity of subculture within the discourses of description and self-identification around dance cultures remains perhaps an obstacle in the development of its academic treatment.

In our various attempts to sort, record and analyse the dance music of the 1980s and 1990s, there are still vestiges of subculture theory. In his essay, 'Rave Culture: Living Dream or Living Death?', Simon Reynolds considers the notion of dance culture as 'a way of life'.[84] He ends his piece with a statement and a question: 'It's still the best thing we've got going in this country. But is it enough?'[85] The implied answer is, 'of course not'. Reynold's article is both an appeal and a riposte to the evocation of dance music and the attendant practices of youth activity and style as *culture*. The assertion that dance music and its associated culture represents *a way of life* – the notion of its sufficiency as a complete horizontal system that expands to fill one's entire social and personal space – may be an act of overburdening on a massive scale, but it is one which Reynolds and a number of other writers are still tempted to invoke.

The suggestion that youth subcultures, such as mod or punk, comprised complete and entire sets of activities, values and participatory codes feeds the nostalgia which permeates the treatment of contemporary cultural movements (forever looking for the new punk or the new rock 'n' roll). Though the single discrete dance *culture* as molarity was a mythical ideal even during the heyday of acid house, writers and participants still yearn nostalgically for a moment of primal unity, and oneness – a unity that is quickly revealed to be a valorization of the small scale, of the nascent dance forms and the lives, values and activities of a small élite vanguard of producers and consumers.

The appeal of subculture was built on the notion of *homology*.[86] The term identified what emergent cultural theorists saw as a symbolic equation in the experiences and values of particular youth groups and their acts of consumption – clothing and music choices primarily – which together comprised a stable semiotic code that could usefully be mapped. Parcels of identification, however transient or temporary, became pledges of allegiance: subcultural affiliation was *a way of life*. This concept was important to those attempting to construct a new academic field of engagement around the study of youth and its culture, from whose patterns of consumption and display could be obtained significant 'readings'. Yet, instead of enabling the investigation of connections between various acts of consumption and social activity among the young, the notion of homology was taken to imply that one social activity such as dance connoted one particular set of tastes, activities and values – an implication that flawed many of the accounts which took it to heart, as academics became obsessed with producing taxonomies of dubious value, sorting and labelling, freezing the cultural continuum for a little while and then moving on.[87]

Subculture's most well-known theorist, Dick Hebdige, quickly complicated the notion by emphasizing the importance of distinction. Hebdige asserted that, in terms of their comparative value at least, youth cultural homologies *were not* equivalent. In his book, *Subculture: The Meaning of Style*, he considered the thesis expounded by Stuart Hall and Paul Willis – that it is possible to account for youth cultural formations in terms of structural homologies between their styles, musics and values – and suggested that the radically disruptive aesthetic of punk destabilized such simple structural ascriptions. Hebdige stressed the polysemous nature of subcultural discourse: not all subcultures and signifying practices were the same. His key theoretical innovation was to apply the Kristevan notion of *signifying practice* to the study of everyday life. In his perception of style as a signifying practice, as an *active* intervention on the part of subcultural subjects rather than as a passive self-insertion into a fixed structure of meanings, he asserted the importance of subjective agency in the study of youth cultural practice.

Unfortunately, Hebdige used this critical mechanism to validate the vanguardist aesthetic of those who initiated and produced punk, at the expense of those who were to encounter and experience it through buying the records, or viewing the style as mediated on television and in the press:

> not ... all punks were equally aware of the disjunction between experi-
> ence and signification upon which the whole style was ultimately based.
> The style no doubt made sense for the first wave of self-conscious

innovators in a way which remained inaccessible to those who became punks after the subculture had surfaced and become publicised.[88]

As it happens, punk's most self-conscious innovator quite agreed.

> Interviewed in New Music News, [Malcolm] McLaren provocatively declares that buying the Pistols' records was never the point of punk. The interviewer suggests that playing the records was the only way that a 'sixteen-year-old kid in his room with nowhere to go' could feel involved.
> MC: 'That's sad, really sad. I would prefer him to play nothing. Kick the TV in, smash his mother....'[89]

The sixteen year old, pogoing around the bedroom, deciding to 'be a punk' after seeing the Sex Pistols on TV, was excluded by both Hebdige and McLaren from their narratives of what constituted, and what should be remembered as constituting, punk. Hebdige's subcultural theory did nothing to uncover his experience, the experience of all those whose identities have been shaped rather than merely expressed by music discourse. It validated the signifying practices of the few, while they were only those of the few, and implied that this value drained rapidly when these practices were adopted by a larger constituency. Punk bridled at the notion of becoming a youth movement and derided those who attempted to shape themselves to its blueprint. The élitism within such a culture did not entail scorning just the 'plastic punks', but scorning all those behind the times, those who were not party to their particular cultural dislocation or their sense of sardonic ennui. In its adherence to codes of exclusivity and value, punk appeared no different from previous youth cultures that invoked cachet by fiercely guarding their marginality.

A similar tendency was expressed by some of the progenitors of acid house as club culture ballooned. They displayed open contempt for the 'acid teds', the supposedly clueless hangers-on who bought into the icons of acid house too late: proudly parading their smiley T-shirts and bandannas long after the movers and shakers had donned crystals and white denim. The Liverpool band The Farm put a sheep in Kickers on the front cover of their single 'Stepping Stone', a dig at those who slavishly followed the styles of the savvy few. Many protagonists within acid house sought to continue a particular neo-modernist impetus, passed down through punk, which considers itself antipathetic to the 1980s 'Sunday supplement' notion of style. For such élites, lifestyle is mere consumption, tainted by capital, whereas their brand of style occupies a different ontological space. It is, they imply, more real – lived rather than bought off the shelf. They mock those whose experience was subsequent to theirs rather than simultaneous with it – those who came to be aware of acid house through its representation in the mainstream media, particularly by means of tabloid shock-horror stories,[90] rather than by word of mouth.

While the tabloids' often fantastic tales of debauchery and wasted youth in turn amused and annoyed, the fanzines, specialist music magazines and style magazines whose relationship with dance culture seemed more benign, were engaged in constructing and mediating the canons and categories, hits and misses, aesthetic categories and value judgements within this new sphere. Both music and style journalism had been influenced by the 'new journalism' as championed by such writers as Tom Wolfe and Nik Cohn, particularly its cultural romance with the street. Cohn's history of style, Today There Are No Gentlemen, concerned particularly with the authenticity of class, was highly influential in the development of both subcultural theory and style journalism.

> Ethnic styles were aimed principally at disguising the wearer's origins, their basic middle-classness, and perhaps that explains why Hippie dress has always seemed so half-baked by comparison with the equivalent working-class cults. The latter, whether Teds or Rockers or Greasers, Mods or Skinheads, have always been an expression of a real situation and identity, while Hippie has been a charade, an imitation of an American imitation. Working class uniform has said I am; Hippie has said I wish I was.[91]

This journalistic framework remained in place for twenty years. Throughout the 1980s magazines like The Face and i-D were subcultural outposts in journalism, gleefully plotting and inventing existing homologies, and later moving the goal posts – complicating, mocking or flatly denying they had ever existed. Their titles declared their alliance with the new politics of identity, and its history in the proud allegiance to 'style' in mod culture: the term 'face' was mod slang for a 'top boy', one of the élite, the stars of a scene. In the early 1980s they took their job as theorists and custodians of youth style and culture very seriously:

> Youth Culture now represents not a rebellion but a tradition, or rather a series of traditions that date back to the advent of the teenager and continue to grow along a compound continuum of action and reaction.
>
> Imagine a spiral that begins with a birth out of affluence and post-war liberation and moves through time propelled by its own mythology and its own contrariness and is affected by technology and whimsy and economics. It is cyclical, but the circle is never completed because it is also evolutionary, therefore patterns repeat but they are never quite the same.[92]

This intensity relaxed considerably as the decade progressed: after acid house, for a while at least, writers realized that the rabid generic multiplication of music styles which followed rave could not as easily be mapped on to an accompanying set of sartorial and lifestyle markers. Journalists began to play with their inheritance; although maintaining a fondness for the old model, they were far more ready to ridicule and undercut the categorizing and organizing processes which had formerly been considered sacrosanct.

By the late 1980s subculture had become history – its resonance among those who valued the authenticities of the past made it a useful marketing tool. Certainly, many of the progenitors and participants of acid house, and subsequent dance music cultures in the UK, have been happy to allude to, or affiliate themselves with the historical cachet of subcultural forms, from punk to northern soul. The Back to Basics club in Leeds distanced itself from the neo-psychedelic iconography of rave by using the punk graphics of Sex Pistols' designer Jamie Read, and reviving the 'Never Trust a Hippy' slogan; four years later Heavenly Records' Sunday Social club revived some of the stylistic markers (not to mention many of the records) of northern soul. The mythic resonance of the running battles which took place on the sea-fronts of southern English towns in 1964 is still held dear. In a recent interview, British DJ and record producer Justin Robertson joked about the lack of interest in subcultural affiliation in contemporary youth:

> I think young people have got really bland. There are no gangs anymore. When I was about twelve you had to be a mod or a punk or whatever – you don't see deep housers being chased down the road by drum 'n' bass kids.[93]

For those like Robertson, subcultural affiliation and hostility to those who do not adhere to your homological inclinations is a badge of commitment; a means of signifying a degree of passion and involvement. He implies here that there is no discrimination on the part of today's youth; discrimination as *affiliation*, as the active intervention in the formation of identity. We would suggest rather that the various acts of discrimination and identification made by audiences, fans and consumers are often more supple and malleable than the shorthand categories still used to categorize and encapsulate them. If simple homological ascriptions *ever* did justice to the complexities of practice, then they are even less certain today.

Critics have recently begun to reconsider the analysis of practices of distinction in popular cultures. In rejecting what he terms the 'depth-model' of subcultural theory, Steve Redhead acknowledges the effectivity of media discourses in delineating identification, engagement and disengagement and thereby constituting 'subcultures'.[94] Rather than viewing styles and music as the outward signs of a subculture or as the tools used by *bricoleur* members of those subcultures, Redhead problematizes the distinction between authentic and inauthentic (sub)cultural experience, disrupting the terms of that discourse which invalidates the experience of the 'passive' bedroom-bound sixteen year old.[95] Similarly, Sarah Thornton has pointed out that within the popular cultural arena hierarchies operate as rampantly as within 'higher' art cultures:

> Studies of popular culture have tended to embrace anthropological notions of culture as a *way of life* but have spurned art-oriented definitions

of culture which relate to *standards of excellence*. .... High culture is generally conceived in terms of aesthetic values, hierarchies and canons, while popular culture is portrayed as a curiously flat folk culture.[96]

In dance music and other popular cultural forms, distinction inheres not only in both the aesthetic and formal planes, but also in the modes by which we engage with aesthetic items and cultural practices: the way in which dance cultures are experienced and participated in. Authenticities are grounded on the evaluation of patterns of practice. It is clear that some participants within youth cultures such as dance, whether DJs, music producers, record buyers or clubbers, value a particular mode of engagement which they consider more *active* than other modes of popular cultural consumption. Like the members of many other such cultures, academia included, they privilege notions of commitment (regular attendance in a particular club, involvement in the promotion or organization of a night, DJing, the accumulation of a record collection), and the acquisition and display of knowledge. The implication is that just going out to dance is not sufficient in terms of cultural capital.

The existence of strata of distinction within the consideration of the agency and activity of those processing and using the objects and practices of popular culture has, Thornton suggests, only recently been acknowledged. Fan cultures always seem to create such hierarchies of fandom and commitment; differentiating between various groups and individuals by reference to the period of involvement, their displayed degree of knowledge, social connections and activities within their respective groups. Writers on cultural audiences and modes of reception have commented on the ways in which fans differentiate between active and passive modes of reception,[97] and discriminate between those who seem likeminded, who share the taste choices that are made all the time, who are in possession of sufficient cultural capital – and those who fail to make the grade and are sometimes excluded as a result.

This is another reason why certain protagonists in club cultures have been attracted to subcultural notions and neo-mod values. The nascent clubs of acid house were small, and the cultures that surrounded them were characterized by their love of the small-scale, of gangs, firms and fanzines. If they had an ideology it was one that simultaneously advocated individual agency ('do it yourself'), exclusivity ('do it with your mates') and hedonism ('do it without stopping for days on end'). Small clubs guaranteed exclusivity which in turn guaranteed control. These club cultures aestheticised what were originally economies of scale and bemoaned any kind of expansion or massification beyond a certain point; the irony was that at the same time these economies of scale fuelled the expansion of club culture in the UK after acid house, as popular demand outstripped supply.

As the popularity of the new club culture soared so new clubs opened across the country to cater for the demand. Those who initially 'did it themselves' represent only a small minority of today's club constituency, but the clubs and the attendant cultural development and discourses they inspired are widespread, beyond any localized sphere of influence. Club culture exploded in the UK after 1990. As Kodwo Eshun has pointed out, after acid house 'night swallows the everyday'.[98] The people who promoted and mediated the increasing popularity of dance music and clubbing did their best to offer so many options and opportunities to partake in the new nightlife that cultural theorists could be forgiven for thinking that every young Briton between the ages of 15 and 25 was out 'having it large'. Since 1990 licensing has been extended, clubs have offered longer opening hours, and a progression of all-dayers and all-nighters, festivals and bank holiday specials have created calendar periods within which the really dedicated can party for anything between 30 and 72 hours. Notions of deviance, or subcultural marginality are hard to maintain in the face of the post-rave explosion of UK club culture.

As we have suggested, subcultural authenticities were actually discursive constructs:

> 'Authentic' subcultures were produced by subcultural theories, not the other way around. In fact, popular music and 'deviant' youth styles never fitted together as harmoniously as some subcultural theory proclaimed.[99]

Despite the fact that detailed histories of supposed subcultural allegiance reveal their inconsistencies and contradictions rather than neat homologies, some cultural analysts have been more than happy to consider acid house as just another subculture, greeting it with the same social outrage that accompanied rock 'n' roll, mod and punk, or akin to an updated version of northern soul, with obscure black American electronically-generated dance music replacing obscure black American soul music. Such accounts fail to recognize the heterogeneity of acid house and rave. Over a three-year period (1988–91), dance culture in the UK managed various acts of semioclasm; the fissure of traditional and notionally discrete subcultural forms – an uneasy and drug-related syncretism of the most unlikely collections of youth: hoolies, hippies, crusties, casuals, and more besides. A quasi-utopian view of rave is suggested by the heterogeneous chemical alliance formed by its participants. In this respect, acid house and the rave movement it spawned represented instead what Deleuze has termed a *singularity*, an example of systemic self-organization when previously disconnected elements reach a point at which they begin to co-operate (or oscillate) as a larger molarity. In Deleuze's non-linear philosophical schema such agglomerations are difficult to predict and, importantly, are transient: they coalesce for a limited time and then disperse, leaving traces, affective ripples in the cultural waters.[100]

The musics which fed into acid house and the developing culture were various too; the heterogeneous sounds of the 'Balearic beat' which helped define it did not constitute a discrete musical genre, but an unholy mix of, among other things, hip hop, house, Mediterranean pop and indie rock. DJs' playlists temporarily situated highly disparate musics beside one another. Musical miscegenation reunited several of the dance forms that had emerged after disco, mixing American and European dance musics. Though house music was the dominant mode, the rapid proliferation of styles and sub-genres which followed in its wake, for a short time at least, kept dancefloors moving to a range of grooves. Moreover, style, the single most important determining quantity in the continuing Hebdigean project of youth subcultural analysis, was short-circuited by acid house, as Antonio Melechi has suggested:

> The more general problem for critics who would attempt to read youth and club culture was the emergence of a scene without stars and spectacle, gaze and identification. Those who sought to understand this culture in terms of a politics of usage and identity completely missed the point; the spaces which club culture occupied and transformed ... represent a fantasy of liberation, an escape from identity. A place where nobody is, but everybody belongs.[101]

Melechi here alludes to the inadequacy of employing a vocabulary familiar with a youth culture based around pop and rock music, to deal with a cultural manifestation which eluded concerted attempts at homology. The initial utilitarian preference for baggy or unshapely clothing that allowed comfortable dancing when on drugs, destabilized the predominance of the 'gaze', both in the culture of acid house and of those who wished to analyse it.

Acid house, despite its small-scale beginnings in urban clubs, also ended up destabilizing the axis between subcultural narratives of authenticity and metropolitan space. The metropolitan has always featured strongly in discussions of popular music cultures: Iain Chambers, in his seminal book *Urban Rhythms*, famously described the city as pop's 'fundamental stage' and as 'the place of the contemporary imagination'.[102] As one of the sites where white people first experienced specifically black musical forms, the city street represents an important location within popular culture and is the milieu to which its products consistently refer. This formulation was in part an ironic re-territorialization of literary modernism with its thematization of the urban as the location of the future-in-the-present. Many intellectuals, from anthropologists to style journalists, have constructed themselves as *flâneurs*, moving through the streets, describing and evaluating the varied forms and fashions which they encounter.

There are problems with the continual invocation of the city within accounts of pop music and youth cultural activity: namely in its perceived 'authenticity' and the accompanying fact that this discourse almost inevitably results in bolstering the political and cultural monopoly of the capital city, traditionally the home of the cultural élite. When metropolitanism talks of the 'city', it does not include Birmingham, Leeds or Cardiff: it means London. Pop music culture in Britain has traditionally been dominated by London, home to the vast bulk of the record industry and the media. London is the place where musicians from the provinces, or from Scotland, Wales or Northern Ireland, would come to further their careers.

Though many of its protagonists commuted in from the suburbs of South London, Malcom McLaren's punk made the King's Road, the river Thames and Oxford Street the main sites of its expectorations. The bullish cultural mood that is prevalent in the late 1990s in Britain has been refracted through the capital city, rather than through an increasingly regional United Kingdom, with the dusting down of the cringe-making phrase 'swinging London' invoking the 1960s once more.[103]

What marked out acid house, and the wider rave movement which followed it, was its rapid expansion beyond the confines of a metropolitan 'underground' club culture into many other locations and spaces formerly occupied by more familiar pop and rock forms. Historians of acid house, like Matthew Collin, identify a history of British dance musics that has not been located exclusively in metropolitan space; and neither has the capital monopolized the development and propagation of dance musics. It is sometimes overlooked that London was not the sole originary location for house music's dissemination within the UK. The cultural exchange between black America and young Britain showed no marked respect for the capital – indeed many London DJs ignored the house records that were gaining in popularity in clubs in Nottingham and Manchester, preferring instead to play slower soul music.[104] Acid house burgeoned in the north-west of England as it did in the south-east, quickly spreading to Yorkshire, Scotland and the Midlands, tumbling out of clubs and warehouses into the peripheral, orbital spaces around cities and towns. The styles and generic developments which have followed have never been slaves to the capital, but have looked both nearer and farther: Sheffield, Bristol, Paris, Detroit, and Kingston, Jamaica.

The schism between suburban/rural rave and urban clubbing is analogous with the divide between the town and the country, or the capital and the provinces. As Eshun describes, rave severed itself from the city:

> they [ravers] regarded urban clubbing as another paragraph of the same old subcultural pop narrative: trads, teds, mods, rockers, hippies, punks, clubbers. They scathingly argued that clubs were segregationist, the unwitting dupes of the establishment. Ravers saw themselves as the first ever trans-youth unity movement ... such London clubs as Boys Own, still aristos at heart, accused Rave of encouraging and exploiting a mass uniformity on a scale never before seen in England.[105]

Between 1989 and 1992 hundreds of raves and parties took place well beyond the suburbs, into rural England and Scotland. When thousands of ravers danced beneath the shifting tinctures of the open sky, what began as American urban dance musics became entangled within a skein of pastoral imagery (captured by records like The Beloved's 'The Sun Rising'). The cover of The KLF's album Chill Out showed a gentle rural landscape dotted with sheep, a small joke (at the expense of Pink Floyd) which marked the striking aesthetic shift in the traditional surroundings of youth culture.

Rave went some way to destabilizing the perceived axis between urban location and authenticity, or at least it managed to validate new locations for youth music cultures. The authenticities of urban locale were (and are) still prevalent in the discourse around dance, though, in its fondness for originary location for example. The metropolitan prefix attributed to the various styles of black American musics – Chicago house, New York garage, Detroit techno – indicated that they were still discursively tied to notions of urban authenticity. Certain journalists were quick to apply this trope to home-grown music when they got the chance. When breakbeat techno collided with Jamaican ragga, the resultant musical offspring, jungle, provided just such an opportunity. Excited at a radical new 'home-grown' sound, the press began to herald the UK's first 'authentic' urban music culture. Its origins were of course more complex: 'hardcore', a frenetic breakbeat-driven product of the suburban rave movement, taken up in combination with the reggae-derived dance forms of the Afro-Caribbean. Its producers, some of whom were from a range of urban centres such as Bristol, Birmingham and London, were black and white. But the act of critical placement and preferment within an urban culture failed to acknowledge a partially suburban history in favour of a familiar authentication of the 'street'. Faced with an exciting new musical combination some middle-class journalists reverted to old cultural romanticisms.[106]

Ten years on, contemporary manifestations of rave identify more with counter-culture derived rock festivals like Glastonbury, where we began this chapter. Autonomous dance festivals (along with the dance areas linked to established music festivals) reflected both the initial success, and the ultimate demise of rave as 'one' music. Promoters like Paul Shurey of Universe had made their living out of breakbeat and techno parties in the suburbs and the provinces: outside the subcultural squabbles of city clubbing. They quickly realized that the only means by which their activities could expand, as the generic fissures in post-rave dance music continued, was to promote larger scale, across the board events. The first dance festival of this type was billed as a 'gathering of the dance tribes'. The pastoral imagery of rave was transmuted into an appeal to the exotic Other of Native America, the belief in dance as ecstatic ritual and spiritual activity, the name playing on the cultural implication of 'primitivism' attributed to certain pop music forms and the youth cultures that adhere to them.

Tribal Gathering invoked the imagery of subcultural difference – the anthropological accounting for dance cultures as primitive/immature – while representing an admission that acts of taste discrimination within youth music culture no longer involved internecine conflict. Whereas the ideology of tribal identity would appear to be one of *essential* difference – translated into the notion that you listen to one kind of music and that makes you what you are – the Gathering actually represented an admission that these post-rave taste choices did not equal a way of life. This is while maintaining a central tenet of rave ideology – the residual belief in the transcendence of difference in the act of coming together to dance *en masse*. In fact, Tribal Gathering's festival format offered a great range of delights, a smorgasbord of musical options, participation in which required no subcultural commitment, no passport, code word or correct vintage of trainer: all one needed to do was to purchase a ticket from a record shop or over the phone. Once inside the venue the punter could choose whether to listen to drum 'n' bass, the techno of America or Europe, epic house, big beat or whatever else was on offer.

Tribal Gathering, like rave before it, and disco before that, recognized that

> Dance involves the loss of contact with one's own earthy root (or 'culture') and an ecstatic movement outward towards difference and alterity – or at least community. This is the postmodern condition in its most basic aspect; the orientation toward alterity ... it is not any final product which is of major concern but the seduction of the dance itself, its ability to seduce one into the loss of one's own identity or self-hood.[107]

Twelve years after the advent of house we are presented with the opportunity of an other Saturday night: the possibility of alterity replacing the yearning for novelty. The insatiable appetite for the new at the heart of much pop discourse, the need for 'fresh sensation, another explosion'[108] – a modernist desire for perpetual revolution – disregards the manner in which popular cultures have seemed to coalesce and to reconstitute themselves in the information age. Theories of the postmodern suggest that we address this cultural proliferation and commixture, rather than always waiting for the next phase or the new wave, as Iain Chambers elegantly affirmed before house was even born:

> The co-presence in the late 1970s of virtually all the most important musical styles that have gone into the making of British pop ... marks the practical end of any attempt to view pop as the linear movement of new, more complex, musical forms replacing and obliterating older, simpler ones. This idea, once central to progressive music, is now lost among the multiple directions of a heterogeneous present.[109]

If we consider the many forms which currently make up the 1990s dance scene – disco, old-school hip hop, house, techno, breakbeat, drum 'n' bass – we can recognize the simultaneous co-existence of all the musics which have occupied the dancefloors of the last twenty-five years. Dance music, like rock 'n' roll before it, has not been concluded or 'sorted', despite all the discursive activity which has occurred in the late 1990s, and the continuing desire to create narratives of musical and popular cultural progress; rather it has bifurcated, multiplying its enormous potential for affect.

Some intellectual accounts and discourses around dance and youth music cultures refuse, however, to give up their teleologies, their diagnoses of cultural vitality and decline. They should acknowledge that there might not be – or have ever been – a kernel of 'authentic' truth or identity at the heart of dance; that instead there might be a space, an absence, an otherness, and that the opening up of this space, beyond the subject, for however transient a moment, might be all that its participants require. In terms of it being 'a way of life', dance music and its culture can be something in which we participate and which participates in us; perhaps only for six months, a couple of years, or periodically for twenty years or more. This experience, while representing an epiphany for some, for others forms just another option within a wide range of choices. Like other popular and communal cultures it has been, and will continue to be, intensely vital, but we should not assert that it has necessarily to be the central pillar of any existence, nor maintain that to achieve cultural validity leisure must be transformed into sacrament.

Fourteen years ago Chambers wrote that 'music is not an "escape" from "reality", but an interrogative exploration of its organising categories'.[110] In this sense dance music cultures have not merely comprised strategies for asserting identity, but means of deliciously slipping through the gaps in preordained identities, into the temporary occupation of new zones of experience which leave the participant revivified and imperceptibly altered. As we have suggested in this chapter, we believe the same should be true of the words woven around them.

Notes

1 Quoted in Pascal Bussy, *Kraftwerk: Man Machine and Music*, (Wembley, S.A.F., 1993), p. 19.
2 NME, 22 April 1978, p. 20.
3 The song can be found on Pulp's album *Different Class*, Island Records, 1995.
4 *The Observer*, Preview magazine, 4 February 1996, p. 9.
5 Matthew Collin, with contributions by John Godfrey, *Altered State: The Story of Ecstasy Culture and Acid House* (London, Serpent's Tail, 1997), p. 297.
6 An estimate in the *Guardian* added the number of deaths reported in the media during 1995 to official figures up to 1994, and gave the total as sixty. 'Sorted or distorted?', the *Guardian*, Friday Review, 26 January 1996, p. 2. Figures such as these are always a matter for conjecture, as the ways in which deaths are linked to Ecstasy use vary considerably; from very rare allergic reactions (such as that which killed Clare Leighton, a sixteen year old who died at the Haçienda in 1989), to more common cases of heat stroke or water intoxication, and even accidents with vehicles while under the influence of the drug.
7 In Steve Redhead *et al.* (eds), *The Clubcultures Reader* (Oxford, Blackwell. 1997), pp. 102–11.
8 Greil Marcus, 'Note on the Life & Death and Incandescent Banality of Rock 'n' Roll', *Esquire*, August 1992; reprinted in Hanif Kureishi and Jon Savage (eds), *The Faber Book of Pop* (London, Faber, 1996), pp. 739–52.
9 Ibid., p. 741.
10 Reynolds, 'Death of Rave', in Redhead *et al.* (eds), *The Clubcultures Reader*, p. 102.
11 Richard Leppert, *The Sight of Sound: Music, Representation and the History of the Body* (Berkeley, University of California Press), p. 41.
12 Collin, *Altered State*, p. 8.
13 Ibid., p. 124. Collin points out that it has as much to do with changes in media perception of the game accompanying its increasing gentrification.

14 In a review of a cover of 'Last Night a DJ Saved My Life', Barron wrote that the 'lifestyle transformation' of acid house was bound to have 'political repurcussions': 'I'm told that Ecstasy is virtually impossible to get hold of in Northern Ireland. Why? Perhaps because if the Prods and the Catholics got loved-up the stalemate of sectarian violence would go all wobbly and there are too many people with a vested interest in keeping the strife going.' 'Singles', NME, 30 June 1990, p.14.

15 Nicholas Saunders, E For Ecstasy (London, Nicholas Saunders, 1993), p. 38.

16 As we consider in Chapter 7, the political relevance of such occurrences as rave was not wholly contained in the wilder claims as to the benefits of E or the fleeting utopianism that accompanied its early stages.

17 Collin, Altered State, p. 8.

18 John Macready, in Jon Savage (ed.), The Hacienda Must Be Built (London, International Music Publications, 1992), p. 61.

19 Fierce Dancing: Adventures in the Underground (London, Faber & Faber, 1995).

20 Ibid., p. 33.

21 Sadie Plant, The Most Radical Gesture: The Situationist International in the Postmodern Age (London, Routledge, 1992), p. 147.

22 'Intellectuals and Power', in Donald F. Bouchard (ed.), Language, Counter-Memory, Practice: Selected Interviews and Essays (Oxford, Blackwell, 1977), p. 207.

23 Postmodern Times, a one-day conference held at London's City University, 1 July 1995. Gilroy spoke on a panel titled, 'Rap, Race and Postmodernity'.

24 Andrew Ward, 'Dancing Around Meaning', in Helen Thomas (ed.), Dance in the City (Basingstoke, Macmillan, 1997), pp. 3–20.

25 Ibid., p. 7. Ward is quoting R. Burt in The Male Dancer: Bodies, Spectacle, Sexualities (London, Routledge, 1995), p. 44.

26 See Andrew Ross, No Respect: Intellectuals and Popular Culture (London, Routledge, 1989), p. 5.

27 H.B. Gilmour, Saturday Night Fever (New York, Bantam Books, 1977), p. 1.

28 See Gordon Burn's introduction in Nik Cohn, Ball the Wall: Nik Cohn in the Age of Rock (London, Picador, 1989), p. xvi.

29 New York magazine, 7 June 1976. Reprinted in Cohn, Ball the Wall, pp. 321–42.

30 Albert Goldman, Disco (New York, Hawthorn, 1978), p. 154.

31 'A band appeared in blue denim suits embossed with silver studding. Blacks from Crown Heights, who played as loudly and as badly as anyone possibly could, grinning, sweating, stomping', Cohn, Ball the Wall, p. 329.

32 Holleran, Dancer from the Dance (London, Jonathan Cape, 1979).

33 'There were girls. But they were not Faces, not truly. Sometimes, if a girl got lucky, a Face might choose her from the crowd and raise her to be his steady, whom he might one day marry. But that was rare. In general the female function was to be available', Cohn, Ball the Wall, p. 327.

34 Ibid., pp. 326–7.

35 Ibid.

36 Disco-derived dance forms could still be considered to maintain this homosociality, with its emphasis on bodily discpline. See Walter Hughes, 'In the Empire of the Beat', in Andrew Ross and Tricia Rose (eds), Microphone Fiends: Youth Music and Youth Culture (London, Routledge, 1994), pp. 147–57.

37 Cohn, Ball the Wall, p. 326.

38 Ibid.

39 Ibid.

40 Ibid., p. 338.

41 Paramount Pictures, 1977, directed by John Badham, screenplay by Norman Wexler, based on a story by Nik Cohn.

42 Kureishi and Savage (eds), *The Faber Book of Pop*, p. 378.
43 Hanson, *Disco Fever*, p. 166.
44 Directed by Gene Kelly and Stanley Donen, 1949.
45 '[*Saturday Night Fever*] speaks the truth despite itself. It unwittingly demonstrates how totally fulfilling it is to dance alone', Goldman, *Disco*, p. 11.
46 Cohn, *Ball theWall*, p. 345.
47 See Jack Villari and Kathleen Sims, *The Official Guide to Disco Dance Steps* (London, Hamlyn, 1979); and Carter Lovisone, *The Disco Hustle*, (NewYork, Sterling, 1979).
48 Michel Serres asserts that 'dance has no memory – nowhere is it printed', *Genesis*, trans. Genvieve James and James Nielson (Michigan, University of Michigan Press, 1995), p. 47.
49 Angela McRobbie has said that 'dance seems to retain at its centre a solid resistance to analysis', 'Dance and Social Fantasy', in Angela McRobbie and Mica Nava (eds), *Gender and Generation* (London, Macmillan, 1984), p. 131.
50 This image is taken from Michel Serres' essay on geometry and the development of western mathematical knowledge, 'Mathematics and Philosophy: What Thales Saw...', in Josué V. Harari and David F. Bell (eds), *Hermes: Literature, Science, Philosophy* (Baltimore, John Hopkins University Press, 1982), pp. 84–97.
51 'Dance, Gender and Culture', in Helen Thomas (ed.), *Dance, Gender and Culture* (London, Macmillan, 1993), p. 13.
52 Ibid., p. 12.
53 See Villari and Sims, *The Official Guide*; and Lovisone, *The Disco Hustle*.
54 Goldman, *Disco*, p. 11.
55 Ibid., p. 13.
56 Lovisone, *The Disco Hustle*, p. 6.
57 Paul Spencer, 'Interpretations of Dance in Anthropology', in Spencer (ed.), *Society and the Dance* (Cambridge, Cambridge University Press, 1985), p. 1.
58 Ibid., pp. 1–4.
59 Ibid., p. 6.
60 ' "Saturday Night Fever': An ethnography of disco dancing', in Thomas (ed.), *Dance, Gender and Culture* (London, Macmillan, 1993), pp. 112–8.
61 'Dancing in the Dark: Rationalism and the Neglect of Social Dance', in Thomas (ed.), *Dance, Gender and Culture*, pp. 16–33.
62 Ibid., p. 28.
63 Ward, 'Dancing Around Meaning', p. 18.
64 Hanson, *Disco Fever*, pp. 8–9.
65 Cohn, *Ball theWall*, p. 333.
66 Wayne Anthony, *Class of '88* (London, Virgin, 1998).
67 For a thorough survey of this field and its connections with wider debates around the study of popular culture, see Ken Gelder and Sarah Thornton (eds), *The Subcultures Reader* (London, Routledge, 1997).
68 This interlude is based on an article Thornton originally wrote for *New Statesman and Society*. 'Club Class', *New Statesman and Society*, 16 November 1990.
69 Sarah Thornton, *Club Cultures: Music, Media and Subcultural Capital* (Cambridge, Polity Press, 1995), p. 89.
70 Ibid., p. 92.
71 'I see how club organisers, DJs and journalists – the professional clubbers – get lost within the excesses and irresponsibilities of youth', ibid., p. 91.
72 Ibid., p. 2.
73 Dick Hebdige, *Subculture:The Meaning of Style* (London, Methuen, 1979).
74 Steve Connor, *Postmodernist Culture: An Introduction to Theories of the Contemporary* (Oxford, Blackwell, 1989), p. 196.

75 Cohn, *Ball the Wall*, p. 342.
76 'I didn't learn much … I made a lousy interviewer: I knew nothing about this world, and it showed. Quite literally, I didn't speak the language…. So I faked it. I conjured up the story of the figure in the doorway, and named him Vincent … I wrote it all up. And presented it as fact', *New York* Magazine, 8 December 1997, p. 36.
77 We first became aware of it from three postings on Entertaiment News websites.
78 Cohn, *Ball the Wall*.
79 Ibid., p. xvi.
80 Ibid., pp. 383–98.
81 Ibid., p. 398.
82 See Goldman, *Disco*, p. 153.
83 Andrew Holleran, *Dancer From the Dance* (London, Jonathan Cape, 1979), p. 38.
84 Reynolds, 'Rave Culture', pp. 102–11.
85 Ibid., p. 111.
86 See Lucien Goldmann, *Towards a Sociology of the Novel*, trans. Alan Sheridan (London, Tavistock Publications, 1975); and Paul Willis, *Profane Culture* (London, Routledge, 1978).
87 See Brian Longhurst, *Popular Music and Society* (Cambridge, Polity, 1995), pp. 210–25.
88 Hebdige, *Subculture*, p. 122.
89 Simon Reynolds and Joy Press, *The Sex Revolts* (London, Serpent's Tail, 1995), p. 39.
90 It was certainly the case that tabloid coverage, hysterical and tempting in turns, fuelled the rapid career of the rave movement from 1988–90, as Jane Bussman points out: 'In autumn 1988, the tabloids announced a drugs for drugs' sake free-for-all: just turn up and pop a pill. Prompt and keen as only the young can be, a million British kids did what they were told and trooped out to take drugs in the places where they were told they could get them … the real Mr Big of acid house was Rupert Murdoch.' (Bussman, *Once in a Lifetime: The Crazy Days of Acid House and Afterwards* [London, Virgin, 1998], p. 33). For more on the tabloid mediation of Acid House, see Steve Redhead and Antonio Melechi, 'The Fall of the Acid Reign', *New Statesman and Society*, 23 December 1988.
91 Cohn, 'Today There Are No Gentlemen', *Ball the Wall*, p. 307.
92 Robert Elms, 'Hard Times', *The Face* September 1982, in Kureishi and Savage (eds), *The Faber Book of Pop*, p. 547.
93 'The Second Coming of Lionrock', *DJ* magazine no. 10, vol. 2, 14–27 March 1998, p. 48.
94 Redhead (ed.), *Rave Off: Politics and Deviance in Contemporary Youth Culture* (Aldershot, Avebury, 1993), p. 23.
95 Angela McRobbie has discussed the sexism implicit in this discourse, pointing out that for younger girls most subcultural activity revolves around a culture of the bedroom. See 'Settling Accounts with Subcultures', in Simon Frith and Andrew Goodwin (eds), *On Record: Rock, Pop and the Written Word* (London, Routledge, 1990), p. 77.
96 Thornton, *Club Cultures*, p. 8.
97 See, for example, Henry Jenkins, ' "Strangers No More, We Sing" Filking and the Social Construction of the Science Fiction Fan Community', in Lewis, *The Adoring Audience*, pp. 208–36.
98 Kodwo Eshun, 'Outing the In-Crowd', in Kureishi and Savage (eds), *The Faber Book of Pop*, p. 737.
99 Steve Redhead, *The End of the Century Party: Youth and Pop Towards 2000* (Manchester, Manchester University Press, 1990), p. 25.
100 See Manuel de Landa, *War in the Age of Intelligent Machines* (New York, Zone, 1991).
101 Antonio Melechi, 'The Ecstasy of Disappearance', in Redhead (ed.), *Rave Off*, p. 37.

102 Iain Chambers, *Urban Rhythms: Pop Music and Popular Culture* (London, Macmillan, 1985), p. 210.
103 See Jeremy Gilbert, 'Blurred Vision: Pop, Populism and Politics', in Perryman & Coddington (eds), *The Modernisers' Dilemma* (London, Lawrence & Wishart, 1998), pp. 75–90.
104 In 1989 Haçienda DJ Mike Pickering (as T-Coy) made a record called 'North', partly to remind London DJs that they had initially 'missed the boat on house'. 'Get on the Mike', *NME* 7 January 1989, p. 20.
105 Eshun, 'Outing the In-crowd', in Kureishi and Savage (eds), *The Faber Book of Pop*, p. 738.
106 See David Bennun, 'Judge Dread', *Melody Maker* 5 August 1995, pp. 28–30.
107 Thomas Docherty, *After Theory* (London, Routledge, 1990), p. 6.
108 Cohn, *Ball the Wall*, p. 339.
109 Chambers, *Urban Rhythms*, p. 194.
110 Ibid., p. 209.

2

MUSIC, MEANING AND PLEASURE

From Plato to disco

Pleasure means not having to think about anything, to forget suffering even when it is shown. Basically it is helplessness. It is flight; not as it is asserted, flight from a wretched reality, but from the last remaining thought of resistance. The liberation of which amusement promises is freedom from thought and from negation.

Adorno and Horkheimer, 'The Culture Industry'[1]

'Dance music' is an odd, if now ubiquitous phrase. When we talk about dance music we tend not to be referring to the waltz, or to jive or ceilidh music, or to rock, despite the fact that all of these music genres are, or have their origins in, forms intended mainly for dancing to. So what is it exactly that defines those forms of music usually grouped under the heading 'dance'? What is it that makes house, techno and their variants so specific and unique? Perhaps the most obvious answer is that these forms stand out in the history of recorded 'popular' music in that they eschew verbal meaning. Most house and techno tracks have no lyrics. Vocal samples are used as pieces of sound rather than as meaningful phrases. The fact that dance music is a new form of popular *instrumental* music is what makes it so striking: it is a music which is not based on songs.

Western popular music traditionally consists of songs, with a strong emphasis on the importance of melody combined (almost invariably) with romantic lyrics. Even disco, with its strong melodies and romantic themes, failed to break radically with these formal conventions. By the same token, these musics emphasize their particular status as musics to dance to: in house and techno, the beat has become all important in a way never before seen in western music.

There are reasons why all of this matters, reasons which are not confined to the recent history of disco and its musical progeny. There are reasons why instrumental popular musics face greater resistance from powerful institutions than song-based forms. There are reasons why rock remains the dominant strand of popular music despite the influx of revolutionary dance music, and these reasons are not only to do with the conservative tastes of corporate executives. There are reasons why the British state appears to be more hostile to contemporary dance culture than to any previous form of music culture, reasons which do not simply have to do with drugs. This chapter will look at some of those reasons by examining the history of ideas behind them. In particular we will look at the ways in which music for dancing to – which does not claim to be much else, which has a beat but no lyrics – constitutes a threat to the central values of western culture. In order to do so, we need to consider in some detail the ways in which we think about music in general, and what other ways there might be to think about it.

Words and music

What is music? In one respect, this is a contentious question. Exactly what forms of organized sound constitute 'music' will always depend on the cultural contexts we inhabit, and even when these are taken into account there can never be one simple answer. So, to rephrase the question: how does music work? What is the nature of music's effects? And how are those effects achieved? Most attempts to formulate an answer to these questions, from any number of philosophical schools – from ancient times up until the present day – concern themselves one way or another with the problem of distinguishing between and accounting for two different types of effect which music can have. On the one hand, music can be understood as possessing or producing *meanings*.[2] Some attempts to understand the way in which music works theorize its effects entirely in terms of meaning; they ask what the meanings of particular pieces of music are to particular people at particular times, and how those meanings are constructed. On the other hand, as well as having *meanings*, music can be thought of as producing *affects*, which cannot be explained in terms of meaning. In other words, music can affect us in ways that are not dependent on us understanding something, or manipulating verbal concepts, or being able to represent accurately those experiences through language.[3] It is this non-verbal aspect of music's effectivity which has given rise to its strange status in western thought.

It's notable that western music tradition has its origins in the same place as western philosophy: ancient Greece. This is where the beginnings of western musical notation and European models of harmony and melody are found. At the same time, we can see in early philosophy the beginning of the history of anxieties over the relationship between meaning and affect. The problematic nature of their relationship is cause for concern in one of the founding texts of western philosophy, Plato's *Republic*. Within it we find an approach to music which is at once aware of and frightened by its peculiar power. Plato regards music's ability to induce apparently direct affects with deep suspicion, and we can see from the words he places in the mouth of his mentor, Socrates, the first manifestation of a mistrust of music's apparent ability to subvert ordered meaning which continues to the present day. Plato was suspicious enough of *all* types of affect – as well as all forms of representation – to portray Socrates as wanting most forms of music banned from his ideal Republic. In this perfect city, ruled by a caste of philosopher-kings, most forms of music would simply be disallowed. Modes suitable for the passionate intensity of mourning would be rejected: 'even women, if they are respectable, have no use for them, let alone men',[4] as would be the 'relaxing ones' inclined to encourage 'drunkenness, softness or idleness'.[5] Socrates wants only simple, conservative music which will encourage sobriety, military courage and self-discipline. Having rejected all music apart from that which 'will best represent sound courage and moderation', Socrates goes on to dismiss all musical forms characterized by complex rhythms and to make redundant the manufacturers of all musical instruments 'of many strings or wide range'.[6]

There are a number of issues here, but most obviously we can see that music is specifically devalued for Plato/Socrates when it is associated with physical pleasure or intoxication. Already we see emerging the idea that musics associated with revelry, with physical luxuriance, with the pleasures of the body, are inherently bad. Socrates is not satisfied here, however. After he has prescribed the only acceptable range of musical forms, he then demands that they must only be deployed in such a way as to conform to the dictates of verbal meaning. Music, Socrates declares, must be composed so as to fit words; words cannot be composed to fit music, and the idea of purely instrumental music is not even referred to. 'We shall then adapt the beat and tune to the appropriate words, and not the words to the beat and tune.'[7]

This may seem like a slight enough gesture, but as we shall see, it is one which continues to be replicated in the discourses of western culture up to the present time. Not only are most forms of music banned altogether from the philosophers' Republic, but even in the case of 'good' forms of music which Socrates wants to encourage, it is demanded that music's capacity for affect be subjugated to the demands of linguistic meaning. In fact, music itself – as opposed to music which exists as a mere accompaniment to words – is treated with the utmost suspicion. Unless it is tied down by words, given a fixed and ordered meaning by language, music is viewed as an inherently dangerous, destabilizing force. As we will see, this is not a view limited to one old man in ancient Athens.

If Plato's work traditionally marks the birth of western philosophy, then modern philosophy's most significant landmark remains the moment of the Enlightenment, at the end of the eighteenth century. Here once again, we find key figures expressing quite similar views on the nature and status of music.

Jean-Jacques Rousseau in his *Essay on the Origins of Language*, provides an interesting discussion of the nature of music, which both looks to earlier accounts and sets the terms for the dominant discourse which was soon to emerge. What is particularly interesting is that Rousseau offers an account of the nature of music based on a specific definition of the nature of *sound*.

> The beauty of sound is natural and the effect purely physical. It derives from the diverse particles of air that are set in motion by the sonorous body and its aliquots – possibly to infinity.[8]

However, Rousseau distinguishes between music and mere sound, and argues that music only acquires value when it *transcends* sound's physicality:

The sounds of a melody do not only act on us as sounds but as signs of our affections and feelings. Thus do sounds excite in us the emotions which they express and which we recognise.[9]

So Rousseau explicitly distinguishes between music as representation, as mental experience, and as something experienced at the level of the body. He distinguishes, that is, between music as affect and music as a source of meaning, and he specifically identifies the former with bodily pleasure, in a very similar way to Plato. This idea was developed further by the most important philosopher of the Enlightenment, Immanuel Kant.

In Kant's reflections on the aesthetic status of music, we find Rousseau's terms reproduced and refined. Kant is concerned with the problem of how far music can be said to belong to his prized aesthetic category, the 'beautiful',[10] and how far it must be understood as having the much inferior status of the merely 'pleasurable'. The former, more privileged description Kant attributes only to the 'fine arts'; those which are appreciated through reflective judgement rather than mere sense experience. The 'pleasurable' are those arts with merely physical effects. Exemplary among these for Kant is the practice of

banquet *Tafelmusik*, an odd convention which is supposed to entertain by providing a pleasant accompaniment to put the guests in a cheerful mood, encouraging relaxed conversation between neighbours at table without requiring them to devote any attention to the music itself.[11]

Kant raises an important issue here; for him, the relative status of music as an art object is a question not just of its nature in itself, but of what we do with it. As long as music exists largely to make us feel good – its sonorous textures caressing our bodies but not our intellects – rather than to provide us with an object of rational contemplation, it can never aspire to his category of the beautiful. It is remarkable how consistent Kant is with Plato, who wrote thousands of years before him. Both writers display a distinct uneasiness about music in general, and are particularly quick to marginalize forms of music associated with idle pleasure and physical sensation. Kant may not want to ban them, but he is keen that they should not be valued as highly as the more 'rational' artefacts of fine art. The implication for Kant's comments, like Rousseau's, is that music which has identifiable and analysable meanings is more acceptable than music which merely affects us on a level inaccessible to language.

Thus the philosophical tradition seems remarkably consistent in its attitudes to music. However, we can only get a true sense of how deeply ingrained these ideas are in western discourse on music if we consider the extent to which they were shared by someone who might normally have been thought to stand radically apart from this tradition. Theodor Adorno was one of the most eminent Marxist cultural critics of the twentieth century, and the one to write most extensively on music. More importantly perhaps, he was one of the first thinkers of the twentieth century to explicitly question the value of the Enlightenment project[12] with which Kant – and, in a somewhat paradoxical manner, Rousseau – has always been associated. And yet in his writings on music there is a fundamental similarity with the ideas of Plato, Kant and Rousseau.

Adorno's classic essays on Schoenberg and Stravinsky set out to argue for the importance of the project of Schoenberg's serial music, partly in terms of its authenticity as the continuation of a certain critical tradition going back at least to Beethoven and German Idealist philosophy, and partly in terms of its challenge to the conservative terms of the bourgeois musical discourse of the early twentieth century. While Adorno makes many incisive points concerning the radical potential of modernist music, while he pursues a relentless critical opposition to the bourgeois music discourse of his day, in key ways he actually replicates the terms of that dominant discourse. The most telling passage for our purposes is that wherein Adorno insists that:

> the objective consequence of the basic musical concept, which alone lends dignity to good music, has always demanded alert control via the subjective compositional conscience. The cultivation of such logical consequence, at the expense of passive perception of sensual sound, alone defines the stature of this perception, in contrast to mere 'culinary enjoyment'.[13]

Here, Adorno replicates precisely the terms shared by Rousseau and Kant, his derided 'mere "culinary enjoyment"' equating to Kant's 'pleasure rather than ... beauty' and Rousseau's 'sounds only considered as having effects on the nerves'. In all cases aesthetic cognition is distinguished from and declared superior to mere sensory pleasure.

Adorno does not simplistically perpetuate the discourse of bourgeois music. In valorizing a complete break with conventional tonality, in advocating a return to the polyphonic techniques of counterpoint, he engages in a critical project which is still met with violent reactions by those with strong investments in conservative musical discourses: many upholders of the great classical tradition still abhor the music which he advocated. However, on the issues that concern us here, Adorno is firmly located within the dominant western tradition.

We can see, then, that the western tradition has tended to construct and discuss music in largely coherent and consistent terms, and that that tradition is larger and longer than the accepted canon of philosophy (to which nether Rousseau nor Adorno can be said to belong in any unproblematic sense). Music is understood by this tradition as being problematic in its capacity to affect us in ways which seem to bypass the acceptable channels of language, reason and contemplation. In particular, it is music's apparent physicality, its status as a source of physical pleasure, which is problematic. By the same token, this tradition tends to demand of music that it – as far as possible – be meaningful, that even where it does not have words, it should offer itself up as an object of intellectual contemplation such as is likely to generate much meaningful discourse. Even those forms of modernist music which have aspired to pure abstraction (in particular the tradition of serial music), have been written with an emphasis on complexity and a deliberate intellectualism which foregrounds the music's status as objects of rational contemplation rather than as a source of physical pleasure.

Around the end of the eighteenth century and the beginning of the nineteenth century, however, German philosophy (the central strand of European philosophy of the last two centuries) radically reconsidered the status of music. Philosophers from Schopenhauer onwards began to take a very different view of music to their predecessors. Indeed, Schopenhauer writes that 'the composer reveals the innermost essence of the world'.[14] In his detailed study of nineteenth-century German aesthetics, Andrew Bowie describes this moment:

> Music comes to be seen by key nineteenth-century German thinkers as the highest form of art. For this to be the case a substantial shift in the dominant view of music has to take place. The significance of this has philosophical resonances which we are still feeling. For reasons both to do with developments in music, and with developments in philosophy, music which is not accompanied by a verbal text, or which does not accompany a text, often comes to be regarded as more important than music with a text. From *a union of music and language, where language is the senior partner*, emerges a divorce, in which the formerly junior partner becomes autonomous and is no longer bound to represent what a verbal text can express.[1] (Our emphasis.)

Bowie rightly observes that music discourse underwent a fundamental change at this time, a change in which the cultural identity of music can be said to have altered. From something which the mainstream of western philosophy sought to suppress, it became, in some cases, its most privileged term. While Bowie sees this as indicative of a major change in the nature of philosophical discourse, we would suggest that what is really crucial here is the extent to which such a change accompanied fundamental shifts in the structure, composition and consumption of music itself. It was not the basic terms of western philosophy which changed; it was music itself which changed in such a way as to comply with those terms. Beethoven's symphonies, which one listened to in a darkened concert hall, neither moving nor speaking throughout, were an entirely different experience from the pleasant *Tafelmusik* of, say, Bach or Telleman, or to pieces of music intended for dancing to or inspired by dance forms. This interpretation is borne out by the observation that *dance* (always the most obvious indicator of music's physicality) also underwent a radical cultural devaluation at this time. Judith Hanna writes that:

> The French and industrial revolutions (in the eighteenth and nineteenth centuries) dealt serious blows to the prestige of dance, sending it from the epitome of royal male performance to the nadir of 'inferior' female

performance. Among the sociopolitical elite, activities of the body became associated with moral laxity and impediments to economic productivity.[16]

Although Hanna's work is largely concerned with performance dance, she points out that the very delineation of a sphere of performance dance separate from more generally participative types was part of the process whereby dance became a devalued activity. If we consider music in terms of its social usage and the way in which this has related to changes in musical form, then it is possible to argue that the changing status of dancing has been a crucial factor in western musical history. The classical tradition itself was defined, in a way, by the gradual detachment of music from the dance. In the various changes in form and composition which mark music from the sixteenth to the nineteenth centuries, we can hear the shift of the principal site of music's consumption away from the dance-floor to the concert hall. The gradual move away from dance-related forms, from cyclical repetition and rhythm towards melody and complex harmony as sources of musical pleasure, all bear witness to this process.[17] Within the dominant culture of western Europe, dance became an increasingly devalued activity during these centuries, as the body and its pleasures were increasingly devalued too.[18]

In many ways, philosophical ideas about what is good and desirable and what is frightening and dangerous in music have remained consistent throughout western musical history. These ideas became consolidated as part of hegemonic discourse on dance and music at the end of the eighteenth century, a moment when so much of the modern world was born. How do these assumptions compare with contemporary ideas about the nature of music, or ideas which do not strictly derive from the philosophical tradition? The following section will consider these questions.

Body music: The materiality of sound

Contemporary understanding about the way in which music affects us may vary, but it rests on a common and generally indisputable observation: that is, that music is *sound*. Music is constituted by waves of sound that vibrate through the air, vibrating the eardrum in specific patterns which are registered by the brain. But, importantly, it is not only the ear which registers these vibrations; deaf people can learn to play and 'hear' music. These vibrations are registered on some level *throughout the body*. No one knows this better than today's clubber. When a 25kW bass-line pumps through the floor and up your legs, you know that music isn't only registered in the brain.

It will be central to our arguments here to observe that music – like all sound – is registered on a fundamentally different level to language or modes of visual communication, just as the philosophical tradition has always suspected (and feared). This difference can be explained in terms of the fundamentally physical, corporeal nature of musical experience, which in turn is a result of what we term the *materiality of sound*.

First, let us consider the point that music is specifically registered throughout the body, it is not simply a matter of mental cognition. This aspect of musical experience is manifested most vividly in the case of dance music; the dancer receives music through the body in a manner whose directness is manifested in the very act of dancing. But it is also important to understand that to some extent *all* music must function in this way. As sound, the vibrations of all musics are capable of being communicated to the whole body.

It is for this reason that many people – including cultural theorists – have tried to answer the question 'how does music work?' by highlighting music's *corporeality*. Robert Walser, commenting on the feelings of empowerment which listeners can derive from heavy metal, writes that:

> The music is felt within as much as without, and the body is seemingly hailed directly, subjectivity responding to the empowerment of the body rather than the other way around.[19]

This observation has been extended and elaborated on with regard to music in general by a range of commentators. Writing in the 1960s, Lévi-Strauss suggested that:

> Below the level of sounds and rhythms, music acts upon a primitive terrain, which is the physiological time of the listener.... The inner, or natural grid, which is a function of his brain, is reinforced symmetrically by a second and, one might say, still more wholly natural grid: that constituted by the visceral rhythms.[20]

The corporeality of musical experience has recently been of particular concern to two of the most prominent writers working at the boundary between popular music studies and critical musicology, Richard Middleton and John Shepherd. In an essay written in 1993, Middleton proposes a 'theory of gesture', arguing that 'how we feel and how we understand musical sounds is organised through processual shapes which seem to be analogous to physical gestures'.

Middleton draws on the work of a number of theorists, anthropologists and musicologists in order to articulate a model of musical experience as inseparable from the listener's experience of their own body. Referring to the work of the Hungarian musicologist Janos Maróthy, Middleton explains his theory that rhythm, which Maróthy regards as 'the basic principle of reality', can be used as a basic analytical category for the analysis of music on such terms.

> Maróthy has eloquently described the permeation of the whole spectrum of musical parameters (and beyond) by rhythmic principles. The physical spectrum of periodicity zones (lungs-heart-feet-fingers-speech

organs-vocal chords-ear drum – ultra-sound perception – electro-chem-ical neural circuits – eye (light waves)) is mapped (or partly so) by the musical spectrum covered by the frequency zones of rhythm (in the strict sense) and pitch, which together cover the distance from pulsations occupying several seconds each, up to a frequency of approximately 20,000 pulsations per second. This gives a theoretical basis to the idea that 'gesture' occupies a spectrum, with relationships to obvious corporeal movements at one end and neural pulsations at the other.[21]

This account provides a basis for understanding the 'corporeality' of music in a scientifically-grounded sense. Compared to writing, or to other forms of visual communication, music possesses a *literally* visceral quality, relying for its effects not just on the neural registration of light waves but on the resonance of sound waves throughout the organs and the body tissues.

We should note that the implication of the model which Middleton draws from Maróthy is that this distinction is ultimately quantitative rather than qualitative, sound waves merely vibrating more slowly than light. However, the fact that light waves vibrate too quickly to be registered by any part of the body apart from the eyes while sound waves vibrate slowly enough to resonate throughout the body, means that our actual physical experience of the two types of vibration is qualitatively different. It is for this reason that music can be said to, as Robert Walser suggests, 'hail the body directly'. At the same time, this observation should lead us to consider the fact that even 'sound' is not a fixed quantity; some sound waves vibrate more slowly than others. Another phenomenon which is illustrated more vividly in the case of dance music than anywhere else is that it is precisely the bass end of the frequency spectrum – comprising of the slowest vibrating sound waves – that provides listeners and dancers with the most *material*, most directly *corporeal*, types of experience. It is the bass and the sub-bass which are *felt* at least as much as they are heard.

This brings us to our second point: the comparative materiality of *all* sound. Physicists have known for the best part of a century that the difference between matter and energy can be expressed as a simple difference between the speed at which particles vibrate; the particles which make up 'matter' vibrating more slowly than those that make up 'energy'. This has two key implications. On the one hand, it means that *all* 'materiality' is basically relative. On the other, given that sound vibrates that much more slowly than light, we can say that in some quite concrete way, music can be regarded as having a *degree* of materiality which other forms of communication apart from physical touch do not. What is more, as we have just seen, it is possible to speak of different sounds as possessing different degrees of materiality, with the bass being the 'most material' end of the sound spectrum.

If the notion that music is capable of affecting the body directly is central to our understanding of what music is and what it does, then this should quickly turn our attention to the relationship between music and dancing. Nowhere is the physical reality of music made more obvious than on the dancefloor, where particular configurations of sound (i.e., records) are judged by their success or failure in 'making us' dance. While the tradition of choreographed performance dancing is obviously a site at which ideas about the relationships between the body and music have been played out for centuries, it is in musics designed to encourage and facilitate 'social' dancing (i.e., group dancing for lay people, rather than performance dancing by professionals for the benefit of an audience) that music's physical effectivity is manifested most clearly. While we clearly cannot make a rigid distinction between 'physical' and 'mental' experience in any case, dancing does appear to present itself as the manifestation of an experience of music which is physical more than it is intellectual. As the anthropologist John Blacking has said:

> Although music and dance are forms of non-verbal communication, they are always social facts, and so they can never be completely free of the verbal concepts and constructions of reality that predominate in different societies.... Nevertheless it can be shown ... that there are forms intrinsic to music and dance which are not modelled on language. As conscious movement is in our thinking, so thinking may come from movement, and especially shared, or conceptual, thought from communal movement.[22]

Scholarly writing on music – 'classical' or 'popular' – has been astonishingly neglectful of the importance of the relationship between music and dancing. We shouldn't be surprised by this. This tradition, which we have already seen exemplified in the writings of philosophers, has tended to shape the thinking of most writers and thinkers in all fields of western thought. The dislike of music's apparent physicality has led it to barely even acknowledge an important relationship between music and dance, let alone to give that relationship serious consideration, even though it is the case that this relationship has existed for as long as human beings have produced 'music'. With regard to more recent developments, if we consider the importance which the philosophical tradition places on having meaningful words to accompany music, we can then see the significance of the rise of forms of popular music – house, techno, drum 'n' bass, trance – which often have no words at all. Musics whose primary purpose is to move our bodies via the materiality of the bass, which often do not offer linguistic meanings, would seem to epitomize everything that philosophical tradition dislikes and distrusts about music.

Mind and body

In the philosophical writings outlined here, the traditional western dichotomy between body and mind has been mapped on to ideas about the effectivity of music; music, we are told, can affect the body on the one hand and the mind on the other. This dichotomy is in itself notoriously problematic, however. There is not, as many commentators have pointed out, a simple distinction between the body and the mind. Our experience of our bodies is always culturally determined; the very way we stand and sit varies from culture to culture. Similarly, it is impossible to speak of music simply affecting our bodies 'directly' since the ways in which we respond to certain sounds are always culturally coded. As an example, consider how difficult it is for some people to dance to certain kinds of music to which others can hardly keep still. There cannot therefore be a simple distinction between our physical experience of music and the meanings which we attribute to it. The interaction between sounds and our bodies will always be in part a result of learned responses, of personal and/or cultural dispositions. This observation follows from our assertion as to the *relative* materiality of music, emphasizing that this materiality – in comparison to other modes of experience and communication – is only relative. As we have already pointed out, the implication of our quasi-scientific explanation of this relative materiality of sound is to problematize altogether the distinction between the material and the non-material, and this in turn problematizes the distinction between mental and physical experience.

There are a number of overlapping issues here. At their centre is the question of what exactly we mean and understand by 'the body'. Can we really distinguish between music as experienced 'by the body' and music as experienced 'in the mind'? Can we really distinguish between physical and mental experience? If not, how can we therefore talk about 'the body' as a site of 'direct' experience, somehow separate from intellectual and discursive experience?

We will not be taking the idea that there is a rigid demarcation between the body and the mind, between mental and a physical experience, very seriously here. Such an assertion belongs to the realms of theology and metaphysics. Rather we will argue with those philosophers and theorists who see this distinction as a culturally specific one, a socially and historically determined aspect of our experience of ourselves. In fact, even the relative distinction between 'mind' and 'body' is an unstable one, always culturally determined rather than natural or inevitable. Further, we would argue that the active *maintenance* of this distinction along particular lines is one of the central projects of the dominant tradition in western thought. Modes of experience which make obvious the problematic nature of this division between mind and body, between interior and exterior experience, are therefore among the most prohibited and policed modes of experience within western culture.

Various writers have tried to engage with the issue of the relationship between music, the body and society.[23] However, in our view none of them has developed an adequate formulation of this relationship, mainly because they have not had sufficiently developed theoretical models of the relationship between the body and discourse to draw on. In our opinion, the most satisfactory way of understanding these issues is presented in recent work by Judith Butler. In *Bodies that*

Matter, Butler is concerned with the theoretical status of 'the body' and in particular the *gendered* body. She is concerned with the fundamental issue of how fixed
gendered identity is, how 'normal' heterosexuality can be said to be. In particular,
Butler takes issue with the 'essentialist' ideology which sees masculinity and femininity as fixed properties, *'essences'*, which all people possess depending on their
genitally-determined gender. Butler addresses a tendency among some essentialist
theorists to write about the body as a *site* of discourse, a thing which can be
inscribed by culture and ideology, but which is not *created* by them. According to
these theorists, one is male or female before anything else, and nothing can alter
that fact. Butler writes against the idea, implicit in any essentialist model, that the
gendered body is a pre-discursive site 'which only bears cultural constructions
and, therefore, cannot be a construction'.[24]

However, Butler also writes against the idea that to oppose such a view is to
adopt a radically idealist position according to which 'everything is discourse' and
there is no such thing as material reality. Rather, she emphasizes the importance of
thinking carefully about precisely what we mean by the terms 'matter' and 'materiality'. Fundamentally, Butler draws our attention to the importance of the
observation that we have already made, and that is made with some force in the
work of such philosophers as Derrida and Irigaray, that one of the central and
most limiting terms of western philosophy is precisely its insistence on a rigid
distinction between the ideal and the material. Butler therefore writes against the
replication of this distinction, implicit as it is in any attempt to draw a rigid
distinction between matter and discourse. Drawing to some extent on Foucault,
Butler argues a position which avoids such distinctions:

> the regulatory norms of 'sex' work in a performative fashion to consti-
> tute the materiality of bodies, and, more specifically, to materialise the
> bodies' sex, to materialise sexual difference in the service of the consoli-
> dation of the heterosexual imperative.
>
> In this sense, what constitutes the fixity of the body, its contours, its
> movements, will be fully material, but materiality will be re-thought as
> the effect of power, as power's most productive effect.[25]

Butler therefore argues that the body itself, and our conception of its 'materiality',
are in some sense cultural constructs. Although she does not use such simplistic
examples herself, it might be pointed out that the simple fact that we have
observed, that even physical posture is culturally variable, would tend to bear out
her thesis. For Butler, there is not a rigid distinction between the materiality of the
body and the culturally-determined discourses on the body. Rather, that very
materiality is thought of as being a function of discourse.

These statements raise the question of what exactly we mean by 'discourse'.
The term 'discourse' has largely been popularized in recent years by the work of
Michel Foucault. Foucault's work is famously concerned with the ways in which
important areas of human experience are discursively shaped. For Foucault, the

ways in which a phenomenon such as sexuality are discussed, written on and legislated for are actually constitutive of its existence. Foucault's project in Volume 1 of The History of Sexuality, for instance, is to challenge the notion that there is such a thing as 'sexuality' as separate and distinct from the ways in which 'sexuality' is discussed. For Foucault, for instance, 'homosexuality' is not a universal phenomenon, but a particular socio-discursive category which only comes into existence once a particular range of sexual activities (i.e., sex with an adult of the same sex) come to be discussed and circumscribed as belonging to a particular, delimited set which can be labelled 'homosexual'. For Foucault it is these regulated sets of statements (for example, 'A man who has sex with another man is a Homosexual') which make up the fabric of social reality.[26]

A further, crucial dimension of Foucault's notion of 'discourse' is its emphasis on the nature of power. Foucault famously deploys the term 'power/knowledge' to designate the functioning of discourse in terms of his view that there is no fundamental distinction between the production of knowledge and the exercise of power. Not only is it true that 'knowledge is power', but 'power is knowledge'. Not only is there no such thing as objective, 'true', detached 'knowledge', not only are those with social and economic power in a position to enforce their view of the world on the rest of society, as Marx suggested; the exercise of power and the delineation of 'knowledge' – of those discourses which are accepted as true – are one and the same thing. Power, according to this model, is a productive force rather than a merely restrictive one. It creates meanings, identities and truths, rather than merely masking or distorting them as most models of power tend to suggest.[27]

Foucault's model of discourse has been taken up and used by many other writers, two of whom are particularly worth mentioning here. First, at the level of political theory, Ernesto Laclau and Chantal Mouffe engage with the question we have touched on already, of the nature of the relationship between the cultural/ideological and the 'material', by addressing the question of the nature of 'discourse' in the work of Foucault:

> Our analysis rejects the distinction between discursive and non-discursive practices. It affirms that a) every object is constituted as an object of discourse, insofar as no object is given outside every discursive condition of emergence and b) that any distinction between what are usually called the linguistic and behavioural aspects of social practice, is either an incorrect distinction or ought to find its place as a differentiation within the social production of meaning, which is structured under the form of discursive totalities. Foucault, for example ... has maintained a distinction – in our opinion inconsistent – between discursive and non-discursive practices.[28]

In other words, just as there can be no firm distinction between the 'mental' and the 'physical', so there can be no pure 'activity', no merely physical 'experience'.

which is not also discursive, in that all activity and experience involves some degree – however slight – of thinking, classifying and meaning. The implication of these comments might be to suggest that the term 'discourse' should not only be taken to refer to linguistic activity, but more or less to any form of organized experience (to which there will always be a linguistic-classificatory dimension).

An effectively identical account of 'discourse' is given by Robert Walser in his discussion of the usefulness of theorizing music as discourse. Walser writes:

> The analytical notion of discourse enables us to pursue an integrated investigation of musical and social aspects of popular music. By approaching musical genres as discourses, it is possible to specify certain formal characteristics of genres but also a range of understandings shared by musicians and fans concerning the interpretation of these characteristics. The concept of discourse enables us to theorise beyond the artificial division between 'material reality' and consciousness.[29]

To say that there is no final distinction between physical and mental experience is also to say that there is no final distinction between the body experienced in its physical materiality and the body 'in discourse', that is, the body as discussed and experienced according to the terms set by specific social and historical contexts. This is the crucial point on which all of these writers implicitly agree.

Conclusions

We can now bring together a range of insights in order to develop Walser's model of music discourse and thereby to help us to conceptualize the relationship between music and the body. We can say, following Middleton, Maróthy, Walser, and Laclau and Mouffe, that there is no firm distinction between the mental and the physical, between the discursive and the non-discursive. One important implication of this conclusion is that the problem of the difference between musical affect and musical meaning more or less disappears. Rather than there being a clear distinction between the two, 'meaning' can be seen as merely one part of a broad continuum of effects which discourse can have.[30]

Further, we can say, following Butler, that the body itself is constituted in and by discourse; 'discourse' here being conceived as including all of the practices, from walking to dressing to having sex, through which we experience our bodies and articulate that experience. Music and dancing are among these experiences. Music as discourse can be conceived as offering us experiences which are at once 'physical' and 'mental'. However, music's medium is sound, and sound is a qualitatively different medium from any visual medium. It is experienced by parts of the body which no other medium can directly affect. As such it offers an experience which is quantitatively more physical than any offered by other media. No form of discourse is wholly physical or wholly mental, but we might say that music, which is registered throughout the body and not only on the brain, is on an important level, it is a more physical type of discourse than others. We might therefore hypothesize that our experience of music is related to the physico-discursive experience of our bodies on some particularly profound level.

This hypothesis forms an important part of our discussion throughout this book. The basic assumption being that our subjectivities, our sense of self – including, fundamentally, our bodies – are shaped by a multitude of practices which we are involved in since birth. Among those practices, importantly, are the practices of listening and dancing to music. Listening and dancing to music can (although it will not necessarily) offer an experience of the body which either stabilizes and reconfirms or disrupts and alters our previous experience of it. In subsequent chapters, we will consider further the implications of this statement.

Notes

1 Theodor Adorno and Max Horkheimer, The Dialectic of Enlightenment trans. John Cumming (London, Verso, 1979), p. 144.
2 See, for instance, Simon Frith, Performing Rites (Oxford, Oxford University Press, 1996), pp. 249–78.
3 See John Shepherd and Peter Wicke, Music and Cultural Theory (Cambridge, Polity, 1997), pp. 7–27.
4 Plato, The Republic, trans. Desmond Lee (London, Penguin, 1974), p. 158.
5 Ibid.
6 Ibid.
7 Ibid., p. 160.
8 From Peter Le Huray and James Day (eds), Music and Aesthetics in the Eighteenth and Early Nineteenth Centuries (Cambridge, Cambridge University Press, 1981), p. 95.
9 Ibid., p. 99.
10 Kant's most prized category was 'the sublime', and later developments in music discourse and aesthetics were to produce a notion of music as the ultimate embodiment of the sublime, but that did not happen at this point in time.
11 Ibid., pp. 220–1.
12 Adorno and Horkheimer, The Dialectic of Enlightenment, trans. John Cumming (London, Verso, 1979).
13 Theodor Adorno, Philosophy of Modern Music, trans. A. Mitchell (New York, The Seabury Press, 1973), p.13.
14 Quoted in Andrew Bowie, Aesthetics and Subjectivity: From Kant to Nietzsche (Manchester, Manchester University Press, 1990), p. 210.
15 Ibid., p. 179.
16 Judith Hanna, Dance, Sex and Gender (Chicago, UCP, 1988), p. 123.
17 See, for instance, Wilfred Mellers, The Sonata Principle (London, Barrie & Rockliff, 1962), pp. 1–9.
18 See Hanna, Dance, Sex and Gender.
19 Robert Walser, Running with the Devil: Power, Gender and Madness in Heavy Metal Music (Hanover, Wesleyan University Press, 1993), p. 45.
20 Claude Lévi-Strauss, The Raw and the Cooked (London, Pimlico, 1994).
21 Richard Middleton, 'Popular music analysis and musicology: bridging the gap', in Popular Music vol. 12, no. 2, 1993, p. 179.
22 John Blacking, 'Towards an anthropology of the body', in Blacking (ed.), The Anthropology of the Body (London, Academic Press, 1977).

23 See Richard Middleton, *Studying Popular Music* (Buckingham, Open University Press, 1990); and John Shepherd and Peter Wicke, *Music and Cultural Theory* (Cambridge, Polity, 1997).

24 Judith Butler, *Bodies That Matter* (London, Routledge, 1993), p. 2.

25 Ibid. p. 2.

26 Michel Foucault, *The History of Sexuality Volume One*, trans. Robert Hurley, (London, Penguin, 1978), p. 9.

27 Ibid., p. 94.

28 Ernesto Laclau and Chantal Mouffe, *Hegemony and Socialist Strategy* (London, Verso, 1985), p. 107.

29 Walser, *Running with the Devil*, p. 28.

30 For a useful reflection on the issue of meaning and affect, see Brian Massumi, 'The Autonomy of Affect', in Paul Patton (ed.) *Deleuze: A Critical Reader* (Oxford, Blackwell, 1996). We might also suggest a similarity between our position here and those problematizations of the distinctions between meaning, affect, effect and performativity offered by Austin, with his notion of 'illocutionary force': J.L. Austin, *How to Do Things with Words* (Oxford, Oxford University Press, 1962).

3

THE METAPHYSICS OF MUSIC

Introduction

In the previous chapter we made some important observations about the ways in which music has been discussed over the centuries and the ways in which it can be discussed today. In this chapter we will consider in more detail the discursive formations which have dominated western thinking and how they have shaped the ways in which music has been talked about. Most importantly, our task here will be to account for and at times to deconstruct the aesthetic and ideological priorities of the dominant music discourses of the west.

Richard Middleton has offered a lucid account of these priorities in his discussion of mainstream musicology's failure to engage adequately with popular music, pointing out that while it may pass itself off as an objective way of understanding music, classical musicology represents a sedimented set of very particular and exclusive practices, a musical ideology which universalizes and glorifies a tradition of music specific to nineteenth-century Europe. As Middleton makes clear, classical musicology is at best of little value in the study of popular music because of its formal and notational obsessions with tonality and harmony and its relative neglect of such issues as rhythm, timbre, micro-tonality, and so forth.[1]

What does classical music discourse's particular and arbitrary set of priorities amount to? We will argue in this chapter that they amount to much the same thing as the prescriptions offered by the philosophers we looked at in Chapter 2; an attempt to suppress the materiality and physicality of music. If we consider what it is that classical music discourse privileges in music on the one hand, and what it suppresses on the other, we can clearly discern an attempt to efface the materiality of sound-sources (be they vocal or instrumental) by removing any trace of them from the sound produced. This denigration of materiality and corporeality has been crucial to musical theory and practice at least since the time of Beethoven and German Idealism, the key moment in the articulation of that music discourse which is usually today called 'classical' (but which, while pursuing developments that began in the sixteenth century, technically did not begin to define itself fully until the emergence of the Romantic movements of the early nineteenth century).[2] During the period from the early nineteenth century to the early twentieth century a particular Germano-centric notion of what constitutes 'great music', of what composers belong to the canon of great music, and of what theoretical and notational tools are appropriate to the analysis and recording of this music, was articulated, sedimented and became hegemonic. Although this discourse has from time to time been challenged, it continues to dominate attitudes to music in those institutions which control the preservation, production and dissemination of music in the public sphere. We will also argue later in this chapter that although it may contest the terms of 'classical' music discourse on some levels, the dominant strands of western 'popular' music actually replicate many of them also.

So far we have looked at some of the ways in which music and dance have been discussed by the 'western philosophical tradition'. In this chapter we will consider in more detail the nature of some of the discursive formations which continue to determine the ways in which music and dance are regarded in western culture. As we have already seen, one of these is the old and powerful system of ideas which has its most obvious manifestation in the writings of the philosophical tradition. However, this tradition and its ideas would have little relevance if the ideas discussed within it were merely the concern of a handful of obscure old men (and a few obscure young ones). It is our contention here – although hardly an original one – that the philosophical tradition is only one particularly articulate manifestation of a tradition of thought which continues to inform much of our cultural, social and political life. Not just philosophical ideology, but also political, legal, economic, aesthetic and religious ideas have been shaped by these particular mode of thought. Perhaps most importantly, our common-sense notions of meaning, identity and truth continue to be shaped by ideas which we can identify as belonging to the same coherent set of ideas as the philosophical texts which we have already discussed. Importantly, this is a set of ideas which is specific in what it allows us to do, think and say. There is always much which is either excluded from it altogether, or which it actively marginalizes. What we are considering here is the idea of a coherent dominant strand of thought – indeed, a coherent dominant *way of thinking* – in the west.

There are a number of different ways of understanding and refining this notion of a dominant tradition. One way, which tends to concentrate on philosophical texts, is that informed primarily by the work of Jacques Derrida and contemporaries like Luce Irigaray. Derrida provides a frame of reference according to which a dominant strand of thinking in the west can be identified in the work of apparently diverse and contradictory thinkers. This strand of thinking is usually called 'metaphysics'.[3] Derrida himself builds on the work of earlier philosophers such as Heidegger and Nietzsche, and is close to the ideas of other poststructuralist thinkers such as Barthes, Deleuze and Irigaray, but his concept of 'metaphysics' is more or less unique.

Metaphysics is usually seen as being at least as old as European culture itself. Often closely related to this concept is the concept of patriarchy. This is a central concept in almost all feminist writing, naming as it does the system of ideas and practices and the structures of power which at least since ancient times, and in most parts of the world, has defined women and femininity as inherently inferior to men and masculinity. From a feminist perspective, the most important thing to understand about the dominant tradition in the west is that it is patriarchal and phallocentric, perpetually marginalizing women and feminine experience.

Other ideas that concern themselves with western culture and society tend to focus on a somewhat shorter time-frame. Ideas derived from the work of Marx concern themselves with society since the emergence and development of capitalism, which is usually identified as having emerged at some point between the beginning of the sixteenth century and the end of the eighteenth century. Operating on a similar time scale, but with very different concerns and emphases, are theorists who consider the most useful category for understanding the experience of western culture since the Middle Ages to be that of 'modernity'. In both cases, what is at issue is the effect of the rapid and intense changes which society, technology and culture – at first in Europe and then across the world – have undergone over the past five centuries. Marxist perspectives tend to place the greater emphasis on the importance of the development of the capitalist mode of production: the system of production, distribution and exchange based on the private ownership of industrial capital by individuals and corporations. The emergence of modern modes of manufacturing production and the consequent changes to the social structure are seen as having a determining effect on the emergence of new forms of social and political organization, new cultural forms and new ways of thinking. Most importantly, the struggle between the owners of capital – whose aim is to maximize their profits at the expense of the workforce – and the workers – whose aim is to maximize their share of the wealth which they generate and to minimize their working time – is seen as the driving force behind social and cultural change in recent centuries. The category of 'modernity' on the other hand, while being by no means incompatible with a Marxist perspective, tends to see these changes not as the simple effect of one determinable cause (for example, economic change), but as part of an overall and more or less integrated process.

What is interesting here is the fact that from the point of view of a concern with the cultural status of music and dance, these various categories often appear to overlap, allowing us to perceive a dominant tradition with a very specific set of terms, values and priorities which are reinforced by the combined effects of metaphysics, patriarchy, capitalism and modernity. In very broad terms this tends to involve the valorization of a series of related terms – reason, self-presence, the mind, masculinity, sight, individuality, and so forth – at the expense of their 'opposites' – irrationality, diffidence, the body, femininity, touch and hearing, sociality, and so forth. We will see in this and subsequent chapters how these several different ways of understanding the sources of the 'dominant tradition' break down and overlap.

Derrida and John Shepherd: Deconstructing music

Derrida's early work is particularly concerned with the relative status ascribed to speech and writing in western philosophy. He looks closely at a range of key texts of western thought, from Plato to Freud, and asks why it is that *speech* is so often accorded a privileged status as the guaranteed medium of truth, whereas writing – from Plato to Saussure – is so often treated at best as an untrustworthy and parasitic derivation of speech, and at worst as a black art. Derrida characterizes western philosophy and – at least by implication – western culture in general, as *logocentric*. This word derives from the Greek *logos*, meaning 'word'. Western culture, Derrida argues, privileges modes of thought and experience which occur in the medium of verbal language, which thereby have clearly identifiable and analysable meanings. Derrida adds a further observation that logocentrism is usually expressed in terms which explicitly or implicitly privilege speech as the ideal medium for verbal language. Derrida designates this preference for speech with the terms 'phonocentrism' and 'phonologocentrism'.

One has to be extremely careful when using Derrida's work: that the work is not simply an engagement with a handful of philosophical texts, but an attempt to examine some of the terms according to which almost all thinking occurs, at least in western culture. While the term metaphysics designates a specific and identifiable tradition of thought, it is also a tradition of thought which we are all, to some extent, embedded in. The project of this book – to offer coherent, classificatory accounts of given cultural phenomena (however tentative) – is arguably by definition a metaphysical one. To write as we do of 'metaphysical discourse' is problematic precisely because the very concept 'discourse' derives from the metaphysical tradition itself. In what follows we will use the term metaphysics in a highly delimited way, to designate a particular set of philosophical priorities which have dominated western thinking since classical times, and which can be clearly identified and to some extent sidestepped and overturned. It is nevertheless crucial to bear in mind that a book such as this one can never hope completely to step *outside* of metaphysics, attacking it from without, as we are all to some extent always already within metaphysics, within the western tradition of reason. Throughout the rest of this book, we will discuss the extent to which forms of music pose severe problems for this tradition of thought. However, it is important to remember that it is also the case that music as we know it only comes to exist at all *within* that tradition. A music which somehow managed to be *completely* unmetaphysical would have to exist in such a radical state of disorganization as to be not music at all, but pure texture; white noise.

Derrida's account of phonologocentrism has particular resonance for a discussion of music because it involves in part a consideration of the status of sound in the discourse of western philosophy. Derrida identifies the figure of *hearing oneself speak*, thus experiencing a wholly unmediated self-presence, being at one with oneself, as one of the fundamental organizing tropes of western philosophy. To hear oneself speak is to experience the ideal state of being-as-presence, a state of undifferentiation to which *writing* is always inimical, constituted as it is by an irreducible materiality, a constitutive *spacing*, a relation of *exteriority* to the reading/ writing subject.

In his essay 'Tympan', Derrida considers the place of the ear in this schema:

> indefatigably at issue is the ear, the distinct, differentiated, articulated organ that produces the effect of proximity, of absolute properness, the idealising erasure of organic difference. It is an organ whose structure (and the suture that holds it to the throat) produces the pacifying lure of organic indifference. To forget it – and in so doing to take shelter in the most familial of dwellings – is to cry out for the end of organs, of others.[4]

It is not difficult to see that this is what we saw Plato, Rousseau, Kant *et al.* bid us do in the previous chapter; to forget the ear. Or rather, to forget the ear *as organ*, as anything other than a pure immediacy which allows cognition to go untroubled by the materiality of sense experience. Is the specific denigration of music's physicality not itself an appeal 'for the end of organs'? It is precisely an ideal of sound as ideality which constitutes one of logocentrism's basic terms. And yet music must also pose a particular problem for this discourse, for to hear music is inescapably to hear sounds which come from outside oneself, that occupy an external space which can be shared by others, and thus must problematize that ideal, undifferentiated interiority which the subject-hearing-itself-speak knows. Thus, the discourse of metaphysics is forced into the double gesture of both acknowledging music's sensuality, it's physicality and exteriority, while at the same time seeking to denigrate these characteristics and to valorize an ideal of music experienced as pure interiority, without the mediation of organs.

The issue which this observation raises is one which Derrida deals with at some length and in several publications. In much of his early work, Derrida is concerned with the problematic relationships between sense, interiority and exteriority.[5] Derrida's deconstruction of these apparent oppositions is echoed by the music theorist John Shepherd in an essay concerned with the nature of musical experience:

> Sociality, then, is as manifest in the private, internal world of individual awareness as it is in the external, public world of shared behaviour. The two put each other in motion, and are never static, either in themselves, or in relationship to one another.[6]

Here, as in Derrida, the distinction between the interior and the exterior, the individual and the world of others, is radically questioned. Also as for Derrida, a consideration of the status of *sound* is central to this questioning. Shepherd continues:

it is a fundamental experiential characteristic of sound that it lifts off the surface of its material source to occupy the space not only between the source and the listener, but also around the listener.[7]

Shepherd emphasizes the degree to which music can be said to be character-ized by an inescapable exteriority/sociality. He links this quality to the irreducible materiality and physicality of sound. Yet at the same time he continues to high-light the degree to which music (and sound in general) can problematize the very distinctions between physicality/exteriority and ideality/interiority. With regard to Derrida's account of phonologocentrism, we should remember that sound – conceived in a particular way – *can* be the medium of apparent self-presence. The very fact that it resonates throughout the body can lead it to be experienced as pure interiority; it is not *necessarily* experienced as exterior. Shepherd therefore describes sound/music as a site of exchange, a shifting boundary *between* the 'inner' and the 'outer'.[8]

We can thus bring Derrida's account of phonologocentrism and Shepherd's account of the sociality of music together in a coherent account of metaphysics' treatment of music. Metaphysical discourse, in defending the integrity (the *propriety*) of the unified and self-present subject, must seek to close off that space of exteriority which music partially exists in. This is what motivates the texts of Rousseau, Kant and even Adorno to denigrate music's physicality, its relation to the materiality of the body and its organs. This itself requires that they maintain a rigid distinction between the sensory-corporeal and the intellectual. Music's power to problematize this distinction, and thus to problematize the terms of metaphysical discourse itself, must be held at bay.

This account also provides us with an explanation for classical musicology's two great lacunae: timbre and rhythm. As Middleton has pointed out, the musical and theoretical discourses of classical music simply cannot accommodate timbre as a musical issue.[9] The textural and microtonal qualities of sounds, as distinct from melodic, harmonic and tonal qualities, are not registered by conventional music notation. Classical music training, on whatever instrument, valorizes 'purity' of tone; overtones must be expunged, tonal accuracy must be perfect, the listener must not be aware for even a moment that the possibility of textural varia-tion in the way the instrument is played exists at all. Timbre, we argue, is thus suppressed precisely because to engage with timbre as a musical issue is to engage with the materiality of music and its sources. That this suppression is a fundamen-tally logocentric gesture is further suggested by Derrida's comment in 'Tympan' that, 'Timbre, style and signature are the same obliterating division of the proper. They make every event possible, necessary and unfindable'.[10]

As well as confirming the metaphysical nature of classical musicology's suppression of timbre, the deconstruction of the *proper* can explain the other key blind-spot of classical music discourse: rhythm. It has often been observed that 'classical' music pays little heed to rhythmic issues (this is bound up indissolubly with the increasing distance between 'serious' music and dance music from the

Renaissance onwards), and that conventional notation can only register rhythm in a crude and simplistic manner. This observation brings us back to Middleton's use of Maróthy to articulate a model of musical gesture. There we find an idea of rhythm as the primary category for the analysis not just of music but of existence itself to be fundamentally connected with an idea of music as essentially corporeal. Middleton has made this explicit link elsewhere,[11] pointing out that in the musical discourses of various cultures, and in the competing discourses of different twentieth-century theorists, rhythm and repetition are always associated with physicality, and the denigration and/or valorization of rhythm and repetition always goes hand-in-hand with the denigration and/or valorization of bodily pleasures.

This observation makes Maróthy's notion of rhythm as 'the basic principle of reality' seem very close to Derrida's suggestion that iterability (repeatability) and spacing are constitutive elements of all experience. This in turn can lead us towards a better understanding of the nature of metaphysics and the reasons for the suppression of rhythm in classical music discourse. Rhythm, we might say, is part of a series of terms which logocentric discourse suppresses; this series includes timbre, spacing, iterability, exteriority, physicality and materiality. It is the operation of this metaphysics in music discourse which motivates the simultaneous suppression of sensory pleasure, the material, the physical, timbre and rhythm in that discourse.

Deconstructive dance

This set of priorities and suppressions inevitably leads to the specific denigration of dance. Dance is an undeniably *physical* experience. It involves a relationship to music which radically problematizes such key metaphysical terms as the distinction between internal and external experience. When we 'feel' music enough to actually move in time to its rhythms, the distinction between 'outside' (where the music comes from) and 'inside' (where the music is felt), is radically problematized. Dance is a definitively liminal experience. In addition, it is an experience of *affect* which often seems to be as devoid of coherent *meaning* as musical experience can get. It should come as no surprise, therefore, that dance often appears to be one of that series of terms which logocentric discourse denigrates. On the one hand, the classical music tradition regards dance as a negligible activity; even Strauss' waltzes are today treated largely as concert pieces rather than as dance music. On the other hand, what more extreme refusal of all of metaphysics' priorities can we imagine than a rave? A crowd of people immersing themselves in a collective experience of the materiality of music, each individual losing themselves in a shared ecstasy whose medium is bass and rhythm; an experience of music not at all as an object of rational contemplation but as affect itself, whose chief mode of expression is a wordless cheer; there could hardly be any more direct refusal of logocentric imperatives.

But it is not only the classical tradition which has this attitude. Much contemporary 'popular' music discourse also marginalizes dance as an activity and marginalizes those forms of music associated with it, as we have seen. Rock music in particular is generally defined today in opposition to dance forms. Johan Fornas has written illuminatingly of the struggles which go on at the borders of the genre of 'rock', pointing out that, 'The rock/pop field is a contested continuum. The notion of authenticity is frequently used to distinguish rock from pop, as rock ideologists defend the value of folk and/or art ingenuity against commercial substitutes'.[12] One of the key terms by which forms excluded from the generic field of 'rock' are designated today is simply 'dance'.

The prevailing demarcations of popular music genres can be read off from the ways in which record shops and music papers catergorize the various sections of music. Perhaps nothing could illustrate many of the arguments in this book more vividly than the fact that record shops still tend to divide themselves up according to the boundaries 'rock/pop' and 'dance/soul', etc. In other words, a range of musics which appear to have nothing in common apart from the fact that in their various ways they all manifest traditional European logocentric priorities (emphasising lyrics and melody) are distinguished from a range of musics – soul, hip hop, house, techno, and so forth – which appear to have little in common apart from the fact that they don't. Publications which make some claim to represent a comprehensive selection of genres almost always privilege rock over other forms, assigning 'dance' musics a few, specially-identified pages.[13] On the other hand, magazines which prioritize 'dance' musics tend to sell themselves as specialist publications, thus ignoring other types of music altogether.[14] In all cases, conservative types of 'rock' and 'pop' are defined as being, or at least as being closer to, the norm of popular music, while 'dance' musics are defined as something specific, and divergent from that norm. Looked at objectively this might seem rather bizarre; what is popular music for if not for dancing to? Why is 'dance' music defined as somehow not belonging to the mainstream of popular music? What we can see in the implementation of this normalizing hierarchy of terms is precisely the hegemony of logocentric discourse even within 'popular' culture.

A simple consideration of grain

One of the most read, if least explored critiques of the dominant attitude to music in the west is that offered by Roland Barthes in his essay 'The Grain of the Voice'. In it he considers the implications of giving more thought to the significance of timbre in the understanding of musical pleasure. Ostensibly a critique of the aesthetic priorities inherent in the practice and evaluation of bourgeois singing, Barthes gestures towards a critique of that whole musicology which legitimates those techniques. Barthes praises a particular singer for deploying a style which foregrounds the materiality of the voice and of the language in which it sings, rather than concentrating on clarity of expression. In the essay he draws heavily on the work of Julia Kristeva. Kristeva's work in the early 1970s was concerned with analysing 'signification' as a process which could be accounted for in terms of two main components: the *symbolic* and the *semiotic*. We can understand this distinction to some extent in terms of the distinction between meaning and affect. The symbolic is that aspect of signification which produces meaning as such; the order of coherent classification. The semiotic is the order of pre-linguistic affect, of the unconscious drives as they organize and disrupt the subject and its experience of its body. Kristeva is primarily concerned with the analysis of literary texts, for the purposes of which she offers a distinction between what she terms the 'genotext' and the 'phenotext':

> What we shall call a *genotext* will include semiotic processes but also the advent of the symbolic. The former includes drives, their disposition, and their division of the body, plus the ecological and social system surrounding the body, such as objects and pre-Oedipal relations with parents. The latter encompasses the emergence of object and subject, and the constitution of nuclei of meaning involving categories: semantic and categorical fields....
>
> We shall use the term *phenotext* to denote language that serves to communicate, which linguistics describes in terms of 'competence' and 'performance.[15]

Barthes draws on this distinction as follows:

> 'grain' is ... the materiality of the body speaking its mother tongue; perhaps the letter, almost certainly *signifiance*.
>
> Thus we can see in song (pending the extension of this distinction to the whole of music) the two texts described by Julia Kristeva. The *pheno-song* (if the transposition be allowed) covers all the phenomena, all the features which belong to the structure of the language being sung, the rules of the genre, the coded form of the melisma, the composer's idiolect, the style of the interpretation in short, everything in the performance which is in the service of communication, representation, expression, everything which it is customary to talk about, which forms the tissue of cultural values (the matter of acknowledged tastes, of fashions, of critical commentaries), which takes its bearing directly on the ideological alibis of a period ('subjectivity', 'expressivity', 'dramaticism', 'personality' of the artist). The *geno-song* is the volume of the singing and speaking voice, the space when significations germinate 'from within language and its very materiality'; it forms a signifying play having nothing to do with communication.[16]

He continues:

> The 'grain' is the body in the voice as it sings, the hand as it writes, the limb as it performs ... the simple consideration of 'grain' in music could

lead to a different history of music from the one we know now ... were we to succeed in refining a certain 'aesthetics' of musical pleasure, then doubtless we would attach less importance to the formidable break in tonality accomplished by modernity.[17]

For Barthes the role of 'grain' in singing is to open up *signifiance*, that often pleasurable process – characteristic of Kristeva's 'semiotic' – which derives from the action of the signifier itself, beyond, superfluous to and independent of the act of signification, making 'grain' something much more than merely timbre. At the same time, his point is not far from one we have already made: that the musical and theoretical discourses of classical music cannot accommodate timbre as a musical issue. As we have already seen, whether in the case of vocal music or instrumental music, the dominant discourse of the west dislikes and devalues music's materiality and physicality. For Barthes, this suppression is inseparable from a suppression of *signifiance*.

But what kind of alternative is there? In 'The Grain of the Voice', Barthes tells us now much he likes throaty singers, but we can certainly extend his arguments – as he himself suggests – to cover other types of music. The logic of their arguments is such that many types of music could be seen as foregrounding 'grain'; microtonal musics, musics which rely on textural and drone effects, musics which rely on percussive effects more than melody and tonality, would all fit the bill. In the case of dance music, we could certainly see some types of music foregrounding 'grain' more than others. The classic example which we discuss below is acid house, which was based on the definitively 'grainy' sound of the Roland 303 bass synthesizer. Various types of house and techno use harsh textural effect. We might also think of the ways in which in the production of electronic music, various types of 'grain' are left in place as part of the overall sonic effect; for example, the scratches and crackles heard on samples obviously taken from old vinyl records, or the 'imperfect' sound quality deliberately sought after by producers using old analogue synthesizers and recording equipment rather than 'cleaner' sounding digital equipment.

On the other hand, we could on one level see *all* dance music as exploring the territory of 'grain' which Barthes points towards in his essay. Even the 'cleanest' sounding commercial house tune is produced in such a way as to give relative prominence to the bass and the drums. As was discussed earlier, an emphasis on bass and percussion is always an emphasis on the tangible, physical, material qualities of sound, those qualities which Barthes uses the concept of 'grain' to help us think about. Compared to most other types of music in the west, even the least 'grainy' 'dance' musics rely on these qualities a great deal. However 'light' the sound is, dance music is after all *dance* music, and as such always emphasizes the corporeal dimension of musical experience. The physical, textural, material qualities of sound are always emphasized, even when the actual sounds used are not particularly rough. And there is still another sense in which we can see almost all dance music as working on the same plane as Barthes' 'grain'.

Jouissance: The nature of ecstasy

In his book *Queer Noises*, John Gill writes that:

> Dance music as it is perceived now – soul, disco, funk, techno and the many mansions of house – is, I believe, the one form of music which, even in its most degraded form, is bound up in something that closely resembles Roland Barthes' notion of *jouissance*, that is, rapture, bliss or transcendence.[18]

As Gill points out, everything about the contemporary dance music-drug experience is organized around the pursuit of a certain kind of ecstasy: waves of undifferentiated physical and emotional pleasure; a sense of immersion in a communal moment, wherein the parameters of one's individuality are broken down by the shared throbbing of the bass drum; an acute experience of music in all its sensuality – its shimmering arpeggios, soaring string-washes, abrasives squelches, crackles and pops; an incessant movement forward, in all directions, nowhere; the bodily irresistibility of funk; the inspirational smiles of strangers, the awesome familiarity of friends; the child-like feeling of perfect safety at the edge of oblivion; a delicious surrender to cliché.

Gill rightly suggests that the term *jouissance* might designate this experience more accurately than any other. The concept of *jouissance*, derived from psychoanalytic theory, is central to the poststructuralist work of both Barthes and Kristeva. The French word (one of whose more common meanings is, simply, 'orgasm') takes on slightly different meanings in the work of these two writers and in more orthodox Lacanian psychoanalysis, but in all cases it designates a type of extraordinary sensation which derives from the moment before the human child leaves its state of comfortable bliss, a state usually associated with still having access to the mothers' breast, (*pace* the work of the pioneering psychoanalyst, Melanie Klein). It is at the moment that it falls from this state of grace that the child enters into the symbolic order of social relationships, gendered identity and language.

The pre-linguistic state is conceived as one in which the child does not perceive a distinction between its own self/body and that of the mother and, by extension, the rest of the world around it. The moment of entry into subjectivity, of the acquisition of identity, is thought to be at one and the same time the moment at which language is acquired and the moment when the social meaning of gender is realized in the Oedipus complex and its partial resolution.

As it is fundamentally a moment of *separation* (from the mother, from the world experienced as an undifferentiated whole, from those others whom the child must now relate to as a discrete individual), this moment is thought of as one of irrecoverable loss; the sense of completeness, the fullness of pure *jouissance*, can never really be returned to without that loss of humanity which is a descent into psychosis or autism. Its loss is the price we pay for becoming human. However, although this pure state can never be recovered, that form of pleasure associated with it – a pleasure which can never be adequately described precisely because it is pre-linguistic, pre-subjective – can be experienced in situations in which our normal relation to the symbolic order is disrupted. *Jouissance* is the name given to this pleasure. *Jouissance* is often thought of as a pleasure which operates particularly at the level of the body's materiality, being associated with that moment which is characterized at once by pre-linguistic experience and by the child's effectively unmediated relation to the mother's body. Barthes and Kristeva therefore tend to think of *jouissance* as being accessed at moments when the materiality of the means of signification interrupts meaning; precisely those moments which are designated by the terms 'semiotic', 'significance' and 'geno-text'. Barthes refined his notion of *jouissance* somewhat in his short work, *The Pleasure of the Text*, drawing an unstable distinction between *jouissance* (rendered in this translation as 'bliss'), that excessive and unmasterable pleasure which spills over the boundaries of sense, and *plaisir*, ordinary pleasure constituted within the horizon of meaning.[19]

Although Barthes, like Kristeva, was largely concerned with literature, these comments are actually rather easier to understand with respect to music than to writing. A Barthean aesthetic would clearly value a certain excessive (and *regressive*) *jouissance*, which would be made available by music which actively foregrounds its materiality, its corporeality, that maintains a direct relationship with the body. What music does this more explicitly and successfully than dance music? It is worth bearing in mind here that although for Barthes it generally appears to be a form of pleasure, according to the psychoanalytic theory of Lacan, *jouissance* is actually often experienced as unbearable pain, as the eruption into subjective experience of that which subjectivity by definition cannot tolerate. Think of the fact that sounds with harsh textures, reminding us of the hard materiality of their sound sources – the ear-splitting whine of uncontrolled electric feedback, the noise of heavy machinery, the sound of nails scratching a blackboard – are almost always *unpleasant*; think of how close these noises are to sounds which are generally thought of as pleasant – the throb of a bass drum, the ecstatic flight of an electric guitar, the impassioned growl of a soul singer – and we have an illustration of the principle of *signifiance* giving rise to a *jouissance* which can be experienced as either pleasure or pain. Perhaps a Barthean aesthetic must therefore be thought of as valorizing a specific experience of *jouissance as pleasure*, an experience which dance music is precisely calculated to induce.

What Gill and others suggest is that dance cultures are almost all – one way or another – about the pursuit of *jouissance*. Not that one can ever really talk about a pure and simple pursuit of *jouissance*. Barthes' distinction between *jouissance* and ordinary pleasure can be very useful to us in understanding more precisely the types of pleasure which dance and other cultures offer. When people use the trappings, sites and slogans of dance cultures in order to make identities for themselves, to define themselves in relation to the world, to carve out subcultural spaces, then they are certainly pursuing something more like *plaisir*; a way of articulating and reinforcing their identities rather than breaking them down. Almost any time that lyrics serve to organize the ways in which we relate to a piece of music, it is *plaisir* which is being experienced. We might think of those vast numbers of house and disco tracks which have lyrics with no more purpose than to exhort us to dance, to 'feel the rush', to chase ecstatic moments, as operating at the very border between *plaisir* and *jouissance*, pointing us quite carefully from one realm of experience to the other, generating as such their own very specific types of pleasure. Most pieces of music might be thought of as operating to some extent on both levels at the same time, through their simultaneous combination of geno-song and pheno-song. However, it must certainly be the case that it was the dance music revolution of the late 1980s, which saw the geno-textual instrumental track become the norm for house music rather than the relative novelty it was for disco, which saw youth culture transformed by a drug *named* after the experience with which *jouissance* is almost synonymous – Ecstasy – and which saw the development of a culture which places more emphasis on the pursuit of *jouissance* than any other in living memory.

The anglophone music critic whose work has been most influenced by that of Barthes and Kristeva is the writer and journalist, Simon Reynolds. Reynolds has for years been concerned with the themes of *jouissance* and *signifiance* in music, of the pursuit of regressive Ecstasy through such diverse means as drone rock and hard-core techno. In 1992, Reynolds penned this elegy to the then-new phenomenon of 'hardcore', the frenetic 150 beats per minute sound of free parties, working-class rave clubs and pirate radio stations, which was to mutate in a way few other than Reynolds would have predicted into the self-conscious avant-gardism of drum 'n' bass:

> No narrative, no destination: 'ardkore is an intransitive acceleration, an intensity without object.... Does this disappearance of the object of desire, this intransitive intensity, make 'ardkore a culture of autistic bliss? Certainly, sex as the central metaphor of dancing seems remoter than ever. Rave dancing doesn't bump and grind from the hip; it's abandoned the model of genital sexuality altogether for a kind of polymorphously perverse frenzy. It's a dance of tics and twitches, jerks and spasms, the agitation of a body broken down into individual components, then re-integrated at the level of the entire dancefloor.... It's pagan too, this digital Dionysian derangement whose goal is to find asylum in MADNESS. (Hence the slang of 'mental' and 'nutty', sound systems with names like Bedlam, groups with names like Lunarci, MCs chanting 'off my fucking tree' – pejoratives turned into desirable states-of-mindless-ness).
>
> It's emotionally regressive too (as all the musically progressive genres of the last decade – rap, oceanic rock, noise – have been): hence the infantilism of ravers' dummy-sucking or bubble gum chart hits like 'A Trip To Trumpton'.[20]

Reynolds here points towards an aspect of *jouissance* which is central to any real understanding of the concept. *Jouissance* is a *regressive* experience, related to a moment in the pre-history of the subject before gendered identity is assumed. It therefore possesses an eroticism which is in some sense pre-sexual. This is why, for Barthes, the body of *jouissance* seems always to be curiously ungendered. Indeed, Barthes says as much himself in *The Pleasure of the Text*: 'The text ... grants a glimpse of the scandalous truth about bliss: that it may well be, once the image-reservoir of speech is abolished, *neuter*.'[21]

We might conclude from this discussion that dance music should be seen as tending to induce an ecstatic experience of *jouissance* which is – if only partially and temporarily – an escape from gender itself, a return to a moment when there was no 'I' and specifically no 'I'm male' or 'I'm female'. We might say, in fact that this is precisely how the central experience of 'rave' works; it offers us ecstasy by liberating us from the demands of the symbolic order, the demand to be male or female, the demand to speak and understand, the demand to be anything at all. It is significant then that this is not only an abstract conclusion drawn from an application of the work of some French literary theorists. It is in fact an interpretation which has been offered by many people, including many participants in those cultures themselves, at least since the moment of acid house. The relative desexualization of the dancefloor was a common topic of conversation among those (male and female, gay and straight, ourselves included) who found this one of rave's most liberating effects on British night culture. The loose clothes and infantile or psychedelic imagery which accompanied rave culture through many of its mutations (acid house, hardcore, trance) all helped to emphasize the status of raving as a means to access an asexual *jouissance*, a childhood state. This has been a common theme among academic commentators as well,[22] and has to be understood as one of rave and post-rave dance culture's most striking features. While disco may have provided space for the articulation of non-hegemonic sexualities, especially for gay men, its spaces, its rituals, and the lyrics of its songs all served to constitute it as a resolutely sexual space. Despite the fact that rave and post-rave clubs and spaces have always been places where people were likely to meet sexual partners, it is undeniable that one of rave's major effects was to constitute a space in which the ecstatic pleasure of dancing could be experienced according to terms which did not make the expression of sexuality its primary aim. Given the arguments which we have pursued in the preceding chapters, it's not surprising that the soundtrack to this change should have been instrumental musics with a repetitive beat.

The argument that such music can liberate us from gender sufficiently to grant us the experience of neuter *jouissance* is deeply problematic, however. The logic of our argument thus far would be that it is purely the physical, corporeal, timbral qualities of music which, via their *significance*, offer us access to *jouissance*. Such musics seem inevitably to subvert the symbolic order. However, a consideration of the issues involved in a wider context will demonstrate that this proposition is in certain cases very difficult to sustain. Let us return to the issue with which we were recently concerned: the significance (or signifiance) of vocal grain in western music.

Different voices

A great deal of our discussion so far has looked at the different ways in which writers on music and culture in general have treated the actual and metaphorical status of the voice.[23] On the one hand, we have looked at Derrida's account of that phonologocentrism which regards the voice as the site of unmediated truth. On the other, we have looked at Barthes' account of the 'grain' of the voice. At first glance, what we might seem to have here are two quite different attitudes to the status of the singing voice. However, we can see that in fact these two ways of looking at the issue converge precisely. For just as we saw that the metaphysical tradition is antithetical towards instrumental music except when such music manages to render itself metaphysically desirable, an object of pure contemplation, so we can see that the classical tradition only valorizes the voice when it does what metaphysics expects of it. When the voice ceases to present itself as the means of unmediated communication which philosophy so often wants it to be, when it allows it physicality and materiality to interfere, when it does not strip itself of 'grain', then classical music discourse is largely hostile towards it. The implication is that it is not a question either of the metaphysical-classical tradition or its poststructuralist critics believing that either instrumental music or song are in themselves good or bad. Rather, it is a matter of understanding the ways in which the former tradition privileges a particular set of *values* which it usually sees manifested in a particular *ideal* notion of the voice as pure breath, untrammelled by the body.

Similarly, Barthes' account of the relative significance of the voice with 'grain' and without cannot be simplistically mapped on to contemporary music. For over the past twenty years, the 'grainy' male voice has in fact become one of the key elements of dominant music discourse. Where it is a novelty in the classical tradition about which Bathes writes, the gravelly, textured, idiosyncratic voice is typical of most forms of rock. But the *use* to which vocal 'grain' is put in rock is very different to the implicitly deconstructive use of it described in Barthes' essay. Within contemporary rock discourse, the 'dirty', untrained sounding voice has come to signify sincerity, authenticity, truthful *meaning* of a kind which a trained singer (supposedly) might not be able to produce. Bob Dylan, Mick Jagger, Iggy Pop, Bruce Springsteen, Ozzy Osborne, John Lydon, Joe Strummer, Bob Mould, Michael Stipe, Liam Gallagher, even Mark E. Smith – the rock vocalist almost invariably uses the 'grain' of his voice to signify the corporeality of his music, not in opposition to an ideal of immaterial, 'pure' meaning but in opposition to the perceived contrivance and technologically-mediated inauthenticity of 'pop'. This is a case of music's relationship to the body being foregrounded, but precisely *in the service* of a phonologocentric ideal of the voice as the site of unmediated truth, of natural authenticity. In this sense rock discourse is deeply informed by folk

ideologies, with all of their hostility to technology and 'artificiality'.[24] It is important to note here that the 'grainy' rock voice is almost always *male*. As we will
discuss in the next chapter, when considering the relationship between music and
the body, we have to pay attention to the different *types* of body that exist.

What we can learn from this consideration of the status of vocal grain in rock
discourse is that even 'grain' which foregrounds the textural, material qualities of
music and the physicality of its sources, can be deployed in the service of metaphysical ends when it functions within the context of a discourse which
privileges the voice in the *particular* way that conventional rock does. We will see
shortly what happens when 'grain' is deployed in a context which displaces that
privilege.

It has not always been the case that rock music was thought of as something
different from 'dance' music. In fact, in the beginning, dance music is exactly
what it was. Rock 'n' roll (which may or may not have been black American slang
for sex) was a term which specifically designated the rhythmic *movement* which
such music was supposed to accompany. Today, however, we are used to there
being a firm distinction between rock and dance musics. Whether we call them
something general like 'dance' or 'pop' or label them with ever more specific
generic names (soul, disco, house, progressive house, and so forth). This is not to
say that people *don't* dance to rock music in specific ways, but a glance around any
record shop will make clear that music defined as 'dance' is clearly thought of as
separate from 'rock'.

The question is, how did this distinction come about? How did a form of
dance music, with its roots in black blues and an enthusiastic audience of white
teenagers, turn into a music which is more often than not defined in strict opposition to dance? The story of rock's separation from dance is precisely the story of its
becoming respectable, of its move from the margins to the centre of contemporary culture, and of its rearticulation in terms of the dominant values of western
culture. During the 1960s rock became the music of educated white middle-class
men; aspiring to art-status, to literacy, to various types of complexity. If the story
begins anywhere, then it begins with Bob Dylan's electric turn. The hero of the
American folk protest movement first embraced rock 'n' roll in 1964, at exactly
the same moment that his writing turned from folk-ballad realism to a neo-
symbolist poetry steeped in the American romanticism of Walt Whitman and the
Beats. This was the moment, we might say, at which rock 'n' roll was transformed
definitively from a dance style into a sanctioned art form, and it is no accident
that it did so via the medium of a voice which, for all its celebrated 'grain', was
definitively that of a white man immersed in western literary and biblical culture.
Despite its many mutations, rock was never again treated as dance music by any
but a handful of people. Having bought into the metaphysics of romantic
ideology, with its belief in the value of 'art', its obsession with authorship and
meaningful expression, rock became a music more in tune than out of it with the
metaphysical prioritization of voice, brain and sense over body and dance.
'Dance', like 'pop' (and for similar reasons) became one of the terms normally

excluded from the field of 'rock'. By the time of house music's emergence in the 1980s, the idea that rock could be dance music was considered revolutionary by some (the ideologists of the 'baggy' dance–rock crossover, in particular), unthinkable by others (everyone who wrote obituaries for rock in-between the moments of acid house and Britpop[25]).

What this illustrates is precisely the enormous pressure which the governing discourses of our culture can place on cultural forms. This might be an odd image to use in the case of rock 'n' roll; nobody forced Bob Dylan to invent rock as we know it, just as nobody forced everyone from the Beatles to Black Sabbath, in their various ways, to follow him. The adoption of rock 'n' roll by white men, and their transformation of it into 'rock', was a project in which artists and audiences alike were enthusiastic participants. But a price was paid. The black R & B performers who originated the sound, to this day receive little of the credit and even less of the money that might be thought due to them for the invention of modern popular music. The same process which transformed a dance form into a genre reproducing almost all of the key terms of western musical metaphysics indissolubly turned a black music into a white one, and while it would be dangerous to draw a firm distinction between 'white' and 'black' musics, or to argue that black culture exists simply outside of western modernity rather than in a complex relation to it,[26] the story of rock illustrates some of the dubious political effects of the continued hegemony of metaphysical music discourse.

In the case of musics less wholly articulated within the terms of western music discourse, the pressure which that discourse can exert is more obvious. In the example of house and techno, it has clearly been the case throughout their history that records which possessed a strong melody and vocals have more easily been granted air-play, and consequently more exposure, than records which did not. This might not seem particularly important, but if we consider the fact that such musics did not begin as specifically *vocal* genres, and that it has generally taken records which in their deployment of vocals and melody are far more in tune with the dominant musical discourse than their instrumental forebears to dent the charts (with some honourable exceptions), then we can conclude that there is a strong external pressure on dance musics to become more song-oriented, more meaningful, less rhythm/body/dancefloor centred than they might otherwise be. This is not an argument for house purism or against songs, but it is important to understand the mechanics of a culture which clearly privileges the one over the other. It's this pressure which has resulted in the rather strange phenomenon of certain types of popular music being specifically designated as 'dance musics'. Those types of music which most resist rearticulation with the terms of classical music discourse, which refuse to suppress their status as dance musics by becoming songs, anthems, units of meaning, are all labelled under this broad but also uniquely specific category (few other labels tell you so precisely what you're supposed to *do* with the music in question, as the label 'dance' does).

As long as the dominant values of a culture remain informed by metaphysical imperatives, then there is always a strong pressure on its musics to conform to those imperatives. The tension between the demands of meaning and melody on the one hand, rhythm and materiality on the other, can be seen as having informed much of the recent history of popular music. Most obviously, for instance, we can ask why it is that vocal music remains the dominant form of popular music. Why it is that the radio mix of a dance single always gives prominence to the vocal. Indeed, why has the popularization and mass marketing of a dance genre invariably involved a shift in its production values, away from an emphasis on bass and drums towards an emphasis on treble, melody, vocals? The answer, in part, is that these remain the dominant musical values of our culture.

We have to be very careful here. There is a long tradition of dance music fans preferring the more esoteric sound of musics which eschew the 'mainstream' musical priorities of melody and verbal language, eschewing the more popular sounds as 'plastic disco', 'handbag house'. The point of our analysis is not to condone or support this kind of dancefloor élitism, but to understand in a more considered and objective way just what might be at stake in such arguments. While it is true that in the context of western music discourse, musics which privilege rhythm and bass while eschewing verbal music are in some sense more 'radical' than other kinds, this does not mean that they are necessarily better. Deconstructing received notions of meaning, truth and identity can often be liberating but can just as often be completely disempowering; without meaning, how do we think? Without identity, how do we act? The ecstatic experience towards which such music and its attendant dancing can lead us, where we literally lose ourselves in an oblivious obliteration of self, can be a liberating and challenging experience. It can also be terrifying, disempowering, or a literally mindless escape from problems which we might need to deal with.

By the same token, nothing we say here should be taken to imply that there is something wrong with enjoying a song. Enjoying the sense of (real or fantasized) identification with a singer, the pleasure we can take from melody and musical narrative, are irreducible aspects of our musical life. The point is not that there is something wrong with them, but that the dominant musical values of our culture tend to permit and enable those pleasures while actively suppressing others.

To sum up some of these arguments: the dominant values of western culture privilege a particular set of terms and priorities at the expense of others, but these philosophical priorities can manifest themselves in a variety of ways at different times and in different places. All music possesses the qualities of physicality and repetition which metaphysical discourse seeks to eradicate from it, but in some instances these qualities will be foregrounded while others will be highly limited, even suppressed. The singing voice can manifest metaphysical priorities as the site of pure meaning; it can also problematize them through the intervention if its own materiality, its irreducible 'grain'. On the other hand, even the 'grainy' voice can come to participate in metaphysical discourse when it becomes the site of authentic and self-present meaning rather than the site of its problematization. Instrumental music was traditionally considered suspect by the philosophical tradition until transformation in the practice of music at the end of the eighteenth

71

century made it possible for instrumental music to manifest metaphysical priorities with often greater ease than could vocal music. By the twentieth century, of course, modernist composers who were the most committed to a metaphysical eradication of all physicality and sociality from their music, for the most part eschewed vocal music altogether as being the most tainted by those qualities. On the other hand, in the field of popular music, the singing voice generally (but by no means always) remains the site of meaning and full subjectivity, the point at which metaphysics most powerfully shapes music.

We can see many examples of this phenomenon in contemporary music culture. The traditional dominance in the pop market of forms of rock and soul which absolutely prioritize melody and a clear vocal line as their central elements can be understood in these terms. More specifically, it is possible to map the field of dance music as a whole in terms of the framework which we have established here. Dance musics after acid house have taken many forms, some of which push further its rejection of dominant musical values, some of which bring dance music into different types of accommodation with them. It might be useful to consider some of these generic distinctions here.

Acid house

British dance culture could be dated as beginning at just about any time. 'Ravers' did not invent the practice of dancing all night with the aid of illegal stimulants; northern soul fans, among others, were doing that in the early 1970s. Northern soul itself grew out of the mod culture, obsessed as it was with black American dance music and pharmaceutical speed. Disco enjoyed widespread popularity in the late 1970s, as schoolchildren the length and breadth of the land were taught the dance steps to Village People's gay anthem 'YMCA'. In both cases there had been examples of non-vocal dance music achieving relative popularity (for example, the early SalSoul Orchestra records of the mid-1970s and countless pioneering disco instrumental tracks). The anti-rock tendencies of rave ideology can be traced at least to the moment of post-punk's transmutation – via a moment of fascinated flirtation with funk and disco – into the 'New Pop'. But popular memory – and, most importantly, media memory – currently considers 'dance culture' as we now know it as beginning with the emergence into the British musical consciousness of a particular sound and the culture which quickly grew up around it: acid house.[27] Ten years after 'Anarchy in the UK', punk was little more than a historical footnote; acid house, a variant of an obscure American club music, invented by accident,[28] is still remembered as the beginning of 'where we are now'.

After our examination of the history and terms of the dominant discourse on music in the west, it is hard to imagine a sound which could overturn the priorities of that discourse more completely. Acid house was probably the most self-consciously repetitive form of western music to have emerged since the development of recording. Its hypnotic beat appealed to the body of the dancer while making no concession to classical demands for narrative meaning or harmonic substance. More even than other types of early house records – which shared acid's insistent repetition – it eschewed melody in favour of *texture*. The TB-303 'squelch' which it made famous, is unique for its capacity to be *felt* by the listener/dancer across a very broad frequency range; able to reach deep down into the bass octave, or shriek into resonant squeals of higher frequency sound. In the roughness of its timbre, it is pure electronic *grain*.

Of course, the *use* to which this music was put was crucial in determining its importance. Despite the existence of earlier pharmacologically-motivated dance cultures, no genre had so explicitly advertised its status as music for dancing all night to on illegal drugs. But it is not as if any music could have served this purpose, and it is not easy, on the other hand, to imagine such music having any other primary purpose. Inscribed in the very sound of acid house, in its emphasis of bass, rhythmic repetition, in its exploration of texture before melody, was a refusal of the metaphysical priorities of western music discourse.

Musically, acid house constituted an eruption of refusal of the aesthetic priorities of metaphysics.[29] But this does not mean that other kinds of music have not and will not continue to resist those imperatives. At the same time, no music can be seen to be completely opposed to 'metaphysics'. No sound can refuse *completely* the demand for ordered coherence, for some kind of meaning, however slight. The simple fact that a listener recognizes a particular set of sound *as music* means that some kind of ordered communication is taking place. It is important to keep in mind, therefore, that in applying the kind of analysis which we have been developing here, we are always dealing in matters of *degree*. All musical texts have both geno-texts and pheno-texts.

House

The roots of acid can be found in Chicago soil. The house music which grew there in 1985 and 1986, was a minimal four-to-the-floor dance music, reminiscent of disco, but stripped to its bare essentials, raw and machine-driven. It retained disco's emphasis on rhythmic repetition, and on the centrality of the bass-line, while decentring more 'conventional' melodic, vocal or song elements. Compare a typical house track with a standard rock, pop or even soul number, and one can see how much further it is – at least in the terms set out here – from the values and priorities of the dominant western discourse. Whereas such musics are almost always based around distinct songs, with lyrics to be understood and sung along with and several stretches of extended melody, the Chicago house which influenced so many later forms was organized around a bare minimum of bass line and drums, with sparse keyboard parts, and the occasional sampled or repeated vocal line. Often those elements of melody and vocal that were present, like the all-important bass and drums, are experienced not as part of an extended whole but as repeated bursts, elements of *rhythm* before anything else. Rather than constructing its melodic lines according to conventional methods of extended development and triadic harmony, house tends to use short bursts of melody, using pentatonic melodic techniques which, significantly, locate it firmly outside the dominant musical discourses of the west. Its sampled snippets of sung or spoken vocal do not add up to coherent verses, rather instead becoming part of the rhythmic syntax of the track itself. Its ability – by means of the sampler and the sequencer – to turn *any* sound into a rhythmic element, remains the basic template for most contemporary dance music. The foregrounding of bass and percussion, the insistent use of repetition, and the overriding emphasis on its *functionality* as dance music, all mark a definitive break with logocentric music discourse.

This not to say that songs and vocals do not figure at all. A primarily black/gay club culture, adapting technologically a disco tradition, could hardly, after all, *ignore* the voice. Some Chicago house, and in particular the New York form of house 'garage' (named after the legendary New York club, Paradise Garage), made a point of using house rhythms and Philly soul and gospel derived song structures. Moreover house itself did produce its share of memorable songs – Frankie Knuckles' 'Tears', Joe Smooth's 'Promised Land', Ten City's 'That's the Way Love Is', to name but three. House rhythms were of course also 'taken up' by pop, and used as a new mode of backing/arrangement for more 'traditional' song elements with varying degrees of success. There are a few points of note here – first, that in the mix and arrangement of vocal house tracks, as in disco, the rhythm is not subsumed, or de-emphasized by the presence of a vocal or song, and the song structure is often 'opened out', extended beyond four minutes of verse, bridge, chorus. Second, in practice the ratio of 'songs' to more minimal 'tracks' and 'dubs' has always been low on the house dancefloor – they have tended to be played at the end of the night, or at the end of a set – the successful ones canonised as end-of-the-night anthems. Third, vocal house, and in particular garage, has always offered at least one 'dub' mix (usually several) – that is a mix where the vocal is shattered, effected, and used but in part, rhythmically, in the manner we have discussed above – in the knowledge that, while the radio is more likely to play a song, 'dedicated' dancefloors and the DJs which serve them, prefer the minimal stripped-down tracks.

Techno

The word 'techno', one of dance music's most complex generic designations, began as a spin-off of Chicago house, was intended to describe the particular products of nearby Detroit's club scene, which had been producing a somewhat icier, more futuristic take on its neighbour's minimal recomposition of disco. When asked for a definition of this new dance sound of Detroit, DJ and producer Derrick May described it as the sound of 'George Clinton and Kraftwerk stuck in an elevator'.[30] This comparison of European and American musical traditions was entirely appropriate: black American techno musicians, such as May, Juan Atkins and Carl Craig, were greatly influenced by the European practitioners of new wave rock and synth-pop, and their attendant neo-classical musical traditions (a fondness for string and piano sounds was demonstrated by May's enormously influential single 'Strings of Life'). Yet at the same time, as May's choice of artist name – Rhythim Is Rhythim – suggested, the insistence of the dancefloor, and Afro-American musical priorities were still being actively upheld.

Techno joined house in inspiring and invigorating the popular musics of Europe in a way that was unheard over the past twenty-five years. It proved massively popular in the UK and Europe, inspiring new strains of rave music like 'hardcore', as such producers as Joey Beltram and Jeff Mills toughened its timbres and drove tempos faster. While techno as a club music form now spans the Atlantic, residing in European cities such as Berlin, Ghent or Glasgow, as much as in Detroit, and in any number of manifestations, the word itself now is often used indiscriminately to describe any pop record which contains an abrasive or machine-driven dance component (bands from The Prodigy to Republica have been referred to as 'techno' acts, much to the vitriol of fans of the 'original' Detroit sound).

The term itself and the music it designated drew on an iconography of the future, and a machine-driven sound which began in the electro forms of the early 1980s. In their initial interviews with mostly UK journalists,[31] techno's creators, Juan Atkins, Kevin Saunderson and Derrick May (who had all attended the same high school in Belleville, Ypsilanti), repeatedly referred to the influence of their immediate surroundings: 'techno' as a label alluded to the (problematic) industrial heritage of the 'Motor City', and its double valuation of technology, as both negative and positive. The black musicians working within Detroit had grown up with the harsh fact of technology's necessary formulation within a tough socioeconomic context. This geo-social context was vital but complex: techno was not the sonic representation of a city splitting, but a newly-opened space within which European glimpses of a robot-cool future collide with rather more dystopic social impetus, within a zone of pleasure in which the rhythm brought relief; a reterritorialization within a zone of urban crisis rather than an act of illustration. Sonically the music played on the received distinction between 'technology' and 'humanity', choosing to forego the disco-derived voluptuousness of house music in favour of a certain coolness, a refusal to force machine-music into shapes and textures which would conform to traditional, humanist notions of 'musicality'.

At times its preoccupation with discourses of the future-in-the-present, a modernist politics of the 'underground', and the implicit avant-gardism pursued by some of its protagonists, has seemed to carry techno almost towards an accommodation with those puritan discourses to which dance culture is normally so hostile. May's reputed revulsion at the Dionysian idiocy of the UK rave scene is ironic when one considers how much it owed to records such as his own 'Strings of Life'. An unfortunate desire to uphold a Detroit 'aesthetic', when techno continued to mutate, alter and influence in Europe, feeding into rave, trance and ultimately such forms as gabber, has sometimes been manifested in a fondness for 'purism' and geographical authenticity (not of course exclusive to techno by any means) in some of the cultures and discourses around it, often by white musicians and journalists on behalf of black or diasporic musical forms.[32] These forget that techno at its most exciting collided American and European traditions, rather than merely retracing narratives of appropriation.[33]

It was the popularity of techno and its iconography of the machine which later inspired the emergence of 'electronica' and 'isolationism', pioneered by Sheffield's techno label Warp and its 'Artificial Intelligence' series of LPs. Despite some fine records favoured as 'chill out' and 'post-club' material by dance fans, the discourses around the movement which ensued appeared to remove techno from the dancefloor and back into the mainstream of the metaphysical tradition; musics to listen to, musics to sit still to, electronic avant-garde music by and for (although not exclusively) white middle-class men. Such unfortunately titled labels as 'intelligent techno' signalled the removal of these musics from the zone of the body towards those of the intellect and 'art'. These genres and discourses were promoted in the UK by magazines like The Wire and the organizers of the Institute of Contemporary Arts' influential club, the Electronic Lounge. Both were instrumental in redeploying a muscular modernist discourse on electronic music, which had more to do with the avant-gardism of Stockhausen than with any kind of dance music, favouring dark abstraction over sensual pleasure. In addition, the seriousness of some of techno's fans, their continued preference for spartan fatigues and functional dress pace rave, and the scene's disengagement from any disco-derived fondness for glamour, at a time when many club promoters were favouring a menu solely comprised of anthemic house, led many to claim (somewhat unfairly) that this was music solely for boys.

This is not the whole story, however. Techno in its several forms remains conscious of its status of dance music, and although some of its textures and timbres have been considered robotic and cold, techno as a genre has kept as much faith with its roots in funk as any other electronic dance genre. As well, techno's asexuality might be seen as a deliberate strategy, a pursuit of neuter jouissance which seeks not simply to regress to a moment before the regulating discourses of sexuality took hold of our beings, but to go beyond them into an imagined cyborg future, a place where the fluidity of cyberspace is the medium for non/identity and the robot exoskeleton is the site of a constructable, engineerable, alterable, androgynous corporeality. The paradigm for this mode of being would be the cyborg of Donna Harraway's classic cyber-feminist 'Manifesto', a being capable of using technology to transcend the limits of gender.[34]

Euro-house

We might consider some of the other issues raised by defining house music as 'definitively deconstructive' if we examine some of its more recent variants. As we noted above, house and techno forms, when they were taken up by European musicians, mutated into a number of other forms: rave, trance, 'progressive' house. Epic house and Euro-house are a further two names given to recent sub-genres of house and techno, mainly originating in Europe, which, while still (usually) lacking vocals, deploy textures and techniques characteristic as much of the western classical tradition as of any other. Typical features of Euro-house include lush, full production, with its lavish deployment of synthetic strings, the piano and similar textures; a penchant for grand (if none the less simple) melodic gestures and the rigidly structured use of musical narrative: rising chord sequences, periodic crescendos consisting of bass drop-outs followed by intense drum-rolls which give way to a return to the central bass line and key melodic theme. In their use of triadic harmony, emphasis on melody and linear narrative structures, we might see very little here which does not conform to the dictates of the classical tradition.

Many dance music fans would not disagree with this observation. Its popularity in European clubs and on provincial British dancefloors has rarely been matched by an endorsement from the dance cognoscenti. Some critics, fans and DJs have tended to deride Euro-house because of what they perceive as its formulaic character and shamelessly crowd-pleasing tactics. Preferring instead music with a greater emphasis on bass, drums and more inventive explorations of the interaction between rhythmic and melodic elements, some commentators consider Euro-house as more 'mainstream' than their preferred forms, regarding it as closer in form and technique to traditional white pop forms.

In some respects we would suggest that these evaluations are implicitly – and often unconsciously – informed by the kind of arguments presented here in this book. They recognize that musics which emphasize melody and narrative, which use undemanding textures drawn from the classical sound repertoire, are in certain ways more complicit with the dominant musical discourse of the west than those which do not. There is, however, a fundamental irony in this belief. For the terms in which these charges are actually levelled against these extremely popular forms of music should be strangely familiar to us by now. These terms rarely if ever mention, say, epic house's complicity with logocentric metaphysics. What they deplore instead is its lack of innovation and its failure to place sufficient demands on its audience. This music is viewed as being too easy.

On one level these comments must be taken as valid. Such musics do not pose the same difficulties for listeners educated in listening with typical western ears that, for example, acid house or jungle might do (see below). What is more, few of the arguments in this book would make any sense if we did not recognize the value of experiencing a challenge to one's subjectivity in music: an experience which problematizes rather than merely reconfirms the nature of one's relationship to the world, to others, to oneself, to one's body. But to deride musics which do not offer that experience in a distressing and uncomfortable way, to devalorize musics precisely because they offer their listeners too much pleasure, is simply to replicate the terms of the dominant musical discourse absolutely insofar as it itself replicates western metaphysics' suspicion of bodily pleasure.

The discourse which emerges in arguments against the validity of Euro-house therefore tends to take the form of an articulation of an almost Kantian or

Adornoian aesthetic with a certain commitment to its Afro-diasporic counter-discourses. An argument in favour of the importance of rhythm, timbre and bass therefore becomes, in this context, at the same time an argument in favour of music as a rigorously demanding art object. Euro-house is derided for its failure as 'art'.

We can see a complex politics emerging in this argument. For, if we consider the significance of these debates as they go on *within* dance culture, it is obvious that it is not merely to do with nasty puritanical western culture being opposed by fun-loving, pleasure-seeking dance. Even within dance culture there emerge implicit and explicit arguments as to the best *types* of pleasure: the Afro-derived pleasures of rhythm or the European pleasures of melody and harmonic completion?

What the idea of Euro-house as simply a reactionary form tends to overlook is the radical challenge which such music offers to classical notions of how music can be *used*. Music, according to the classical model, should be an object of rational contemplation, not mere sensory pleasure. It certainly is not supposed to be an aid to ecstatic dancing. But this is exactly what Euro-house is. This is the music whose form has been the most completely determined by the utilitarian demands of Ecstasy culture. In 1995 Simon Reynolds commented on 'happy' hardcore's

> cheesy piano riffs, Beltram-style synth-stabs, shrieking diva-vocals and above all the stomping 4-to-the-floor beat (i.e. all the whiter-than-white elements that activate and accentuate the E-rush and encourage the dancers to 'go mental').[35]

Reynolds' observation applies even more accurately to Euro-house. The pianos, strings, trance loops, rising chords and drum rolls are all precisely designed to accentuate particular effects of MDMA taken in a club environment; the tingling anticipation, the big rush cheered by the crowd, the warm bath of lush sensation. From Reynolds' perspective such specifically Eurofied dance music doubtless possesses none of the saving graces of ''ardkore' and its progeny. Herein lies a paradox, however; for an audience whose identities have been more or less unproblematically shaped by western discourse the ecstatic experience of collective *jouissance* is only made available by musics which *do not* radically threaten the terms of that discourse in *every* possible way. In simple terms: if you have grown up on white pop and nothing else, then minimalist techno, stripped-bare acid or manic drum 'n' bass will probably just give you a headache, but a cheesy Dutch trance tune or an Oakenfold anthem might just open some doors. We would argue, therefore, that there is something subversive at stake here. Modernist avant-gardism and the continued influence of residual puritanism may often converge with a taste for drums and bass to decry any aesthetic experience which offers its participants simple enjoyment, but even the most Eurocentric forms of contemporary dance music refuse many metaphysical and puritanical imperatives in offering just this, in presenting themselves as musics which have no purpose other than to be *used*. Indeed it is precisely their deconstructive accommodation with elements of traditional Eurocentric discourse which lends them such utility, making them accessible to a far wider audience than hardcore or jungle or even acid house enjoyed, democratizing the rave experience and making its pleasures of collectivity and shared ecstasy available to many people who otherwise would have no such access. Cultural politics, like any form of politics, is not always about radical refusals and extreme opposition. Often the most successful strategies are those which construct just such negotiated spaces.

Jungle/drum 'n' bass

At the opposite end of the spectrum from Euro-house we can locate the rigorous avant-gardism of drum 'n' bass. Various narratives tend to locate this genre as an 'advanced' descendent of house and techno. More sophisticated accounts see its several variants as produced at a number of intersections between hardcore, hip hop and reggae. 'Ragga' or 'jungle' techno were among the names given to forms of hardcore/breakbeat to which its creators added elements from Jamaican dance-hall and reggae musics. The tempos which had been attained by breakbeat had reached twice the speed of reggae forms, and so allowed the addition of dub-derived bass-lines, reggae samples and toasting (which had already been present in the form of the rave MC). By the time jungle had emerged as a label, the music was already mutating, stripped-down to intense, frenetically percussive sound-scapes deploying little more than multiply-fissured breakbeats and the intense sub-bass which had been popular since the early days of acid house and techno in the UK. Identified as being resolutely marginal, largely – but by no means exclusively – black, certainly working class, coming out of the urban penumbra of London – Brixton, St Pauls, Handsworth and the suburbs of the South East – it initially found little support among wider audiences or the music press.[36] This marginality, combined with a formal disregard for European musical conventions and a quasi-scientific pursuit of potentials of the breakbeat, made it ripe for the attentions of conventional avant-garde art discourse. Ironically this was not the initial outlook – ragga-laden jungle was initially hyped as a new chart-dance crossover, but only came to the attention of a much wider (and much whiter) audience when the rigours of its minimal drum explorations gave way to more 'musical' exposition, the use of techno chord progressions (pioneered by the likes of Photek) ultimately resulting in the semi-ambient jazz-fusions of producers like L.T.J. Bukem. The name 'jungle' – whose connotations had never been popular with some of its practitioners – had by now been dropped in favour of the neutral formalism of the tag 'drum 'n' bass'. Soon afterwards this music was increasingly adopted by white middle-class audiences.[37]

Jungle/drum 'n' bass can be understood as the latest in a lineage of black musics which have occupied a kind of double-space,[38] appealing to audiences at once as black dance musics and to intellectuals and some fan cultures as avant-garde forms which could be fully legitimated in terms of a western modernist discourse. Indeed, drum 'n' bass at the moment of its inception sounded like a deliberate mediation between bebop and hip hop, the two other key musics in the history of black avant-gardism, even if it did later end up sounding like jazz-fusion. Like its forebears, it occupies a paradoxical position in terms of our account of musical metaphysics. On the one hand it seems extraordinarily anti-metaphysical – with its emphasis on rhythm, texture, drums and bass – while clearly manifesting Afro-diasporic aesthetic priorities.[39] On the other hand, it has tended to be legitimated by critics as a 'serious' art form, entirely in terms of its 'complexity' (which inheres in its rhythmic density – an Afro-diasporic imperative that considers tempo to be relative not absolute, and as such is *intra-dimensional*, combining slow bass with frenetic drums at twice the speed) and relative 'difficulty'. The idea of jungle as providing dancefloor pleasure was almost entirely subsumed in some accounts (despite its continued popularity on the dancefloor) as it transmuted into drum 'n' bass, a new jazz for the 1990s.[40]

There is a logic to this transformation; music which is desperately counter-metaphysical, which refuses almost all of the aesthetic priorities of Eurocentric music discourse, sounds incredibly 'difficult' to those audiences whose aesthetic sense has been shaped primarily by that discourse (it is sometimes dismissed as difficult to dance to by those unfamiliar with it, because its tempo – simultaneously fast and slow – is clocked to reggae speeds and their multiples rather than functioning at 120–140 beats per minute like house and techno forms). However, that discourse, particularly in modernist modes, specifically valorizes such 'difficulty', seeing it as preferable to the pursuit of mere sensory pleasure. Hence the easy re-reading of a black dance form as an exercise in modernist avant-gardism. This is not to say that producers themselves were not instrumental in this process, negotiating their newly-acquired status as artists and the cachet it afforded them – nor does it suggest that its audiences have not been aware of the music's implicit avant-gardism. Nevertheless, as jungle became drum 'n' bass and some critical discourses turned a dance form into an 'art' music, we can see a clear manifestation of the hegemonic operation of metaphysical music discourse.

Whatever their generic differences and separate histories, all of these musics at the point of reception share a commitment to the pursuit of a common goal; the creation of a shared feeling of ecstasy and release on the dancefloor. If *jouissance* is the best name for this way of feeling, then we will have to explore – and problematize – that term in more detail than we have done here. This we will do in the following chapter. For now, it is sufficient to recognize that this experience and all of its specific components are deeply feared and frequently opposed by that mode of thinking which has dominated the west. As we will see in Chapter 6, this tradition finds its most acutely individualist manifestation, as well as its most successful actual implementation, under the conditions of capitalist modernity which to some extent we still inhabit today.

Notes

1 Richard Middleton, *Studying Popular Music* (Buckingham, Open University Press, 1990), pp. 104–6.
2 Ibid.
3 See Geoffrey Bennington and Jacques Derrida, *Jacques Derrida* (Chicago, UCP, 1993), p. 38.
4 Jacques Derrida, 'Tympan', trans. A. Bass, in P. Kamuf (ed.), *Between the Blinds* (Hemel Hempstead, Harvester, 1991), p. 156.
5 See 'Speech and Phenomena', in Kamuf, *Between the Blinds*, p. 27.
6 John Shepherd, 'Music as Cultural Text', in J. Paynter, J. Howell, R. Orton and P. Seymour (eds), *The Routledge Companion to Contemporary Musical Thought* (London, Routledge, 1993), p. 145; cf., John Shepherd, *Music as Social Text* (Cambridge, Polity, 1992).
7 Ibid., p. 147.
8 Ibid., p. 149.
9 See Middleton, *Studying Popular Music*; cf., John Shepherd's essay in Ruth A. Solie (ed.), *Musicology and Difference* (Berkley, University of California Press, 1993), p. 62.
10 Derrida, 'Tympan', p. 158.
11 Middleton, *Studying Popular Music*, p. 259. An investigation of the significance of repetition in musical experience might also have to examine it in terms of Freud's identification of a fundamental 'compulsion to repeat' in 'Beyond the Pleasure Principle': see Sigmund Freud, *On Metapsychology*, Penguin Freud Library, Volume 11 (London, Penguin, 1984), pp. 269–339.
12 Johan Fornas, 'Listen to Your Voice!', in *New Formations* (London, Lawrence & Wishart), Winter 1994, p. 158.
13 For example, *New Musical Express, Melody Maker, Select, Q* and *Rolling Stone*.
14 For example, *Mixmag, DJ* and *Muzik*.
15 Julia Kristeva, *Revolution in Poetic Language*, trans. Margaret Waller (New York, Columbia, 1984), pp. 86–7.
16 Roland Barthes, 'The Grain of the Voice', in *Image Music Text*, trans. Stephen Heath (London, Fontana, 1977), p. 182.
17 Ibid., pp. 188–9.
18 John Gill, *Queer Noise* (London, Cassell, 1995), p. 134.
19 *The Pleasure of the Text*, trans. Richard Howard (New York, Farrar, Strauss & Girouux, 1975), pp. 13, 16–17.
20 See Simon Reynolds *Ardkore Archive* on http://members.aol.com/blissout/index.htm. See also Simon Reynolds, *Energy Flash: A Journey Through Rave Music and Dance Culture* (London, Picador, 1998).
21 Barthes, *Pleasure of the Text*, p. 16.
22 See Drew Hemment, 'e is for Ekstasis', in *New Formations* (London, Lawrence & Wishart), Summer 1997; Antonio Melechi, 'The Ecstasy of Disappearance', in S. Redhead (ed.), *Rave Off* (Aldershot, Avebury, 1993); Maria Pini, 'Cyborgs, Nomads and the Raving Feminine', in Helen Thomas (ed.), *Dance in the City* (London, Routledge, 1997); 'Women and the Early British Rave Scene', in A. McRobbie (ed.), *Back to Reality* (Manchester, Manchester University Press, 1997).
23 For an interesting discussion of the status of the voice in popular music discourse, see Simon Frith, *Performing Rites* (Oxford, Oxford University Press, 1996), pp. 183–202.
24 See Simon Frith, 'Art Versus Technology: The Strange Case of Popular Music', in R. Collins (ed.), *Media, Culture and Society: A Critical Reader* (London, Sage, 1986), pp. 263–79.
25 See Greil Marcus, 'Notes on the Life and Death and Incandescent Banality of Rock 'n' Roll', in Hanif Kureishi and Jon Savage (eds), *The Faber Book of Pop* (London, Faber, 1995).
26 See Paul Gilroy, *The Black Atlantic* (London, Verso, 1993), Chapter 1.

27 Both *Time Out* and *Muzik* magazines offered such narratives in their respective celebrations of '10 years of dance culture': *Time Out* June 11–19 1997, *Muzik* January 1988.

28 See Chapter 5 for a fuller history of the TB-303, its inception in acid house and the aesthetics of technological 'mis-use'.

29 The significance of acid house's refusal of vocals was realized early on. See Simon Reynolds, *Blissed Out* (London, Serpent's Tail, 1990), p. 184.

30 Collin, *Altered State*, p. 23.

31 For example, Stuart Cosgrove, 'Seventh City Techno', *The Face*, no. 97, May 1988. Reprinted in Kureishi and Savage (eds), *The Faber Book of Pop*, pp. 677–81.

32 'Original, folk, or local expressions of black culture have been identified as authentic and positively valued for that reason, while subjective hemispheric or global manifestations of the same cultural forms have been dismissed as inauthentic and therefore lacking in cultural or aesthetic value precisely because of their distance (supposed or actual) from a readily identifiable point of origin.' Paul Gilroy, *Black Atlantic*, p. 96.

33 Efforts to police the 'purity' of a genre like techno can usefully be examined and recuperated by considering issues of black musical autonomy, in the political context of a culturally-polarized America. For more on this topic, see our forthcoming work, 'Iconographies of the Future and the Popular Avant-garde'.

34 Donna Haraway, 'A Manifesto for Cyborgs: Science, Technology and Socialist-Feminism in the late Twentieth Century', reprinted in Harraway, *Simians, Cyborgs and Women: The Reinvention of Nature* (New York, Routledge, 1991), p. 150. For a more sceptical reflection on these issues, see Barbara Bradby, 'Sampling Sexuality: Gender, Technology and the Body in Dance Music', *Popular Music*, Cambridge University Press, vol. 12, no. 2, 1993.

35 Simon Reynolds, 'Rave Culture: Living Dream or Living Death', in Redhead (ed.), *The Clubcultures Reader* (Oxford, Blackwell, 1997), p. 103.

36 See Matthew Collin, with contributions from John Godfrey, *Altered State: The Story of Ecstasy Culture and Acid House* (London, Serpent's Tail, 1997), Chapter 7.

37 See Simon Reynolds, 'Sounds of Blackness', *The Wire*, June 1995.

38 See Gilroy, *Black Atlantic*.

39 See Tricia Rose, *Black Noise: Rap Music and Black Culture in Contemporary America* (Hanover, Wesleyan University Press, 1994), pp. 62–98.

40 Reynolds, 'Sounds of Blackness', *The Wire*, June 1995.

4

TAKE YOUR PARTNER BY THE HAND

Dance music, gender and sexuality

Gender and culture

What if music IS sex?

Suzanne G. Cuisick[1]

I'm mair intae the touchin' on E than the penetration.

Lloyd, in Irvine Welsh, *Ecstasy*[2]

In Chapter 3 we considered the fact that despite being a self-consciously physical, raw, timbral music, conventional rock seems in many ways to comply with the deeper demands of metaphysical music discourse for meaning, truth and sincerity emanating from the unmediated voice. But there is a further aspect to the rock voice which makes it very much like the voice of classical philosophy. The rock voice is almost definitively masculine. Even on those rare occasions when women sing music which can be unproblematically defined as 'rock', the vocal style tends to take on the 'masculine' characteristics of traditional rock singing. When this doesn't happen, such music is usually understood to be a compromise between 'rock' and other forms (usually folk or pop). It is not only in the rough aggression of its vocal conventions that rock can be seen to possess certain specifically masculine qualities, and certain critics have argued that rock and the classical tradition share more than just a commitment to authenticity and meaning. Critics and theorists drawing on feminist theory have argued that certain types of music can, at least in certain contexts, be characterized as masculine or feminine, and that both rock and the classical tradition tend to privilege masculine over feminine forms. In this chapter we will explore these ideas, and consider some of the implications of certain types of feminist and queer theory for a deeper examination of some of our key issues, and the impact that those ideas have had on certain types of music criticism. Crucial to our discussion is the observation that within western modernity, dance has tended to be an activity indissolubly associated with the feminine. Within post-war popular culture, dance cultures have been particularly associated with young women and gay men on the one hand, and with the cultures of the

African diaspora and of dispossessed working-class young men on the other. All of these groups for one reason or another have been denied access to full masculine subjectivity as conceived by the dominant discourses of western culture. We will consider in detail some of the reasons why this might be the case.

Any strand of feminism rests on a critique of the imbalances of power between men and women, between masculinity and femininity, which have manifestly existed in most societies at most times. The types of feminism which we will be drawing on here tend to see this not simply as a matter of men having power over women, but of culture in general being shaped according to terms which privilege the masculine over the feminine. More than this, we will be following the work of Judith Butler, for whom even the sexed experience of the body is conceived as a cultural construct. Rather than the common formulation which sees biological 'sex' as an inescapable given and 'gender' as a social construct, Butler argues that the division between 'male' and 'female', masculine and feminine, is itself culturally specific. Indeed, Butler goes so far as to argue that even the division of humanity into 'men' and 'women' might be culturally determined.[3]

We do not have the space here to enter into current debates on the nature of gendered identity. However, we will argue from a position which more or less follows Butler's. In brief, our position is that we must recognize patriarchy as operating at several levels, which need to be distinguished for the purposes of abstract analysis. At the most basic level, patriarchy makes a fundamental distinction between 'masculinity' and 'femininity', and a range of different oppositions are mapped on to this basic one. We might say that it is the simple fixing of the distinction which is patriarchy's most basic operation. The second level is that at which patriarchal discourse specifically privileges masculinity at the expense of femininity. In other words, a set of terms which together are taken to constitute 'the masculine' (i.e., aggression, activity, size, solidity, rigidity) are treated as more valuable, important and desirable than their supposed opposites (i.e., co-operation, passivity, smallness, flexibility). The third level is that at which humanity itself is divided along these lines, defined as either male or female, man or woman. We might also posit as the final and most immediate level that at which genitally-defined 'men' and 'women' are ascribed characteristics which are exclusively 'masculine' or 'feminine'. This is the level at which the effects of patriarchy are most obviously felt by human subjects, the level at which social pressure is brought to bear in every conceivable way to ensure that men remain resolutely 'masculine', and that women remain unproblematically 'feminine'.

There are still deeper implications to seeing a culture as dominated by the masculine. It can be argued that such domination involves not only the privileging of certain forms of behaviour, but of certain modes of thought. In order to understand this process, it is important to have a sense of the meaning of two of the central terms of poststructuralist feminism: *phallocentrism* and *phallogocentrism*. The former is originally derived from certain strands of psychoanalysis. It refers to the fact that patriarchal culture regards possession of the phallus as the guarantee of full human subjecthood. Recent psychoanalytic theory is often at pains to stress the fact that 'phallus' does not simply mean 'penis'.[4] 'Phallus' according to these terms is a far more abstract marker of patriarchal authority which is acquired (or not) by virtue of an individual's location in a symbolic structure. However, for the purposes of our argument it is sufficient to appreciate that *phallocentrism* is the belief that a particular set of terms which can be described as 'phallic' are taken to define desirable normality, and according to which the possession of a phallus/penis is the only guarantee of full humanity, a guarantee which women are clearly denied. The latter term, phallogocentrism, ties together the concepts of phallocentrism and logocentrism. This term is deployed by such writers as Butler and Derrida to indicate that there is a close connection between the dominance of those terms and values which Derrida identifies as 'logocentric' and the dominance of phallocentrism. In fact, it implies that the two are aspects of a single system which defines women and femininity as the 'others' of western metaphysics' most privileged terms. According to the terms of phallogocentric discourse, femininity equals irrationality, fluidity, the sensual, the body. In the rest of this chapter, we will explore the ways in which ideas along these lines can and have informed thinking about the status of music in western culture.

Mother–matter

To begin, let us return to the primary distinguishing feature of metaphysical music discourse. We have seen, from a number of different perspectives, that such discourse seeks to suppress and at best erase the materiality of music. And yet, this seems a strangely sterile point to have reached.[5] We may know that metaphysical discourse suppresses the materiality of music, but so what? Why does it do that? And what are the wider implications of it doing so? In order to address this question from a feminist perspective, we can look to the work of Luce Irigaray. Irigaray, whose work is often close in its objects and interpretations to that of Derrida, has demonstrated the extent to which the maintenance of a rigid distinction between materiality and ideality has been essential to the maintenance of a phallocentric discursive economy since the time of Plato. She frequently points to the fact that the feminine, particularly as it is associated with the *maternal* in western discourse, is equated with a conception of *matter* as inert yet unstable, 'opaque matter which in theory does not know herself'.[6] Femininity is equated with matter: at the same time, matter is denigrated in a fundamental philosophical way. In *Speculum of the Other Woman*, for instance, Irigaray quotes at length the neo-Platonist philosopher Plotinus' discussion of the nature of the distinction between 'form' and 'matter', which – raising the central issue of the etymological link between 'matter' and 'mother' – appears to relegate the feminine/material to a condition at the very edge of ontology,[7] in a gesture typical of western metaphysics throughout its history.

Sound and vision

It is not only Irigaray's discussion of the role of the form/matter distinction in phallocentric discourse which is relevant to us here. Also of interest is her consideration of the privileged place of the scopic in phallocentric discourse. In her examination and deconstruction of the terms of this discourse, she is often led to excavate a series of optical metaphors which play a crucial role in its articulation:

> Within this logic, the predominance of the visual, and of the discrimination and individualisation of form, is particularly foreign to female eroticism. Woman takes more pleasure from touching than from looking, and her entry into a dominant scopic economy signifies, again, her consignment to passivity.[8]

Central to our discussion in Chapters 2 and 3 was the observation that the human experience of sound is fundamentally more tactile than the experience of light. We have seen that metaphysical discourse explicitly suppresses this aspect of sonic experience, attempting to efface the materiality of sense experience and thus to deny those aspects of human existence foregrounded by the musical experience of sound as physical and social. Irigaray's comments suggest that this is part of a process whereby masculine eroticism is normalized and privileged over feminine eroticism. There is a clear connection between Irigaray's ideas and those of Derrida and John Shepherd when she writes that:

> [Woman] is the reserve of 'sensuality' … she is the matter used for the imprint of forms … and also ear-drum faithfully duplicating the music, though not all of it.[9]

Femininity would seem to equate precisely with materiality, with the ear-as-organ, with that which the phallogocentric schema denigrates and/or tries to render unthinkable.

There is in fact a remarkable resonance between Irigaray's account of the specular economy and Shepherd's:

> Vision encourages projection into the world, occupation and control of the source of experience. Sound encourages a sense of the world as received, as being revelationary rather than incarnate.
>
> Sound reminds people that there is a world of depth which is external to them, which surrounds them, which touches them simultaneously from all directions, and which, in its fluidity and dynamism, constantly requires a response. Unlike vision, which is the medium of division and control, sound serves to remind people of their tangible relationship to the natural and social worlds. Sound – unlike vision, which is assimilated

exclusively through the head – is the only major medium of communication that actively vibrates inside the body.[10]

This is very similar to certain passages from the work of Irigaray, wherein femininity is equated with the tactile, which is in turn equated with fluidity,
dynamism and contiguity, as well as a Derridean refusal of self-presence, just as
Shepherd equates sound with the same terms. In another essay, Shepherd has
himself made explicit the suggestion that femininity can also be inserted into this
series of equivalences.[11]

There is thus a clear convergence between the thought of Irigaray, Shepherd
and Derrida. While maintaining an ideal of the self-spoken word as pure presence,
phallogocentric metaphysics suppresses sound as *sense-experience* as figuring materiality, the corporeal, the social, the maternal-feminine, and as radically
problematizing the distinctions between form and matter, interior and exterior,
self and other on which its discourse rests. Consequently it privileges a series of
terms which includes the scopic, the ideal-intellectual, an idea of sound-without-
the-physical-ear (therefore as pure interiority), the phallic-masculine. We perhaps
now have a better idea of what the wider implications of classical musicology's
denigration of materiality might be; it is a gesture which is ultimately motivated
by the suppression of femininity and the perpetuation of phallocentric authority
in the dominant discourses of the west.

The fact that this discourse privileges the *visual* as the purest and most important form of sense-experience is of particular interest for a consideration of the
status of music. As we have already seen, this tradition tends to be suspicious of
music – any music – in general, and this can in part be explained in terms of its
preference for sight over the other senses. As always, however, this is not simply a
matter of a preference for sight *as such*, but what it is that sight tends to represent
in the western imagination, which is truth conceived as immateriality, immediacy
and spirituality. This is precisely because of that relative immateriality of vision as
compared to the other senses, as we discussed in the previous two chapters. And
precisely because – compared to touch or hearing – sight is experienced as *less
physical*, the philosophical tradition tends to prefer it over the other senses. By the
same token, this tradition likes music best when it seems to take on some of the
characteristics of the visual. One manifestation of this tendency is the aspiration of
modernist composers to create 'pure music', music whose rigorous formal
abstraction is such that it is often both meaningless and entirely ineffectual for any
but the most trained listeners. It is no accident that the critical discourses
according to which such music is produced will regard the privileged site of
music's production and consumption to be not the concert-hall or even the
conservatory (certainly not the dancefloor!), but the *score*; the music represented in
visual form. It is no accident either that those discourses tend to take such a
masculinist view of the composer's role as lone hero, as the mighty intellect. As
Irigaray has taught us, the privileging of the visual is almost always bound up
with the privileging of the masculine.

Finally, Drew Hemment has pointed out, that this privileging of the visual is often displaced by the necessarily sonic nature of the experience at the heart of contemporary dance culture:

> On the dancefloor there is a disappearance of language, and a disappearance from language: the subject of enunciation becomes inoperative, and hence so does the force of objectification which it carries. Neither subject nor object exist in music. This adds to music's effect of displacing the primacy of vision and rendering the objectifying gaze redundant. This is not to deny that the floors of many night clubs are filled with spectacular glamour. But this usually represents a recolonisation of the dancefloor by the male gaze and is not an inherent tendency of acoustic space, itself 'boundless, directionless, horizonless, the dark side of the mind'.[12]

Gendered shapes

But this is not the end of the story. Irigaray's conclusions can help us to think about the relationship between music and gender in still further ways. This is made most obvious when we consider the closeness between Irigaray's ideas and those of the leading feminist musicologist, Susan McClary. McClary has in fact suggested that the structures of much 'classical' music can be described as phallocentric, and not merely because of their suppression of rhythm and timbre. McClary highlights the degree to which the narrative structures which organize much of post-Renaissance western music are fundamental elements of patriarchal discourse.[13] She therefore associates the dominant music discourse of post-Renaissance Europe, the metaphysical denigration of woman/matter, *and* traditional western narrative structures.

McClary writes that,

> the tonality that underlies Western concert music is strongly informed by a sort of erotic imagery. The principal innovation of seventeenth century tonality is its ability to instil in the listener an intense longing for a given event: the cadence. It organises time by creating an artificial need.... After that need is established ... tonal procedures strive to postpone gratification of that need until finally delivering the payoff in what is technically called the 'climax', which is quite clearly to be experienced as metaphorical ejaculation.
>
> It is interesting to note that when these two versions of erotic metaphors first emerged, they were distinguished from each other along lines of gender association. The images of pleasure were most often projected onto women ... male characters could also indulge in this

discourse, though when they did so, they indicated that they were giving themselves over to the stupor of erotic transport.[14]

She continues:

> In most post-Renaissance Western music and in virtually all of its critical literature, the climax-principle (like the phallus of the classical Greek column) has been transcendentalised to the status of a value-free universal form.[15]

What is at stake in McClary's critique of post-Renaissance tonality is a particular account of the relationship between music and the *gendered* body. In both cases the very *shape* of certain musics is said to have a direct relationship to phallic eroticism, in both instances conceived as being characterised by a privileging of linearity, power and the climax principle.

This observation brings us back to Irigaray, and her designation of woman as 'the sex which is not one'. The principal effect of post-Renaissance tonality's drive towards narrative up to the nineteenth century was an increasing concentration on musical theme. This culminated in the work of Beethoven, whose iconic status in music discourse has been commented on, and whose last symphony McClary identifies as the archetypal manifestation of phallocentric narrative and the climax principle in music.[16] We have seen that in privileging narrative over non-narrative musical structures, 'classical' music discourse privileges theme and melody over harmony and polyphony (Rousseau claimed that 'in fettering melody, harmony saps it of its energy and expression'[17]). In other words, it privileges music made by one instrument or by a number of instruments acting *as one* over music consti- tuted by a plurality of melodic lines interacting and playing alongside each other. Any music which concerns itself with the strict organization of time – as western music written within the dominant European tradition does – must necessarily be monologic in nature; the interaction or parallel existence of more than one melodic line in any piece of music will make it impossible for the music to have a simple, unilinear direction. We can see this privileging of theme, linearity and monologic narrative as an example of what Irigaray identifies as one of the key gestures of phallocentric discourse; the privileging of the singular over the plural.

Irigaray explains this phenomenon by arguing that the dominant discourse of the west is not only phallocentric, but also phallomorphic; privileging discursive structures which possess an isomorphic relationship with the masculine body:

> [in the phallocentric economy] The *one* of form, of the individual, of the (male) sexual organ, of the proper name, of the proper meaning ... supplants, while separating and dividing, the contact of *at least two* (lips) which keeps woman in touch with herself, but without any possibility of

distinguishing what is touching from what is being touched.

Whence the mystery that woman represents in a culture claiming to count everything, to number everything by units, to inventory everything as individualities. *She is neither one nor two.*[18]

It is easy to see how music can be thought of in these terms. The huge orchestral symphonies of the Romantic tradition, wherein a whole orchestra is often used to play a single tune as loudly and phallocentrically powerfully as possible, might be contrasted with Renaissance music (or even the concertos of Bach), in which polyphonic techniques are deployed to create from a plurality of sources an intricate texture, at once soothing and complex. The former we might define as phallomorphic, masculine. The latter we might see as in some sense feminine, resisting phallocentric discourse.

This hypothesis goes considerably beyond the suggestion that phallogocentric music discourse suppresses considerations of rhythm and timbre, towards suggesting that it can also organize the precise ways in which the whole range of musical elements are deployed. If we accept the validity of this thesis, then we must in an important way revise our account of the nature of that discourse. For in the previous chapters, metaphysical music discourse has merely been described as trying to *suppress* the corporeality of music. Here, however, we would suggest that the structures which that discourse privileges are themselves determined by an isomorphic relation to the masculine body. Thus, this discourse is described as attempting to efface a corporeality which is in fact revealed in its own structures. These gestures may seem contradictory (if music wanted to be anti-physical, surely it would eschew the macho-eroticism which McClary ascribes to Beethoven *et al.*?) unless we realize that in fact both are necessary for this discourse to achieve one of its overriding goals: to *transcendentalize* masculine eroticism, defining it *not* as a specifically gendered mode of being but as a universal one. This absolutely requires that music be organised in terms of a phallomorphic structure while *at the same time* the specificity of its relation to the masculine body must be effaced.

We can argue, then – following, in various ways, McClary, Irigaray, Shepherd and Derrida – that classical music discourse, its terms being more or less precisely those of western metaphysics, is characteristically phallogocentric. It privileges the immaterial, the ideal, the intellectual, the private, and, in peculiar ways, the visual. But it is not only classical music and its discourse which can be read as reproducing these terms. A similar account of the gender politics of rock music has been made by a number of critics over the years. In 1978, Simon Frith and Angela McRobbie discussed the various ways in which popular music discourse helps to construct sexual identities for its participants, demonstrating how rock's uses of timbre and rhythm are deployed as part of a discourse which, while rejecting the metaphysical denigration of the body, none the less perpetuates the terms of a phallocentric discursive economy.[19]

Similarly, in their book *The Sex Revolts*, the most extensive and theoretically informed study of the relationship between rock, sexuality and gender yet published in English, Joy Press and Simon Reynolds account for 'cock' rock's valorization of the lone hero, rebelling against convention, in terms of a fundamentally matricidal discourse, motivated by just that fear of the maternal-feminine which Irigaray identifies as a key term of western metaphysics:

> Male rebellion is a re-enactment of the primal break that constitutes the male ego: the separation of infant from the maternal realm, the exile from paradise. The rebel re-enacts the process of individuation in endless and diverse rites of severance.[20]

The critique of rock as phallocentric is taken further by Richard Dyer in his 1979 essay 'In Defence of Disco'. Writing against the prevailing leftist commonsense of the day (folk and rock – especially punk – good, disco bad), Dyer writes that:

> rock confines sexuality to the cock (and this is why, no matter how progressive the lyrics and even when performed by women, rock remains indelibly phallo-centric music).[21]

Dyer offers an analysis here which is precisely similar to those of McClary and Irigaray. Rock's insistent linearity and its pelvic drive seem to figure a sexuality which is wholly phallocentric. We might add once again the observation that its deployment of timbre is also often limited to a range of distortion effects which are used to create an impression of physical power, and thereby of a masculine authority which can ultimately be guaranteed by sheer physical strength. It seems, therefore, that certain forms of music can perpetuate phallocentric discourse even while foregrounding materiality and rhythm, in particular throughout the phallomorphism of their structures.

We can get a sense of the general applicability of such a framework to various types of music if we consider the similarity between certain points made by McClary about classical music on the one hand and Press' and Reynolds' comments about rock on the other. Since these three writers are the ones who, in their respective fields, have presented the most coherent readings of music discourse from an explicitly feminist perspective to date, the similarities between their readings are strikingly significant. McClary writes that, unlike their predecessors, who 'rarely invented stories that "demand sadism"...':

> Beethoven and Mahler quite regularly push mechanisms of frustration to the limit, such that desire in their narrative frequently culminates (as though necessarily) in explosive violence. This may be one of the factors that cause this latter group to be received as more serious, more virile,

more consequential: they don't pull punches, they go all the way to the mat.[22]

Reynolds and Press who write exclusively about rock music, present a very similar account of the motivation behind the macho rock tradition:

> The rebel's quest for sovereignty, for god-like independence, ultimately leads to de Sade. According to Susan Suleman, 'The founding desire behind Sadeian fantasy is the active negation of the mother. The Sadeian hero's anti-naturalism' – his repeated violation of 'natural' laws incest, infanticide, etc.) – 'goes hand in hand with his hatred of mothers, identified as the source of life' (and thus of death). The rebel also resents the power of the mother, wishes he was self-created, invulnerable, omnipotent. If you follow the rebel impulse to its logical, if not inevitable, conclusion, you end up here: a place where ascent to wholeness only comes with another being's mutilation and annihilation, where ecstasy means someone else's agony.[23]

What the similarity between these two extracts demonstrates is that various types of music occupying various cultural locations can all be read as being structured by the same phallocentric discourse, motivated by a fundamentally sadistic eroticism.[24] The question is, then, is *all* western music – or at least all western music since the Renaissance – implicated in and determined by phallogocentric metaphysics?

Musique feminine

In answer to the above question, not necessarily. In fact, McClary and Reynolds and Press come close together again in their attempts to delineate and discuss alternatives to phallocentric music. In discussing Vandervelde's composition *Genesis II*, McClary uses a series of descriptive phrases which she suggests can be applied to music organized along non-phallocentric lines. *Genesis II* dramatizes an apparent conflict between such music and music written to conform to the terms of phallocentric music discourse. Of the part playing the former role McClary writes that,

> we are presented with a minimalistic 'clockwork' pattern in the piano: a pattern that repeats cyclically but which, because it is internally marked by asymmetries of rhythm and pitch, is endlessly fascinating.... It creates a sense of existence in time that is stable, ordered, yet 'timeless' ... the completion of each cycle yields a sense of satisfaction and security, and we experience the possibility that the pattern might be replicated indefinitely. It sets up no expectation for change....
> It is no coincidence that *Genesis II*'s clockwork is reminiscent of medieval music: both are marked by relatively non coercive modal tech-

niques that delight in the present moment, rhythms that are grounded in the physicality and repetitiveness of dance, and the kind of carefully regulated contrapuntal interplay that Renaissance theorists associated with the harmony of the spheres, of nature and humankind, of soul and body.[25]

McClary rearticulates a set of terms which we have already encountered in several places; the feminine is equated with a refusal of linear time and directionality, an expression of cyclicity.[26]

This is even more clearly demonstrated with regard to rock music by Reynolds and Press. In fact, the explicit project of a good part of *The Sex Revolts* is to divide the whole field of rock music into two categories, each representing one of

> the warring sides of rock's soul: the punk v. the hippy, the warrior v. the soft male. These antagonistic impulses define rock 'n' roll as we know it. They can be traced back to a fundamental conflict in the male psyche – between the desire to break the umbilical cord and a desire to return to the womb, between matricide and incest.[27]

Reynolds and Press locate within the latter category musicians who have refused certain of those characteristics of rock which leads Dyer to define it as phallocentric; musicians such as the experimental German group Can, whose fluid, shapeless, minimal improvisations resist the phallocentric drive of traditional rock form. Press' and Reynolds' 'psychedelic mother's boys' could be located alongside Vandervelde, Reich, Glass, Satie, and the composers of Renaissance music as practitioners of music which refuses phallogocentric metaphysics. This leaves us with a set of terms which further complicate the deconstructive materialist aesthetic elaborated in the previous two chapters. The critical framework with which we are left would categorize pieces of music not just according to the degree to which they foreground or suppress the materiality and corporeality of music through deployment of timbre ('grain'), texture, and rhythm, but also the degree to which their structures privilege or refuse linearity, power, unity and narrative.

The 'gender' of dance musics

We can see how this critical framework might be applied to contemporary dance by considering two very different types of music which have emerged from the field of electronic dance: ambient and gabber.

Ambient

The idea of ambient music is not new. Its roots go back at least as far as Satie's 'furniture music'; and David Toop rightly traces its history even further back than that.[28] We might ourselves refer back to the eighteenth-century convention of

Tafelmusik (see Chapter 2, p 41), music that was intended simply to provide a pleasant *background* to eating and conversation, and which Kant so disapproved of. Indeed, despite Kant's bemusement, *Tafelmusik* could be considered to be a far older concept of music and its purpose than that which has dominated European culture since his day. Kant's disapproval of *Tafelmusik* – which he saw as paradigmatic of music thought of as a merely sensuous pleasure, banal background sound, unworthy of serious philosophical attention – and the fact that his comments could easily be applied to contemporary ambient music, is indicative of the ways in which ambient shares dance music's refusal of metaphysical imperatives; it is a music to be *used*, to soothe, even simply to be ignored.

There is a certain ambivalence in the idea of ambient music. The music of practitioners from Erik Satie to Brian Eno (who first coined the term 'ambient'[29]) and later followers, sometimes seems intended to be radically *ignorable* in the way that Satie, inspired as he was by Dada and its anti-art rhetoric, claimed that furniture music was to be. On the other hand, rather than simply being ignorable anti-music, such work – including that of Satie – often seems to be intended to generate utilitarian music which, like *Tafelmusik*, is supposed to have a specifically relaxing function. In the context of contemporary dance culture, this ambiguity is less marked. Ambient music emerged in the early 1990s as a genre indissolubly connected with dance music, despite its formal differences from it (the presence of a beat defines dance music; the absence of one defines 'ambient' proper), because it was used as the soundtrack to 'chill-out' rooms in dance clubs. In these spaces, set aside for clubbers physically and mentally exhausted by dancing and drug-consumption to rest, smoke, talk and calm down, DJs like Alex Patterson and Mixmaster Morris wove soothing soundscapes, bathing the listener in a wash of sounds, electronic and ethnic, old and new. The KLF titled their seminal exercise in ambient collage 'Chill Out', and music for 'chilling out' to became a genre in itself as 'ambient dub' and 'ambient house' – ambient music set to a beat – emerged as intermediary genres in the work of groups like Patterson's the Orb and Banco de Gaia. Although a specifically dedicated ambient scene did develop around clubs like London's The Big Chill, ambient always remained tied to dance culture, its primary function being to soothe and calm listeners under the influence of MDMA and LSD, enhancing and accentuating their more regressive effects.[30]

Ambient is very clearly a type of 'feminine' music as characterized by McClary *et al*. More obviously, even than the most hedonistic form of dance music, its purpose is to work on the listener to encourage their regression into a state of pre-Oedipal bliss. Although ambient has often been thought of as 'head music' in comparison to 'body music' (which is for dancing to) this is a naïve formulation. Ambient music is not an object of contemplation: it is a source of affect. It may not make us dance, but its effects are just as directly physical as those of other dance musics. It is almost always a music of textures more than melodies, of cyclicity more than narrative. It's not hard to see that in terms of McClary's understanding of music pre-Beethoven (pre-Enlightenment, pre-Romanticism) as generally *more feminine* than the music of the past two centuries, we can understand ambient as a return to that earlier model of what music should be. Ambient is certainly directly related to the work of minimalist composers like Terry Riley and Philip Glass whose work is informed by a self-conscious rejection of the meta-physical agendas of musical modernism.

Hardcore and gabber

At the other end of the scale, there is a line of music running through the early hardcore techno of 1990–91 through to the 'gabber' and 'happy hardcore' sounds which emerged in northern Europe and Scotland between 1994 and 1995. From the EuroMasters' frenetically sampled thrash guitars through to anthems like Sperminator's 'No Women Allowed' and Technoheads' comedy gabber hit 'I Wanna Be a Hippy', this music is characterized by jackhammer beats occasionally exceeding 200 beats per minute and rarely possesses anything discernible in the way of melody or rhythmic variation. Angry, adrenaline-testosterone textures are pressed into the service of pure linearity, speed without content, direction without aim. Incredibly popular in northern Europe (Holland, Germany and Scotland in particular), in the UK its main constituency has been with the remnants of the free party movement. Given the obvious comparisons drawn between the musical priorities of gabber and hardcore punk/thrash metal by Simon Reynolds,[31] this isn't surprising; hardcore punk was the main soundtrack to 'crusty' culture for a long time before its brief intersection with mass rave.

To a large extent it's difficult not to understand this type of music as a pure expression of phallomorphism, its sonic emptiness deriving from the fact that there is simply nothing here but phallomorphism; shape without content. It's perhaps not as simple as that, however. Even at 200 beats per minute – *especially* at 200 bpm – gabber is still drug music, still about the ever-intensifying pursuit of collective *jouissance*. Perhaps the notorious title of Sperminator's hymn to homoso-ciality, 'No Women Allowed', reveals a profound truth about the relational nature of gender which gabber manifests in a very concrete way; one way of achieving the asexuality/post-sexuality of *jouissance* – at least for a man – might be to push oneself into a hyper-phallic state in which there is simply no relation to femi-ninity whatsoever.[32] Where that relation no longer holds, masculinity as such might become meaningless. The difference between a hardcore mix and a Beethoven symphony is that in the former climax is never really reached. The mountain remains unclimbed, the woman un-fucked; it is phallomorphism, but phallomorphism without the aim of mastery over woman.

This is not necessarily a good thing, and is perhaps reminiscent of the homoso-ciality of fascism. Collective *jouissance* is not necessarily a good thing; the philosopher Jean-Luc Nancy has suggested that the fascist logic of total immer-sion, of that *communion* which transforms constituent singularities into a homogenous mass, can be just as dangerous as the atomising logic of pure indi-vidualism.[33] The absolute musical simplicity of gabber, its military regularity, its sheer lack of *space*, all tend to induce a crowd experience in which all difference is erased. Such totalitarianism is by definition one of the possible consequences of a collective pursuit of ego-loss; this observation should serve to remind us that the politics of the ecstatic experience is always dependent on its specific modes and contexts. Breaking down our egos might be just as likely to turn us into something worse as something better. This is not necessarily to say that this is any more likely at a gabber rave than anywhere else.

Dance gender and sexuality

The issues discussed so far in this chapter have far wider implications than simply allowing one to read certain genres of dance or other musics as being 'masculine' or 'feminine'. It could be argued that whatever their generic specificities, dance musics offer the most radical challenge available to the musical priorities of phallogocentric metaphysics. We have already seen some of the reasons why this is so. Their deployment of rhythm and repetition, their eschewal of verbal meaning, are all problematic for the dominant discourses. We will examine this proposition further shortly. But there are also other reasons, the most important of which is the strong association between *dance* and those groups of people who are most marginalized by phallogocentric discourse. Dance has often been thought of as a feminine activity, just as those musical forms which subvert the terms of phallogocentric discourse have so often been categorized as 'feminine'. In the latter part of the twentieth century, a strong association between dance musics and gay cultures has been built.

There are a number of reasons for this. Dance and femininity both belong to that series of terms which phallogocentrism marginalizes. We are not proposing a one-way causal relationship here. It is not simply the case that dance is considered a feminine activity, and so, therefore, it is mostly women who dance. Nor is it the other way around; dance is not considered 'feminine' simply because women dance. Rather, it is that within the imagination of western modernity, 'dance' and 'femininity' seem to belong to the same set of terms.

This has been illustrated in a number of ways by various writers. Judith Hanna writes that 'because the esteemed worlds of work have discriminated against the so-called weaker sexes, women and homosexual men have disproportionately pursued the more tolerant, poorly-paid, low-prestige dance career'.[34] Similarly, in her essay 'Youth Culture and Femininity', Angela McRobbie – who has written elsewhere on the dancefloor as an autonomous cultural space for girls and young women[35] – observes that: 'Dance is where girls were always found in subcultures. It was their only entitlement. Now in rave it becomes the motivating force for the entire subculture. This gives girls a new-found confidence and prominence'.[36] Although for reasons discussed earlier we would avoid characterizing 'rave' as a 'subculture', we would endorse McRobbie's point here, and it has certainly been borne out in the work of Maria Pini.

Pini offers an account of rave and post-rave culture as a space for the autonomous (dis)articulation of femininity which brilliantly balances empirical analysis with theoretical insight. In 'Women and the Early British Rave Scene', she writes that,

> women's lack of involvement at the levels of rave production should not blind researchers to the fact that for many women, rave represents an undoing of the traditional cultural associations between dancing, drugged 'dressed-up' women and sexual invitation, and as such opens up a new space for the exploration of new forms of identity and pleasure. In short, if ... women have traditionally been denied the kinds of 'unsupervised adventures' celebrated within previous youth-cultural scenes, then I am suggesting that rave allows for such adventure. Further, within rave, producing the 'self' out of a relentless drive for the maximisation of pleasure is central. Being 'ecstatic' has in many ways replaced previous youth-cultural 'styles of being': being 'political', being 'angry' being 'hard' and even (certainly at the beginning of rave in London) being 'fashionable'. Physical and mental enjoyment becomes a central point of involvement. In many ways, open displays of 'happiness', auto-erotic pleasure, 'friendliness' and enjoyment of dance are traditionally more closely associated with femininity and gay male culture.... In this sense, rave can be read a challenge to heterosexual masculinity's traditional centrality, and for this reason alone is worthy of attention.[37]

Importantly, Pini finds confirmation for this understanding of dance as a manifestation of femininity, a metaphor for 'non-phallocentric formations', in the work of Luce Irigaray.[38] Finally, it is crucial to add here that most of what Pini says about women's experience of rave also holds true for straight men.[39] They too can experience the rave as a liberation from the strictures of gender, stepping, if only temporarily, outside of the suffocating emotional paralysis, the perpetual state of aggression and fear which often constitutes western notions of masculinity.

So we can see that writers covering different areas and different time-spans have commented on dance as a specifically feminine activity in modern culture, a sphere at once marginal and, in certain ways, protected, and that this aspect takes on new significance in the context of rave and post-rave cultures. It is worth noting that this seems to be a development specific to western modernity. There is a wealth of anthropological research on dance in other cultures, and rarely if ever does it posit evidence of the 'feminization' of dance within those societies. It is not only in these terms that the notion of dance as a feminine/feminized activity is problematic, however. It is also important to note that dance in post-war popular culture has very often been a phenomenon which was not only not 'feminized' in any noticeable way, but which has largely been a male preserve. The succession of post-war youth subcultures which so fascinated the theorists of the Birmingham Centre for Contemporary Cultural Studies (Teds, mods rockers, skins) were famously male-dominated,[40] and all had forms of dance as central to their socio-symbolic rituals.

The striking detail here is that all of these 'subcultures' were largely or exclusively working-class phenomena. In the case of the mods we can see their embracing of black American dance music as of a piece with their enthusiastic, obsessive commodity fetishism; evidence of a desire to transcend working-class English parochialism. But even here, and certainly in the case of those of the other 'resistant' youth 'subcultures', it is easy to perceive the distance between the values embodied in the subcultures and the dominant values of bourgeois modernity. The Birmingham theorists saw the aim of these subcultures as being to win 'space' from the dominant culture, and surely none of the spaces which those groups carved out for themselves was as intensely – if only temporarily – free from the strictures of the dominant culture as their dancefloors.

What this illustrates is that the marginalization of dance in modern culture is not simply a matter of phallogocentrism (or of racism), but of bourgeois hegemony also. It was the English bourgeoisie in their most revolutionary moment, the Commonwealth of the 1650s,[41] who were the first people in Europe to try to ban social dancing. Within English culture dance has traditionally been associated with the aristocracy or with 'the people', and it is telling that the middle classes have rarely engaged in any forms of social dancing which were not supposedly imitations of either one or the other. Even the waltz – the nearest thing to a specifically 'bourgeois' dance form – is thought to have originated from European peasant dances. What is most notable about the dancing of the post-war subcultures, which links them to rave and post-rave dancing and distinguishes them from those types of social dancing of which bourgeois culture has traditionally approved, is that they were not primarily courtship rituals. If the waltz embodied perfectly the ideal bourgeois conception of gender relations – the heterosexual couple within which the man was clearly dominant and eroticism was carefully policed – then the dances followed by these cultures, and indeed most of the dances which European culture borrowed from black America from ragtime onwards, embodied something quite different. It does not seem too far fetched to suggest that these dances manifested for their male participants as much as for their female counterparts a space free from the demands of hegemonic gender roles, and in particular a refusal of those roles constructed at the intersection of class and gender discourses. Dance for dancing's sake can be thought of as almost the opposite of work, a form of labour which is literally unalienable in its non-productivity. Bourgeois culture has always tended to associate productive work with masculinity (despite the immense quantity of work which it has forced from the vast majority of women, normally without credit, recompense or self-determination). A man is supposed to be first and foremost a worker, but this is only a satisfying thing to be for a very privileged few. So dancing in an autonomous space, according to rituals entirely other than those required of the prospective father/husband/patriarch-breadwinner, can be read as an assertion both of anti-capitalism and, at one level, a refusal of gender norms.

We can see from this brief discussion that it is in fact not always possible to distinguish between, for instance, class and gender discourses as determinants on a given phenomenon. The discourse of Puritanism, which has been such a central strand of Anglo-Saxon modernity, has always been constituted by a specific articulation of Eurocentric, phallogocentric and bourgeois terms, and it is only in very specific configurations that those terms have become effective. In this particular instance, it seems that the 'feminization' of dance within the dominant culture was no bar to its adoption by proletarian young men, precisely because the marginalization of dance and its pleasures was experienced (if only implicitly) as part of that bourgeois discourse which they sought to resist. We will return to these issues in Chapter 5.

Drag disco: Deconstructive dancing

There is one even more recent development in modern culture which has to be taken account of when considering the sexual politics of dance culture. Since the early 1970s, with the advent of gay pride and the earliest days of disco, there has been a strong association between dance music culture and gay men. Indeed, one can safely say that dance culture as we know it is largely a gay creation. Mods and northern soul fans may have danced all night on speed, but dancing all night – with the aid not just of speed but a range of stimulants and psychedelics – to a continuous mix of music made with the latest recording technology, has always been the preserve of gay culture. It was American gays, mostly from or with strong links to the black and Latino communities, who did it first and who have done it the most consistently throughout the course of dance culture's mutation through disco and hi-NRG to house and techno. The 'dancing queen' is a modern cliché, a stereotype common to gay and straight communities. As John Gill puts it, 'dancing, dance music and places where people dance have been central to the lives of queers since queers were first invented'.[42]

But Gill raises an interesting question about this situation. Why should it be the case, he asks, that gay men have such a strong identification with dance music, when many of its associations often seem to be more rigorously heterosexual than those of any other genre of popular music? The anthems, ballads and floor-fillers which make up the archetypal gay genre, disco, are almost invariably songs which explicitly celebrate heterosexuality. The lyrics of most dance songs are almost always about romantic love and/or casual sexuality conceived within strictly heterosexual terms: from Motown's catalogue of heterosexual mini-narratives, through the exhortations of various disco anthems to their listeners to participate as actively as possible in the heterosexual market place, to the Spice Girls' insistent and never-problematized heterosexuality. Gill also points to 'the institutionalised homophobia of the dance music field',[43] and to the vexed issue of the endemic homophobia exhibited in many areas of black culture, of which dance music is one.

Gill's comments are not particularly well informed. On a historical level he overlooks the extent to which, for much of the period in between the height of disco's success and the eruption of rave in British and then European and

American culture, dance music was more or less unproblematically identified as gay. Hi-NRG and early house, the twin descendants of disco, both had their homes in predominantly gay night-clubs in American and European cities, and both tended – when they had discernible lyrics at all – not to present themselves as explicitly heterosexual. Perhaps more importantly, Gill's assertion that the dance records to which he and other queers dance to so enthusiastically (Gill is admirably careful not to take up a self-righteous or judgmental attitude to such activities) are in fact anthems of heterosexual oppression is extremely problematic, overlooking as it does the most basic developments in twentieth-century theories of signification. The Marxist linguist V.N. Volosinov put forward the view early this century that meaning was entirely a product of social interaction.[44] In his argument which almost all theorists of meaning would now agree with, Volosinov maintained that utterances are understood only in specific social contexts. This point holds for disco songs as well; their 'meaning' is produced only when they are understood in a particular way, and if they are not heard as hetero-sexist then, effectively, they are not (whatever the wishes of their producers).

Nevertheless, Gill does point us towards an important question: why in the first place were queers attracted to this type of music? Dance musics may have become gay forms by the 1980s, but Gill's comments are far more valid when applied to the music of the 1970s; why did gay culture adopt disco tunes as their own? The difficulty with Gill's analysis is that he addresses his objections to dance music on the basis of the songs' lyrics; whereas we would argue that, especially in the case of dance music, lyrics are not the most important element. It is this unwillingness to consider the importance of sonic experience, a gesture fully in keeping with the logocentric terms of most pop music criticism, which leads Gill to offer such a dismissively cursory reading of the one text which explains fully the problem he finds so confusing: Richard Dyer's 'In Defence of Disco'.

In his classic essay, Dyer explores some of the reasons why disco might appeal to women and gay men. Comparing it to rock, his critique of which we have already noted (see p. 91), Dyer writes that:

> Disco music, on the other hand, hears the physicality in black music and its range. It achieves this by a number of features, including the sheer amount going on rhythmically in even quite simple disco music … the willingness to play with rhythm … rather than simply driving on and on…. This never stops being erotic, but it restores eroticism to the whole of the body and for both sexes, not just confining to the penis.[45]

We should stress here that Dyer is not offering an essentialist account of the inevitable anti-phallocentrism of gay sexuality. He is quick to deny that he sees anti-phallocentrism as the preserve, or even the usual mode, of gay sexuality, the frequently cock-centred nature of which he deplores. Furthermore, Dyer crucially does not propose that disco is necessarily anti-cock; its eroticism can, it seems, include that of the penis, being 'all-body'. It simply is not confined to it. For Dyer, disco's interplay of rhythm and melody, its foregrounding of its own status as a material source of physical pleasure, offers the dancer/listener access to a poly-morphous experience of the body whose pleasure is not confined in simple gender terms.

This is a critical proposition for any consideration of the sexual politics of music, especially dance music. Rather than positing a *feminine* music which would simply *reverse* the privilege granted to masculine forms by phallogocentric discourse, Dyer presents the possibility of a music which would deconstruct the opposition between masculinity and femininity, and he suggests that disco is an example of such a form. This would make disco – or any other musical form which could achieve a similar aim – remarkably serviceable to the project of a deconstructive queer-feminism such as that proposed by Judith Butler. A politics which seeks not simply to reverse the cultural marginalization of women and queers but to disrupt the discursive systems which fix sex and gender according to the binary oppositions man/woman,[46] masculine/feminine, gay/straight, would surely look to cultural forms which operate just as Dyer sees disco as doing.

It is worth bearing in mind that it is not only dance music that might be thought to operate in terms such as these. The musicologist Suzanne G. Cusick, in her essay 'On a Lesbian Relationship with Music', offers a fascinating reflection on what it might mean for her to experience music in the classical tradition from a specifically lesbian perspective:

> The choice I cherish ... is ... to let the music 'do it' to me ... or not. Possibly that is, there are musics which I dis-prefer because they upset a power-equilibrium.... Possibly there are musics to which I respond posi-tively or negatively from the lesbian 'I', as she continually reconstructs herself by her 'sexual' behaviours. But that response is not based on a direct correspondence among, say, Beethoven's insistent rhythms, their possible representation of male sexual thrusting, and my 'rejection' of males as 'sexual' partner. Nor is it based on a direct correspondence between my woman's body's supposedly diffused sexuality and the diffused 'climaxes' of some music. The chain of events in my 'lesbian aesthetic' response, if it can be said to exist, leads to a preference for musics ... with which I experience a continuous circulation of power even when I let the music be 'on top'. Their representations of the tradi-tionally defined 'sexual' acts of traditionally defined genders us secondary to this larger issue of the power dynamic between music and me. For instance, Terry Riley's famously minimalist *In C*, hardy a repre-sentation of thrust, upsets the balance I seek as much as Beethoven's Fifth Symphony does.[47]

What our reading of Dyer and Cuisick seems to be pointing us towards is the possibility of an aesthetic which would go beyond the sexual binarism of some of McClary's writing (although this is not by any means the limit or the extent of McClary's ground-breaking analyses) and Reynolds' and Press' heterosexual dualism. Here we would be looking for musics which confound and problematize the very distinction between masculinity and femininity. Such an argument does not render irrelevant the project of feminist musicology as it manifests itself in the work of McClary or Reynolds and Press, however. We can only understand musics as deconstructing the gender/sex binary if we can recognize the functioning of gendered discourse in music to begin with, and it is the functioning of that discourse in various musical fields that such work draws our attention to. Following Butler, however, we would want to move on from this point. This is precisely what Dyer's account of disco invites us to do. If the body in its very materiality is an effect of repeated practices of which the experience of music is one, then we can say that what a music like disco can offer is a mode of actually rematerializing the body in terms which confound the gender binary. A music which organizes its pleasures through an interplay of elements 'masculine' and 'feminine', both and neither, might offer scope for modes of experience which would have potentially deconstructive implications for anybody, male or female, gay or straight.

This argument brings us back to the idea we derived from the work of Barthes and Kristeva in Chapter 3, the idea that the experience towards which dance music can lead us is somehow a matter of escaping established gendered identity. However, there may be a difference in emphasis between that model of this experience and a model derived from the ideas of Butler. Butler attempts to rethink the psychoanalytic model of the subject being born into the symbolic order in terms of Foucault's model of power/knowledge as *productive* as well as constrictive. For Butler, there is no pre-linguistic, pre-discursive realm of undifferentiated, corporeal experience, no even partially recoverable moment of pre-Oedipal stasis, no well-spring of pure *jouissance* situated in the pre-history of the subject. Rather, it is the symbolic order itself which *creates the idea* of such a 'before', which constructs the notion of the infant–mother dyad as that which it has interrupted, which produces a nostalgic myth of lost plenitude in the mother's body, thereby constructing femininity itself as permanently and irrecoverably outside the order of language and sense. According to Butler's argument, Kristeva's 'semiotic' is itself a *product* of the symbolic. Of course, Kristeva herself recognizes that in an important sense the semiotic can only be understood as having being retroactively, after the institution of the subject in the symbolic. She does not take up the issue in the same way as Butler, however, and does not discuss this mechanism as a particular operation of *power*.

It is important to understand the reasons for Butler's rejection of a simplistic, quasi-Kristevan celebration of regressive experience. For Butler – and it seems difficult to disagree with her – such an aesthetic has the depressing and rather unlikely implication that the only points at which the iron grip of patriarchal, phallogocentric discourse is weakened are those moments of aesthetic experience characterized by the *signifiance* of rhyme, rhythm, glossolalia, timbre, and so forth.

Butler's critique can be applied very usefully to the model of dance music experience which we derived from Barthes and Kristeva. Following Butler's argument, it
would appear that according to that model it is *only* in those intense ecstatic
moments when the experience of the physicality of music offers us access to a
jouissance which refers back to a moment before we were subjects – a moment
which can only be fully recovered in death or madness – that we can escape or
even successfully interrupt the terms of phallogocentric discourse. According to
this model, we can momentarily *escape* the strictures of phallogocentric discourse,
but we can never hope to dislodge it altogether. This may seem like a pessimistic
view. Put in simple terms, going out and getting high on a beat and a tablet might
be a very liberating experience. It may be an experience that the dominant culture
of the west wishes to marginalize, criminalize and restrict. But does that mean we
have to see in it the limit and totality of a progressive sexual politics? Is that all
there is?

In fact, Butler's critique can be taken further than this, as it could be said that
the very idea of those types of experience as marginal/radical/deconstructive is
itself an effect of phallogocentric discourse constructing its own marginal
moments. In other words, to restrict ourselves to these fleeting moments of intensity as the only real way to challenge the dominant discourses, is to accept the
terms of those discourses, and therefore to have given up the struggle for real
social change before it has even begun. Butler's call for queer feminism to intervene in the symbolic order itself might be read here as having various
implications for cultural politics. Might it be, for instance, that celebrating the
dancefloor as a space of liberated femininity/queerness is simply to reinforce the
status of women and queers as people who can only express themselves on dancefloors? Perhaps the more radical gesture is for such marginalized groups as these
to occupy those spaces normally barred to them by the terms of the dominant
culture. In musical terms, it might be not rave but Riot Grrrl and queercore –
musical movements in which women and queers use noisy, punkish rock (music
only normally made by straight men) to express their anger at and resistance to
oppression – that offer the real challenge to patriarchy and homophobia.

An argument such as this exposes some of the weaknesses in any position
which simply valorizes musics which are perceived as 'feminine' or which can
regress us into a state of *jouissance*. Such strategies run a simple but real risk; that by
merely turning the binary values of the dominant culture on their heads, they
leave the conceptual distinctions on which they rest intact. As we have already
seen, queer theorists like Butler, Dyer and Cuisick tend to want to go further than
this, deconstructing the notions of 'femininity' and 'masculinity' themselves.
However, the implication of their arguments would not be a simple matter of
endorsing projects like queercore and Riot Grrrl, either. The problem with *those*
kinds of project is that they can also serve to reinforce dominant cultural values by
their implicit endorsement of conventional notions of masculinity. Riot Grrrl, for
instance, works to some degree by claiming masculinity (strength, aggression,
noise) 'for' women, but in doing so it can appear to endorse the view that such

traits *are* more desirable than those traditionally associated with femininity. The problems is, then, that strategies which *simply* endorse 'femininity' (or 'queerness') can end up reproducing the terms of the dominant culture, and strategies which *simply* reject it can also end up reproducing those terms.[48] The task – if we follow through the logic of Judith Butler's argument – is not either to reject or reverse terms or distinctions produced by the dominant discourses, but to *deconstruct* them, in doing so problematizing the terms themselves.[49] This is, as we have seen, just what Dyer sees disco as doing.

Rethinking *jouissance*

Where does this leave the notion of *jouissance* as the specific form of pleasure to which dance musics offer us access? We would suggest that we can in fact retain a notion of *jouissance* and of Barthes' distinction between *jouissance* and *plaisir* while at the same time rethinking those concepts in the light of Butler's work. Such a notion fits with a model of human subjectivity as constituted not by one single discourse or one decisive moment, but as an intersection of overlapping discourses. The phallogocentric discourse of patriarchy, which demands that subjects take up genders and attempts to enforce both heterosexuality and a rigid distinction between masculinity and femininity, is one such discourse, but it is overlaid and undercut by other discourses; of class, of race, of nationality, of a myriad political and cultural identifications. It is not the all-encompassing origin of subjectivity and identity that orthodox psychoanalysis, or even the neo-psycho-analytic model of Kristeva, would tend to suggest. If *jouissance* is a kind of pleasure which occurs at points where the grip of gender-enforcing discourse is weakened or broken, then, following Butler, it is no longer possible to see this as a simple *return* to a primordial moment.

This need not prevent us, however, from seeing *jouissance* as occurring outside gender. We can visualize this by suggesting that *jouissance* is now not to be thought of as belonging to a moment before gender, but as occurring in a space which is somehow to the side of it. If we visualize the subject as an interference pattern, as that which occurs at the point of intersection and interruption between different discourses, then *jouissance* might be the noise which is generated at the edges and the in-between points. This would give us a quite literal understanding of *jouissance* as ecstasy. The word 'ecstasy', derives from the Greek 'ekstasis', meaning 'standing outside oneself'. The ecstasy of *jouissance*, we are suggesting here, is precisely such a 'standing outside' of the discourses which fix gendered identity. Not that those discourse can be fully escaped; rather they are interrupted at those points where their overdetermination by other discourses creates a space of *underdetermination*, where the energy of *jouissance* is generated at the very points of agency. *Jouissance* thus conceived is a region of experience which is not simply neuter but at the same time polysexual; a sexuality without fixed gender. As one of the women Maria Pini interviewed said of the rave dance experience, 'It's not sexual, but orgasmic'.[50]

Jouissance is therefore conceived here not as an effect of simple regression, but of the interruption and displacement of particular discursive terms. We might say that *jouissance* is what is experienced at the moment when the discourses shaping our identity are interrupted and displaced such that that identity is challenged, opened up to the possibility of change, to the noise at the borders of its articulation. *Plaisir*, on the other hand, can be understood as pleasure which confirms our existing sense of identity, affirming what we already believe ourselves to be, or at least not threatening the discursive material organization of our bodily selves.

Most types of music might be seen to generate both of these two types of pleasure at the same time, to a greater or lesser extent, but it is largely the ecstatic displacement of *jouissance* that concerns us here, and this as we have seen can arise in a variety of ways. Those various forms of music which, in different ways, foreground terms suppressed and marginalized by the dominant discourses of the west, all serve to interrupt the terms of those discourses which continue to shape our identities even at the level of our bodies. Musics which foreground their own materiality through the deployment of timbre and rhythm, musics which seek to articulate a specifically feminine aesthetic, can all give access to *jouissance*. But it would seem, following Butler's argument, that in doing so they will always run the risk of simply confirming the status of materiality, femininity, and so forth, as extrinsic to normal experience. The types of aesthetic experience which are most likely to effect a displacement of the terms of the dominant discourses without leaving those terms fundamentally intact are those which somehow deconstruct the terms altogether. Not feminine music, but all-body eroticism. Not merely 'grain' or pure rhythm (if there could be such a thing), but musics which reorganize the conventional western relationships between rhythm, melody, and so on.

As we have seen, Dyer for one sees disco as an example of such a music. It is interesting, then, that other writers, like Derrida,[51] have used the dance as a metaphor for just that type of displacement of the male–female binary which Dyer sees as happening on the disco floor. Why should the dance be a metaphor for sexual multiplicity? For a start we should emphasize that this association is never *inevitable*. It is clearly possible for there to be forms of dance which are coded as simply 'feminine' or 'masculine'. As noted earlier, there have been moments in the recent history of western popular culture when dance has been constructed as an almost exclusively feminine practice. On the other hand, Dyer points out that there were areas even of gay disco culture which were thoroughly phallocentric, and he regrets the association of much macho disco (his example is the Village People) with gay culture. In more recent times, there have been forms of dance music which were decidedly phallomorphic, and which have appeared to know it (for example, gabber and hardcore techno).

Nevertheless, there are powerful reasons for dance being thought of as offering us access to a mode of experience which deconstructs the gender binary. We have already seen how dance offers a way of experiencing music which cannot help but foreground the materiality and physicality of that experience. We can think about this usefully in terms of Cuisick's description of her lesbian aesthetic, which she describes in terms of its refusal of a clear distinction between *active* and *passive* listening. The distinction between activity and passivity has always been absolutely central to the maintenance of the distinction between masculinity and femininity in western discourse. The notion that masculine equals active/feminine equals passive goes back as far as ancient Greece. As we have already seen, the dominant musical discourse of the west associates femininity with a passive, sensuous, non-rational, non-contemplative mode of listening to music. Cuisick's lesbian aesthetic can therefore be seen as aiming for a deconstruction of the male–female binary by way of a deconstruction of the distinction between active and passive listening. What more radical deconstruction of this distinction could there be than that which takes place when we dance? On the one hand, to dance to music is always (except in the highly circumscribed context of performance dance) to give oneself up to the music, to allow the music *to dance us*. On the other hand, what more active response to music can there be than to actually move one's whole body in time to it? To dance to music is always, in one sense at least, to deconstruct one of the founding oppositions of gender discourse.

At the same time, most forms of contemporary dance music combine 'feminine' and 'masculine' elements to an extent that very few other forms of music can. If driving rhythm and narrative linearity is a hallmark of 'masculine' music, then of necessity most types of dance music have it. On the other hand, the linear narrative of dance records never reaches a phallomorphically climactic conclusion, because it always has to be possible to mix a record in with the next one. Susan McClary defines the difference between masculine and feminine music as much as anything as the difference between music which reaches a single climax and music which is cyclical in nature. House, techno, trance, jungle, and so on, are typically *both and neither*. The continuous DJ mix erases the distinction, creating a distinctively cyclical soundscape of breaks and crescendos, repetitions and returns, but at the same time it is never purely cyclical in that is never simply repetitious. We can get a sense of this just by listening to one, unmixed dance record from start to finish. Such records do not constitute actual musical cycles; they typically change throughout and rarely repeat large sections note for note, but they also do not progress very far, retaining strong elements of melodic as well as rhythmic repetition, and they never really finish. They *stop* as the vinyl runs out, but they never reach a final conclusion. Of course specific sub-genres and individual pieces of music will exhibit some of these traits more than others. The 'epic house' of producers like Robert Miles and BT often produces tracks which come across as mini-symphonies, with quite definite climaxes. A deep trance mix, evoking the early notion of acid house as hypnotic musical experience, can seem to aspire to the status of pure repetition. On the whole, however, the elements which characterize music as 'masculine' and 'feminine' tend to be uniquely displaced and mixed together in contemporary dance music. Although, as we have already seen, there are certainly more or less 'gendered' forms of such musics, the fact remains that the pursuit of a *jouissance* which is outside 'gender' is their almost universal end, and the mixing up and interaction of elements 'masculine' and 'feminine', of immersion and penetration, of narrative and cyclicity, of direction and texture, is the means which almost all of them deploy.

In 1988, Suzanne Moore suggested that those men who toyed with experiences of 'femininity' without having to deal with the dirt, danger and desperation of actual womanhood were guilty of 'gender tourism',[52] in partaking of feminine pleasure while indissolubly colluding with a society oblivious to women's actual pain and oppression. Simon Reynolds has gestured towards the possibility of a similar critique by describing rave as a culture of masculine 'clit-envy'.[53] Would this be a fair criticism of dance culture as it has developed since Moore made her remarks about the New Man culture of the 1980s? Perhaps, but we think not. What we are dealing with in (post-) rave cultures is a set of material practices which deliberately create an experience of gender-displacing *jouissance* and construct it as a mode of pleasure. In a culture wherein, on the whole, both femininity and a general instability of gendered identity are marginalized and negatively-marked modes of being, this is surely some achievement. Dance cultures have established a socio-technological apparatus within which the disorientation and subjective danger, the destabilization of our normal experience of ourselves and our bodies, is routinely experienced as a source of enjoyment rather than as terrified confusion and blind panic (although anyone who has had a bad drug experience knows how fine the line between the two can be).

Even if the journey into *jouissance* can only ever be temporary, the availability of this experience to large numbers of people can only be a good thing. The ecstatic dissolution of the self on the dancefloor, the transformation of ordinary codes of physical and verbal interaction, is still experienced by many as a life-changing experience which encourages and enables new relationships to the body of both self and other/s. It is the possibility of this experience which Richard Dyer heard in disco nearly twenty years ago, and it's this which remains one of dance culture's most concrete sites of political potential. As we will see in the final chapters, however, it is by no means a potential which is always realized.

Notes

1 Suzanne G. Cuisick, 'On a Lesbian Relationship with Music', in P. Brett, G. Thomas and E. Woods (eds), *Queering the Pitch: The New Gay and Lesbian Musicology* (London, Routledge, 1994), p. 78.
2 Irvine Welsh, *Ecstasy* (Vintage, London, 1997), p. 159.
3 Judith Butler, *Gender Trouble*, (London, Routledge, 1990), pp. 1–34.
4 See Jacqueline Rose's introduction, in Juliet Mitchell and Jacqueline Rose (eds), *Feminine Sexuality* (London, Macmillan, 1982).
5 We leave a consideration of the metaphorics of this sentence to our critics.
6 Luce Irigaray, 'Any Theory of the "Subject"...', in *Speculum of the Other Woman*, trans. Catherine Porter (Ithaca, Cornell, 1985), p. 134.
7 We are indebted here to Judith Butler's reading of Irigaray.
8 Luce Irigaray, 'This Sex Which is Not One', in *This Sex Which is Not One*, trans. Catherine Porter (Ithaca, Cornell, 1985), pp. 25–6.
9 Irigaray, 'Any Theory of the "Subject"...' p. 141.

10 John Shepherd, 'Music as Cultural Text', in *The Routledge Companion to Music* (London, Routledge, 1993), p. 148.
11 Shepherd, 'Difference and Power in Music', in Ruth A. Solie (ed.) *Musicology and Difference* (Berkeley, University of California Press), 1993, pp. 52–6.
12 Drew Hemment, 'e is for Ekstasis', in *New Formations* (London, Lawrence & Wishart), Spring/Summer 1997, p. 57.
13 Susan McClary, *Feminine Endings* (Minneapolis, University of Minnesota Press), 1991, p. 14.
14 Ibid., p. 125.
15 Ibid., p. 130.
16 Ibid., pp. 128–9.
17 P. Le Huray and J. Day (eds), *Music and Aesthetics in the Eighteenth and Early Nineteenth Centuries* (Cambridge, Cambridge University Press, 1981), p. 98.
18 Irigaray, 'This Sex Which is Not One' , p. 26.
19 Simon Frith and Angela McRobbie, 'Rock and Sexuality', in S. Frith and A. Goodwin (eds), *On Record: Rock, Pop and the Written Word* (London, Routledge, 1990).
20 Reynolds and Press, *The Sex Revolts* (London, Serpent's Tail, 1995), p. 2.
21 Richard Dyer, 'In Defence of Disco', in S. Frith and A. Goodwin (eds), *On Record*.
22 McClary, *Feminine Endings*, pp. 127–8.
23 Reynolds and Press, *The Sex Revolts*, p. 152.
24 Freud associates 'sadistic anal' eroticism with 'the instinct for mastery' which – insofar as he posits 'masculinity' and 'femininity' as given categories at all – he associates with specifically masculine sexuality. See Sigmund Freud, 'Three Essays on Sexuality', *On Sexuality*, Penguin Freud Library, Volume 7 (London, Penguin, 1977), pp. 33–171.
25 McClary, *Feminine Endings*, p. 119.
26 Feminine music is thereby defined as something like Hélène Cixous' 'écriture feminine'.
27 Reynolds and Press, *The Sex Revolts*, p. 385.
28 David Toop, *Ocean of Sound: Aether Talk, Ambient Sound and Imaginary Worlds* (London, Serpent's Tail, 1995), pp. 1–22.
29 Ibid.
30 Ibid., pp. 33–5.
31 See Simon Reynolds, *Gabber Archive* on http://members.aol.com/blissout/index.htm. See, also, Simon Reynolds, *Energy Flash: A Journey Through Rave Music and Dance Culture* (London, Picador, 1998).
32 Simon Reynolds, 'Rave Culture: Living Dream or Living Death', in S. Redhead, D. Wynne and J. O'Connor (eds), *The Clubcultures Reader* (Oxford, Blackwell, 1997).
33 Jean-Luc Nancy, *The Inoperative Community* (Minneapolis, University of Minnesota Press, 1991), p. 12.
34 Judith Hanna, *Dance, Sex and Gender*, (Chicago, UCP, 1988), p. xiv.
35 Angela McRobbie, *Feminism and Youth Culture* (London, Macmillan, 1990).
36 Angela McRobbie, *Postmodernism and Popular Culture* (London, Routledge, 1994).
37 Angela McRobbie (ed.), *Back to Reality? Social Experience and Cultural Studies* (Manchester, MUP, 1997), pp. 154–5. See also, Maria Pini 'Cyborgs, Nomads and the Raving Feminine', in Helen Thomas (ed.), *Dance in the City* (London, Routledge, 1997).
38 Pini, 'Cyborgs, Nomads and the Raving Feminine', p. 116.
39 As Simon Reynolds has made clear in his 'Rave Culture: Living Dream or Living Death', in S. Redhead, D. Wynne and J. O'Connor (eds), *The Clubcultures Reader* (Oxford, Blackwell, 1997).
40 See Angela McRobbie, 'Settling Accounts with Subcultures: A Feminist Critique', in S. Frith and A. Goodwin (eds), *On Record*.
41 See, this volume, Chapter 6.

42 John Gill, *Queer Noise* (London, Cassell, 1995), p. 134.
43 Ibid., p. 137.
44 V.N. Volosinov, *Marxism and the Philosophy of Language*, trans. Matejka and Titunik (Cambridge, MA, Harvard University Press, 1972), pp. 98, 102–3.
45 Frith and Goodwin (eds), *On Record*, p. 415.
46 Butler, *Gender Trouble*, p. 127.
47 Cuisick, 'On a Lesbian Relationship with Music', p. 76.
48 See Reynolds and Press, *The Sex Revolts*, pp. 323–31.
49 While Butler's call for queer feminism to intervene in the symbolic might be understood as a call for such politics to concern itself primarily with *language*, her problematization of the Lacanian distinction between 'imaginary' and 'symbolic' itself problematizes the possibility of any such prioritization.
50 Pini, 'Women and the Early British Rave Scene', in Angle McRobbie (ed.), *Back to Reality* (Manchester, MUP, 1997).
51 Jacques Derrida, 'Choreographies', in P. Kamuf (ed.), *Between the Blinds* (Hemel Hempstead, Harvester, 1991), pp. 455–6.
52 Rowena Chapman and Jonathan Rutherford (eds), *Male Order* (London, Lawrence & Wishart, 1988).
53 Reynolds, 'Rave Culture: Living Dream or Living Death'.

5

METAL MACHINE MUSICS

Technology, subjectivity and reception

Any attempt to posit a connection between technological change and musical practice comes up against a number of challenges. As Michael Chanan points out, the history of music technology is highly problematic:

> [for] musical instruments stand in the same ambiguous relationship of cause and effect to the development of works, forms and movements as their technological equivalents in the wider world; like the steam engine, for example, in relation to transport systems and the industrial revolution. In each case, the technology is both agent and symptom of change.[1]

Cultural critics who assert a concrete link between technological development and changes in patterns of musical activity are accused of determinism by both social scientists and other cultural critics.[2] While we are hopefully well past the point of positing simple causal relations between technological change and musical (or any cultural) activity, a critical fondness for abstraction still results in the underestimation of technology's potential for creating complex and contradictory meanings and effects.

The problem partly inheres in the way the word 'technology' is frequently employed as shorthand for 'high' or new technology. The presence of visibly technological items is sometimes taken automatically to connote political radicalism or aesthetic innovation and it has been necessary to fire shots across the bows of those who excitedly map formal or aesthetic 'progress' on to technological novelty in this manner. This said, critiquing a techno-optimism which sees technological developments as always enabling creation or subversion should not necessitate a return to a humanist fear and loathing of technology, always the instrument of capital or state power. As Constance Penley and Andrew Ross point out, technology is no more 'naturally' threatening than it is 'naturally' benign:[3] shouting 'halt, friend or foe?' at the first sight of chrome or an LED will only produce one of two equally facile replies.

The critical task now is to chart technology's permeation rather than determination of music practice, in all its complex forms.[4] We must consider technology in a wider sense rather than concentrating on so-called 'leading edge' items, whose cultural impact may consist solely on a rarefied plane. Such approaches neglect the ways in which more mundane items are appropriated and altered – actively recontextualized or reconstituted within changing patterns of social and cultural practice. In hastening after the ever-remote vanishing point of the techno-logical horizon it is forgotten that, for example, innovative or important technological practice often stems from the 'misuse' of 'low' technology items. This first part of this chapter will consider how recent dance music cultures interact with and are predicated on a variety of different technologies, new and old, 'high' and 'low'. The aim is to broaden the range of items/resources which might be said to constitute music technologies, with a view to suggesting some directions for further enquiry. Consequently our remit goes beyond just the musical instruments employed in the production and performance of dance musics: the technologies utilized include various other items, from digital computers to the domestic hi-fi, many of which have not been, or would not be considered instruments by established musical discourse.

Similarly, more work could usefully be done on the many technologies of reception; from the discrete items of 'equipment' used to replay and receive recorded and transmitted music to the private and public spaces in which these musics are experienced, and the chemical technologies which modulate these experiences. Although this chapter is divided up between technologies of produc-tion and technologies of reception, it will hopefully demonstrate the slippery nature of such a division; critics have recently begun to problematize western separation of the fields of musical composition, performance and reception, or rather to point out how musical practice itself problematizes this separation.[5] Popular music forms and practices often make it difficult to maintain strict cate-gories of production and consumption, with their connotations of activity and passivity; this leads us to question the position of agency within, and authority over the creation of musical meanings, and the ideological assumptions that have underpinned them. Examining the cultures of instrumental dance musics in rela-tion to their technologies of reception is also a useful means of relinquishing the consideration of their operation in primarily specular terms; the terms utilised by some of the socio-anthropological treatments of youth music cultures as discussed in Chapter 4, which write these cultures through tropes of dress and display. These are cultures that have to be heard and felt – not (just) seen.

Technology and visibility

Music has always been produced with and mediated via a number of technolo-gies; to assume that it is only during the latter half of the twentieth century, or during the era of the microchip that technology has entered the process of music making is to misread the various histories of the musical instrument as well as those of recording and production. As Alan Durant has made clear:

> Virtually all forms of music-making are dependent upon some kind of deliberately designed and specialised equipment or technology.... The history of musical instruments is always, in this sense, a history of technology.[6]

Yet many discourses around music consider the presence of certain technologies in negative terms; as a marker of the elimination of human agency from the production of music, the 'murder' of music as living creature. Such musics, its critics argue, omit feeling, they are cold, mechanical, repetitive, lifeless. Other forms of music may be considered emotive, warm and authentic, and yet employ just as many technological components in their production. This contradiction is managed by means of the creation of a hierarchy within technology – what we might consider as an *index of visibility*.

In relation to their degree of historical familiarity and the immediate context in which they are operated, some items are considered *more* technological in status than others. In this scheme, a drum machine is more technological than a drum, a synthesizer is more technological than an electric guitar. Such considerations are founded on an order of the real within which aesthetic preferences are transformed into ontological distinctions. In this manner, distinctions between the technological status of various musical instruments are frequently used within the discourses of popular music and criticism when parties make claims for the authenticity and aesthetic superiority of a particular form or practice. It is sometimes claimed by musicians, critics and fans alike that the presence of a synthesizer or computer in the arsenal of a band or producer downgrades the ontological status of the music they produce: it is artificial as opposed to musics which are *real*. Participants and contestants within musical genres frequently fetishize one set of technologies and dismiss others – a rock aesthetic may favour a Gibson guitar or a Marshall stack. Such distinctions almost always proceed by rendering the technological components utilized in their favoured forms *invisible as technologies* – they are more 'real' or 'natural', absorbed wholly into those that play them as expressive extensions of the performing body.

The letters pages of musicians' equipment magazines from the mid-1980s onwards have regularly featured debates about the death of, or the threat to, 'real music' represented by the advent of digital or computer technologies.[7] Some of the writers dismiss the computer-literate kids, DJs and others who have begun to make records by means of electronic technologies as not entitled to the term 'musician'; their argument is that they do not play instruments, instead they manipulate machines, press buttons, point and click. Some of the fears expressed are professional, and follow the industrial pattern of labour of being afraid of being replicated or superseded by new mechanised techniques. Concern was voiced over the advent of the digital sampler, a machine that could supposedly replicate the sounds made by a musician (unlike the synthesizers that had existed up to this point whose sound bore only a distant timbral relationship with acoustic instruments), as it was feared that it would drive many 'real' musicians with slender livelihoods out of work. Such arguments and assumptions about the musical status of emergent technologies run through many different realms of pop criticism and intellectual evaluation – the legitimacy of a particular item of equipment or form of production technology frequently forms the basis for a dismissal or, just as frequently, approval of a particular piece of music. The various technologies involved in the production of 1970s disco were often cited in attacks on the form made by those whose tastes were more 'authentic': this dance music either used too much studio equipment, employing 48-track tape machines to develop the lush tones of severally tracked voices and orchestral instruments, or as in the work of European disco producers such as Georgio Moroder, it introduced a new range of electronic devices to regulate the beat, resulting in a loss of 'feeling'.[8]

In Anglo-American popular music cultures 'real music' can connote one of a number of forms loosely allied in their retention of a folk-derived notion of authenticity in expression, and defined against what are considered reified pop forms, musically inferior, and lacking substance or content – tainted by their complicity with the structures of capital. Pop is produced with machines, whereas rock, folk, soul, jazz or whichever form one wishes to privilege, is played and performed by artists via the medium of their instruments. Such a construction disregards both the actual practices by which contemporary popular music is produced, and the new skills and activities required in the utilization of digital and computer technologies. Despite the fact that most recording studios are heavily equipped with new digital technology, computers, samplers and the like, which are employed in the production of music of all types, claims to authenticity through the demonization of certain technologies and the rendering transparent of others still feature in the discourses around music.

The dismissal of computers or samplers is not a new phenomenon. The irony is that rock's emergence from folk music was characterized by its use of (relatively) recent electric technologies, developed for dance bands and employed by pop musicians. In June 1965, two weeks after the release of his seven-minute electric single 'Like a Rolling Stone', Bob Dylan took to the stage at the Newport Folk Festival with an electric guitar and a full band and began to play 'Maggie's Farm'. He was heckled by many in the crowd for betraying the premiere dictum of folk ideology; that it should be played with acoustic instruments, rather than the electric ones employed in the commercial realm of rock 'n' roll.[9] This has come to be considered a key moment of rock's inception. Those who bridled at the din made by Dylan, including other folk artists such as Pete Seeger (who later said that if he'd had an axe he would have cut the power cables) as well as those in the audience who booed until Dylan left the stage, did not know that rock would go on to retain the aesthetic of authenticity in performance and expression upheld by folk, and to use it to validate a new form, for a generation who would have no problems accepting its electric instrumentation.

Folk music's inherent notion of presence, of physical contiguity between the performing artist and the receiving audience, was retained by musics whose existence depended increasingly on reproducible media. Of course the 'live-ness' of music captured on any medium is now in doubt; as many critics have pointed out (studio) recording has shattered forever the auratic integrity of the musical moment – at the same time many musics have sought to cling on to a narrative of authenticity that is hardly borne out by practice. Classical music labels have enthusiastically embraced studio recording technologies, which have enabled them to seek to create a semi-platonic ideal performance, through the splicing of segments from various takes.[10] In rock, live concert albums are always composed after the event, at the very least remixed from multi-track recordings, and usually composited, over-dubbed and generally touched-up in order to bear the attentive proximity of repeated listenings. When the British Musician's Union conducted a campaign against recorded music in pubs and clubs, whether from jukeboxes or from DJs, with the slogan 'Keep Music Live', it was acting against the pop industry and for a largely folk tradition of musicians whose livelihoods depended on the maintenance of spaces where they could play music to an audience.

While folk musicians may have suffered in the past thirty years, the desire for folk 'authenticities' has remained tenacious despite both technological advances and the onset of television as one of the main outlets for popular music. A recent vogue for acoustic rock spurred the popularity of MTV's Unplugged show where successful acts prove that they can 'cut it' not only live, as opposed to being studio-based, but theoretically without the aid of any electricity whatsoever, using mostly acoustic instruments. There is some irony that a TV channel dedicated to showing back-to-back videos twenty-four hours a day should have a hand in preserving an aesthetic of authenticity which states that certain instruments are more real than others, but not much. As Tricia Rose has pointed out, MTV was attacked for failing to show anything but white rock music during its first years of broadcast until CBS threatened to boycott it unless they started to show Michael Jackson videos.[11] And while rock was massively popular in the 1980s a great deal of its video work simulated the performance space of the live concert.

Similarly, as dance music swept into dominance of the British charts in the late 1980s, the producers of the long-standing TV pop show Top of the Pops issued a dictate stating that any act wishing to perform in the studio would have to sing live, thereby asserting the 'return' of an aesthetic of musical authenticity in performance to a programme where acts had in fact always lip-synched while a young audience looked on and danced listlessly, only perking up when the camera alighted on them. Top of the Pops had never been a haven of authentic rock values: the shifting space of the studio set never resembled a concert venue, but rather an overlit and makeshift disco. From the 1970s onwards its visual references were directed towards club culture, with the studio draped in tinsel and awash with faux-nightclub neon, and for a period before the advent of music videos professional dancers were sometimes used. Dance troupes Hot Gossip and Legs and Co. would perform routines to songs when the acts in question could or would not appear. If the new dictate was intended to 'show up' the ever increasing number of dance acts in the Top Forty after acid house, whose vocal elements often consisted of repeated samples (frequently from old records), or whose telegenic front-person had clearly not been the singer in the studio, it rather went against the spirit (and the iconography) that had long informed the programme.[12]

As rock attempted to reassert folk performance values, music television among other media has thus sometimes acted to privilege musics which retained a notion of being able to, as the phrase goes, 'cut it live'. What is continually implied by such an performative aesthetic is the necessity of discrete subjectivity; that one can play on one's own, produce music using one's own body and nothing more than the approved technologies, considered invisible, or the extension of the body's natural attributes. This aesthetic works to police the borders of the musical subject: what the body is allowed to play with.

Yet contemporary technologies consistently question this conception of the individual as discrete object, altering both our bodily experience and our experience of the body. As Steven Pile and Nigel Thrift point out, the body, 'understood as biological entity, has undergone significant spatial augmentation'.[13] As the potentials and the affective domains of the body are augmented, so the traditional borders and boundaries of the bodily subject become on the one hand more rigorously patrolled and on the other more frequently challenged and indeed breached, both discursively and in material terms. As Donna Haraway has famously pronounced, 'In the traditions of "Western" science and politics ... the relation between organism and machines has been a border war. The stakes in the border war have been the territories of production, reproduction and imagination'.[14]

Recent cultural criticism, tracking the dual histories of technology and the body in twentieth-century music, has made much of the body's *erasure* by recording and reproductive technologies. For example Michael Chanan states that:

> the technique of reproduction – mechanical, electrical or electronic – creates a distance, both physical and psychic, between the performer and audience that simply never existed before ... the integrity of the musical work, its intimate unity with the time and place of its performance, perhaps the most essential aspect of what Benjamin called its *aura*, has been destroyed. Music has become literally disembodied, and the whole of musical experience has been thrown into a chronic state of flux.[15]

Chanan argues that where once musical performer and audience were, by necessity, in varying degrees of proximity within halls, gardens, places of worship, parlours, theatres and opera houses, the introduction of the phonograph and the radiogram have enabled musical communication without the metaphysics of presence. He disregards Walter Benjamin's wonder at the mechanical reproduction of a 'second-order' aura, which democratized the reception of the new arts on the part of the populace.[16] His conclusion that music has 'literally been disembodied' demonstrates a neo-Cartesian tendency to consider the moment of musical conception and emanation over the experience of reception which can *never* be disembodied. Chanan supports the implied hierarchy of composition, performance, reception which we have identified. In answer, we will consider the manner in which producing and receiving bodies are *reconvened* by the technologies of recording and performance, and the zones within which they operate.

We are the robots

'The drum machine don't make mistake like the musician,' says the little powerhouse. 'If you want to be a good drummer, copy the electric machine then maybe you can see Lee 'Scratch' Perry. Better to use a machine than use a human who is unclean. I'd take a drum machine and beat the drummer until he plays like one.'

Lee Perry, interviewed by Ian McCann[17]

It would appear that contemporary music production has allowed bodies and machines to combine in previously unheard fashion; as reggae producer Lee Perry jokes, many recording musicians now live in the age of the 'click track', the externally-generated electronic pulse that one may consider to have made the drummer cyborg, as her cardiovascular system – her heartbeat and pulse-rate – becomes externally calibrated, digitally clocked. Of course, little is as new as it seems: musicians have been 'clocked' mechanically for over two hundred years, since von Maelzel, mechanician to the Viennese court, automotive impresario and constructor of mechanical musical devices, met the inventor D. N. Winkel and subsequently patented and named the Dutchman's latest creation in France, thereby securing most of the financial rewards of the newly-titled *metronome*.[18]

In the latter part of the twentieth century multi-track tape, computer sequencing and hard-disk audio recording have further complicated the notion of 'real time'. Musical recording now unfolds the various instances of judgement that were conjoined in live performance before an audience. Decisions about what should be retained and what should be discarded, about what order the various musical elements will follow, and the hierarchy suggested by their various positions within the mix, can be made at any stage during the writing and recording of music. Performances are composites, enhanced by drop-ins, edits and the process of 'comping' – compiling the best parts from several takes. For sequenced music little 'performance' may be involved in production itself: perhaps adding live effects from the mixing desk as a track is put down. Even this final stage of committing a mix to tape is not necessarily final: a number of mixes can be executed and composites edited from them, or further remixes performed from the tapes and parts at a later date. This does not represent a negation of skill, or an abdication of judgement – rather, these qualities become more vital the greater the amount of options, sounds, processes and effects become available to the producer/musician.

Computer sequencers have allowed the creation of music within a frame known as 'step time' which collides the activities of composition (on the stave) and later performance of 'written' notes. Here nuance can be painstakingly applied, reapplied or erased; the location of notes and beats can be offset subtly or solidly locked within the dictates of a strict temporal grid – a process called *quantization*. These various options facilitate concrete musical and formal effects. Drum 'n' bass, for example, has continued the practice of sampling, disassembling and reconstituting drum breaks that started with hip hop, and was extended (at twice the tempo) by the practitioners of hardcore. The intricacies of its labour intensive programming defy expressive theories of performance and disrupt linear notions of temporal flow. Despite frequently made aesthetic and formal connections with jazz, this music is painstakingly and minutely constructed using computer sequencers – it cannot be improvised in 'real time', and when played 'live' by a drummer (successful drum 'n' bass acts like Reprazent and Metalheadz have taken their music live in order to promote it beyond a 'core' club audience) ironically its materialiaty ebbs. Live drum 'n' bass drumming becomes an organic approximation, shored up by our prior knowledge of the rigorous syntax of formerly programmed beats.

The often painstaking practices involved in contemporary music recording and post-production (even conventionally 'recorded' albums now usually go through extensive computer-based editing and processing using systems like Avid's Pro Tools) might seem to indicate that they represent the triumph of composition above all – the strictures of computer realization negating any further human interference in the communication of compositional intention. Such an interpretation neglects to consider how, as recording and sequencing technologies have managed to conflate and confuse the relationship between composition and performance, performance (as we will see) becomes more important in its relation to the various moments of reception.

The romantic trope of the artist as intending genius is *not* necessarily confirmed by all of this. Improvisational composition and performance techniques are enabled by sequencers' recording functions; moreover, computers are also able to record, and repeat mistakes; they facilitate felicity. The development of the home or project studio (often computer-based) as self-contained writing and recording space has changed the temporal locus of musical production, and has brought with it aesthetic and economic implications. Rather than adhering to the traditional formula of writing batches of songs which are then recorded in expensive studio facilities over a relatively short space of time, groups who have their own means of production can choose to extend the scope of the writing process into the development of new sounds and timbres, deployment of new modes of composition and instrumentation and the ongoing activities of recording, re-recording and mixing. When understood in this manner, writing and recording become process once more, music can emerge through attrition, or sedimentation, rather than as a priori composition, made physical through performance and material via mechanical reproduction.

Technological development and concomitant shifts in practice have meant a change in the perceptions of the division of labour in the process of popular music production. The advent of multi-track recording thirty years ago enabled musicians to play music with themselves: it allowed one person to adopt multiple musical roles, or to juggle a number of previously discrete personalities. The use of computer sequencers, samplers and other such digital technologies has extended this unfolding of performative subjectivity. A musician/artist is now often producer, performer and engineer too – within the domicile and on a relatively small budget of a couple of thousand pounds. A new species of digital auteur exists, who is able to compose and produce music on a single computer and even create a CD of their work at the end of the process. This does not necessarily comprise a new digital onanism: collective composition, collaboration and performance is still allowed. Moreover, working with samples, or enfolding your own repeated performances within those of others creates a type of community of production. In such dance cultures as hip hop and acid house, to paraphrase Deleuze and Guattari, one person, a pile of records and a pair of decks or a sampling computer, could already have been said to constitute 'quite a crowd'.[19] Sampling has allowed the production of music using only previously performed copyright material (old records), or with a range of audio CDs and CD-Roms which present a selection of performances matched for tempo and key, waiting to be assembled into 'complete' tracks, or to form elements of, or backings to new or existing compositions. All of this has placed considerable resources into the hands of musicians operating outside the large advances and recording budgets of the major record industry. In 1996, British songwriter Jyoti Mishra achieved a 400,000 selling number one hit with a single called 'My Woman' (as White Town), recorded at home on an eight-track cassette multi-track costing less than £700.[20] A large number of dance artists from Orbital to Daft Punk have made successful records, such as 'Chime' and 'Homework', using sequencers, four-track tape machines, or cheap DAT recorders in bedroom or home studios.

Some of the discourses around these new technologies have much in common with the values underpinning folk authenticities in musical forms: self-sufficiency, anti-capital, the use of cheap and accessible equipment. The frequent comparison of dance musics to punk is more convincing in terms of political economy – owning and controlling the means of production, issuing records through a profusion of small independent manufacturing and distribution networks – than in an aesthetic or a subcultural sense. Punk had attempted to explode the status of the rock musician as skilled professional that had developed during the 1960s and 1970s, with fanzines like Sideburns invoking the 'democratic' do-it-yourself ethic of three-chord rock 'n' roll, with a famous one-page guitar lesson: 'Here's a chord, here's another, here's a third, now go form a band'.[21] Musical education by traditional pedagogic channels was deemed unnecessary, as was the conscious knowledge of more than a handful of chords or the concept of key signature. In this way computer and digital technologies have continued the long autodidactic tradition which can be traced to pop's inception. Making your own instruments originated with skiffle – by purchasing a cheap guitar and making a rhythm section out of a tea chest and washboard, you too could be Lonnie Donegan. Nowadays some kids build their own PCs – and even if they merely buy one and some software and a soundcard, they already know how to operate it.

Some of these details suggest a new minstrelsy, akin to that proposed by Jacques Attali in his book *Noise*. Attali furnished a description of 'compositional' forms which predicted the return of a unity of author and performer in the form of the *jongleur*, someone who not only writes and plays his/her own music but makes his/her own instrument too.[22] The folk ideology of 'composition' returns us to the realm of marginal and (thus) authentic musical cultures: local and autonomous, made possible by the return of technologies which subvert the established roles of worker and consumer. Susan McClary notes that 'in the scant seven years since *Noise* was published, extraordinary evidence of such tendencies in music has emerged' – her example (in 1984) was of course punk and new wave.[23] Here another sort of authenticity or integrity can be regained from healing capitalism's fissure between body and that which it produces. A folk-politics of instrumental technology and music production have valorized a few dance producers who build or adapt their own equipment. Richard James, an ambient techno producer, better known as Aphex Twin, promoted himself thus during his early career. James, an electronics student at Kingston Polytechnic at the time, described to journalists how he rebuilt or modified his synthesizers, drum machines and processors to produce *original* sounds.[24] Tales such as this one (in a manner akin to accounts of hackers, phone phreaks and other 'techno rebels') provoke the awe of the majority of us who use and depend on a great many technologies that we can neither construct, mend nor even service ourselves.[25]

The playing and programming of synthesizers and, in particular, the use of sequencers and computer music systems has necessitated a shift in what is considered to constitute the 'musical'. Some writers have not happily acknowledged this development. For example, at the end of what is an otherwise excellent essay on the star system and consumerism in the development of rock, David Buxton makes the following comment:

> Another factor in the decline of the star has been the emergence of computer technology in music, which bypasses the relation between musicians and traditional instruments, on which a large part of the star mythology was based. Music making has become an affair of technicians and record producers. Kraftwerk, an electronic group, has pushed this development to its logical conclusion by employing robots as on-stage replacements.[26]

This is a by now familiar repetition of the line that technology has disenfranchised the musician at the expense of the computer boffin, the author failing to recognize that the restructuring of production roles created by technological innovation, the conflation of the musician and producer in the new space of the MIDI studio, might not defeat the need for the 'star'. As we have seen, the important developments incurred by technology can be said to have occurred on a micro-economic level: that state-of-the-art studios create finished recordings from computer memory rather than from multi-track tape should come as no surprise, but that an emerging cottage industry of writer–producer–artists would emerge at the end of the 1980s, working with computers and digital equipment, who not only could sell respectable amounts of records through small distributors (or out of the backs of vans, via mail order or the internet) but make regular forays into the domain of the Top Forty unaided by backing from major labels or vast recording advances, is much more significant.

Though they operated within the major sector of the music industry (EMI promoted and distributed the products of their label KlingKlang), German 'robot pop' act Kraftwerk have been highly influential, perhaps most obviously in their inspiration of various dance musics from electro to techno. They were the first pop group to suggest a connection between emergent shifts in the political economy of pop production and the exclusive use of electronic music technologies, considered by some to be threatening the removal of human agency from the production of music.[27] Somewhat flat readings by such critics as Buxton seem not to recognize that Kraftwerk's stage robots might constitute more than the 'logical' defeat of human performance. The 'robot replacements' to which he refers were automated puppets resembling the four members of the band that first made their appearance on the *ComputerWorld* tour of 1981 (as part of the encore). They represented the development of visual images of automatism initiated on tracks like 'Showroom Dummies', after which the band had exaggerated their uniform image to the extent that actual dummies were used on promotional appearances for their next LP, *The Man Machine* (EMI, 1978).

The robots themselves were a performative conceit – a form of showmanship that played on pop's expectation of live performance and promotion even from musicians whose technology might not require them to 'play' at all. Interestingly, they were continuing an eighteenth- and nineteenth-century European vogue for automata pioneered by itinerant showmen like von Kempelmen, creator of the 'chess playing Turk', and von Maelzel, who later toured the illusion around Europe and America along with mechanical orchestras and other curiosities.[28] Both sets of performances required of the audience an anthropomorphic suspension of disbelief (achieved by a degree of sleight of hand) – a desire to wonder at the power of the machine. The robots' 'self-moving' properties represented an illusory contract between performer and audience, who posited a degree of 'intelligence' in them, simultaneous with the reassuring knowledge that they had been fashioned by man. The human element had not been eliminated from the performance – this was misdirection. Their creators might not be present on stage but both their music and their ironized image were. Kraftwerk's pre-programmed robots served to ironize the constructedness of music and performance, emphasizing the agency which was behind it.

Although this was performance in the theatrical sense, informed by a dry, somewhat camp, humour, their ironic self-representation also hinted at new subjective relations within musical production and performance which band members Ralf Hutter and Florian Schneider have repeatedly discussed:

> It's like a robot thing, when it gets to a certain stage. It starts playing … it's no longer you and I, it's It….
>
> We are playing the machines, the machines play us, it really is the exchange and the friendship we have with the musical machines which makes us build a new music.[29]

As the technologies employed in their musical production are imbued with 'life', so in their mode of presentation and performance Kraftwerk sought to project themselves as but 'components', more machine-like. The *menschmaschine* appeared to extend 'Kraftwerk' beyond the familiar conception of the pop band, towards an aggregation of human members, technological items and studio space, without asserting the usual internal hierarchy which delineated them: 'Sometimes we play the music, sometimes the music plays us, sometimes … it just plays'.[30] Kraftwerk suggested that instruments were not merely passive vessels, containers for the expression of the intending artist. This was (and indeed remains) a widely held position in music discourse, even among musicians who had pioneered the use of synthetic sound. In explaining his use of synthesizers, even avant-garde space-jazz hero Sun Ra resorted to a familiar conception of expressive intention:

> The main point concerning the synthesizer is the same as in all the other instruments, that is, its capacity for the projection of feeling. This will not be determined in a large degree by just the instrument itself, but always in music, by the musician who plays the instrument.[31]

Kraftwerk's Hutter and Schneider suggested that their equipment and the space of their studio were control technologies, but ones which fed back into the process of musical creation. They felt the need to acknowledge the fact that instruments make contributions; they guide or alter what can be performed, providing limits within which the performer or player can operate. Technologies and the discourses which surround them imply or suggest particular uses or practices, which the operator can choose to take up or ignore. Thus instrumental technologies and their patterns of use form part of the guiding parameters by which musical production takes place. This is not to underestimate the ability of the innovative to improvise, to twist items out of their intended trajectories, to recontextualize them within radical new patterns of practice. It is to some of these activities, musically manifested within the use and misuse of often 'low-tech' items, which we now turn.

121

Low technologies

> Talking about the crap that works – how crummy pieces of equipment make magic. I said this was a model of popular culture – where 'base' materials (doo-wop, hula hoops) keep getting transmuted into something magical and powerful.
>
> Brian Eno, diary entry, 19 April 1995[32]

In his essay, 'Sample and Hold',[33] Andrew Goodwin refutes a simple ascription of postmodern aesthetics to contemporary digital pop production (particularly sampling) because he considers that neither the practice, nor the discourses which surround it, bear out a strictly Benjaminian analysis. Goodwin is rightly wary of deterministic accounts which assume that technologies (or the musics which utilize them) are 'inherently' radical or avant-garde – when of course such judgements should be applied (or not) strictly in relation to practice. Much of his argument hinges on how the discourse of musicians themselves often fails to reflect the aesthetic or theoretical claims made for their music by others. In his eagerness to demonstrate that contemporary digital or technological musical practice and the discourse around that practice may still recourse to familiar authenticities (a point which we do not contest), Goodwin fails to consider why some musicians might feel the need to distinguish between their 'authentic' practice and others', beyond the implication that musicians are pretty good at coming up with reasons why what they do is better than what other musicians do.

The aestheticization of technologies of production is a means of conferring value on a particular musical form, and practitioners of dance musics that employ electronic or digital equipment traditionally denigrated by rock's discourse of the real have also employed these strategies in their efforts to validate their activities in relation to prevailing musical discourse. Goodwin observes that dance and other musicians use such terms as 'warmth' or 'feel' in relation to the equipment they employ, terms which by their implicit opposition to machine-like 'coldness' suggest the humanization or vivification of inanimate technologies. We could read this as similar to rock discourse's absorption of musical equipment into the body, rendering invisible the technologies it employs. Conversely we might try to suggest that it echoes the subjective complications suggested by Kraftwerk in their refusal to hierarchize the activities of the human and the machine, with the music emerging from a larger entity or assemblage (sometimes theorized as *cyborg*). It is also important to recognize that musicians delineate the equipment they use in relation to a complex matrix of values, characteristics and associations. Thus when certain items of equipment are spoken of as being 'warmer' or having more 'feel' than other items, this is a recognition that the items in question assist the musician in achieving the result that (s)he wants, that they permit or facilitate the production of particular and concrete musical effects.

In other words, concepts like 'warmth' or 'funk' (which, of course, approves a particular type of 'feel' in black and dance musics) while acting as markers of aesthetic approval have additional and specific musical meanings which, to quote Robert Walser, are 'contingent but never arbitrary'.[34] These connote specifically formal or timbral characteristics with histories and patterns of signification that can be usefully excavated if approached carefully. For example, 'warmth' as a term in music production has a specific meaning as a shorthand for a particular timbre achieved on pre-digital recording, connoting an accentuation of lower mid-range frequencies common to analogue musical technologies. This characteristic was caused by the saturation of magnetic tape with a recorded signal or by the presence of valve components rather than transistors in a particular item. Digital sound produces no such artefacts and, as a result of its ability also to retain the very high frequencies often attenuated by analogue, is conversely sometimes regarded as 'cold'. While notions of 'warmth' and 'coldness' carry significant implication of approval or displeasure, we must remember that not all musicians agree with them or choose to lend them equivalent value. There are many musicians, from 'dark-side' drum 'n' bass acts to the neo-modernist avant-garde, who privilege the equipment that enables them to achieve 'cold' or 'harsh' sonic effects.

Some observers consider it strange that notions of 'feel' and 'funk' could pertain to the realm of machines.[35] One of the means by which dance musics which employ computer technologies have been criticized is that they privilege the coldly regular. When the 'four to the floor' rhythms of disco, pioneered by the likes of Philadelphia International Recordings and the dynamo that was M.F.S.B.'s drummer Earl Young,[36] were translated on to the electronic drum machines which were coming into use during the late 1970s, some critics decried the 'soulless' sound of Euro-disco. Nelson George states that:

> At least the Philly disco records sounded like they were made by humans. Soon, Eurodisco invaded America, initially from Munich, and later from Italy and France. It was music with a metronome like beat – perfect for folks with no sense of rhythm – almost inflectionless vocals, and metallic sexuality that matched the high-tech, high-sex, and low passion atmosphere of the glamorous discos that appeared in every American city.[37]

Not everyone concurs with George's view of the influence of computers in dance music. Others admired the mixture of the human and machinic exactitude reminiscent of that originally intimated by the funk innovators of the early 1970s:

> 'It was a search for perfection,' he [John Cale] says. 'It was in admiration of James Brown's demanding precision. He would say, "If you play the wrong note I'm going to dock your pay one hundred dollars!" There was a kind of mentality of absolute exactitude. The electric metronome came in and it would not change by one iota. It was rigid all the way through.'[38]

The capacities of sequencers and musical computers to alter tempo fractionally, to introduce error, swing or 'feel' into sequenced musical data is constantly being extended,[39] yet the rigidities in timing exhibited by older, 'cruder' sequencers and drum machines have not been abandoned. For many people they have become part of the musical aesthetic of computer-based pop and dance music. The rhythmic precision established by bands like Kraftwerk, and taken up by early electro-boogie producers, is similarly cherished by hip hoppers who refuse to give up the gritty sound of their SP-12 drum sampler, or those house and techno producers who still cherish their TR-808 and TR-909 drum machines. These are technologies that have contributed to the establishment, characterization or actualisation of a musical aesthetic. What were formerly prescriptions or restrictions have become active choices: while technology has enabled musicians to 'loosen up' the beat, many choose not to. In this sense, once again, technologies may contribute to or imply particular uses and practices as they develop, which are subsequently codified as an aesthetic. This is one of the main reasons why old equipment remains popular in the realm of such dance music forms as hip hop and house. It may be more precise, offer less choices and more prescription, but it also contains what is by now part of an aesthetic built in to its ageing hardware. Andrew Goodwin's comment that, 'we have come to equate machines with funkiness,' should perhaps read: 'we have come to consider some machines *more* funky than others'.

Thus, 'funky' as a term of aesthetic approval still carries part of an earlier sense: 'smelly'.[40] A notion of 'funk' has attached itself to the musical products of dance musicians who have been at the forefront of utilizing old and unwanted, failed or superseded pieces of equipment, often doing so out of economic necessity. The widespread use of older analogue technologies in dance music forms like house and techno occurred partly as a result of such economic concerns. Digital synthesizers such as the DX7 entered the market at the start of the 1980s and caused the value of the analogue machines that had existed up to this point to plummet, making them newly accessible to the young producers and DJs who developed house and techno music.[41] The subsequent aestheticization of analogue (which influential critics like Goodwin have failed to refer to in either a political or an economic context) was a function of the new dance music's success and influence; as others attempted to recreate its characteristic sounds, formerly discarded equipment became revalued, and often ended up more expensive than when it was first sold. As dance forms spread and increased in popularity over the course of the next ten years, instrument and equipment manufacturers began to realize that a new market for their products had emerged and subsequently began to create instruments that simulated or alluded to the sounds of these analogue antecedents. The musical equipment market now contains a preponderance of 'virtual analogue' synthesizers and sound generators, whose intended aim is to emulate the characteristic sounds of voltage controlled instruments.

One machine that has found itself recreated in at least five different forms in the past five years is Japanese synthesizer manufacturer Roland's TB-303 Bass Line. Created in 1982, the TB-303 was designed to accompany a small Roland drum machine called the TR-606 Drumatix as a bass-line generator, the two items creating an automated rhythm section for gigging guitarists and other musicians to use.[42] However, its unconvincing electronic sound and difficult programming structure (to create a bass-line entailed entering three sets of information in turn – notes, rhythm and accents – effectively programming it three times) meant it was a commercial failure and it quickly disappeared from both production and earshot. This was until Chicago house producers Marshall Jefferson and DJ Pierre (along with Roy Davis Jnr, Spanky and the other members of an act called Phuture) turned its peculiarities – the haphazard nature of its programming and its distinct sound – into a strength, repeating an enharmonic sequence over the course of ten minutes, while altering its timbre by manipulating the unit's filter cut-off and resonance controls.

The subsequent record, 'Acid Tracks', was a huge underground hit and went on to spawn a thousand imitators both from Chicago and within the UK where house was becoming both a musical and a cultural sensation. Jefferson claimed that this historical moment of inception was unforeseen:

> 'Acid Tracks' was an accident man. When you get an acid machine you don't pre-programme anything. You just hit some notes on a machine, man. DJ Pierre, he was over and he was just messing with this thing and he came up with that pattern.... We played it at the Music Box, man, and everybody was flipping.[43]

This peculiar bass sound became the main timbral marker for a new strain of house music known as acid, and the TB-303 that produced it quickly became known as the 'acid machine'. Over the years it would be deployed in various ways; in the atonal synth-funk blueprints of 'Acid Tracks', Sleazy D's 'I've Lost Control' and Tyree's 'Acid Over', and then, after a four-year absence, in European trance and techno forms at much faster tempos, building multiple layers of amphetamine-friendly synthesized sound. As a result, it has acquired the status of a 'classic' musical instrument; a small, silver plastic box becoming an unlikely cousin to the 1963 Fender Stratocaster and the Stradivarius. The price of an original TB-303 has rocketed, fuelled both by a narrative of authenticity and lack of availability. As we have noted there are now many items on the market specifically designed to do nothing more than reproduce its synthetic timbre. The timbral qualities of the synthesizer itself were not, of course, the sole point. The obtuse nature of the interface and programming structure influenced the atonal result: wildly enharmonic sequences verging on a twelve note series.

The radical innovations claimed for black dance musics such as hip hop and house are often indexed to their use of once cheap or 'failed' technologies like the TB-303. Removed from their intended functions such items often trace very different trajectories. The other famous example of appropriation and recontextualization has been the standard, consumer hi-fi, whose potential for the reproduction, replication and alteration of existing musics has resulted in various

complex cultural effects and manifestations – most notably hip hop. One of the reasons hip hop has been so attractive to theorists is that it utilized techniques previously employed only within avant-garde practice, outside the auspices of high-art institutions – using street-level equipment. What's more, you could dance to the result. The assault on propriety and the discrete integrity of recorded music famously committed by hip hop's 'cut-up' aesthetic, was created using domestic cassette machines and turntables (the subsequent availability of sampling served to aid rap production only after the basic principles of cut-up had long been established[44]). Steinski's 'History of Hip Hop Volumes I, II, and III' was put together using a painstaking amount of tape edits performed using the pause button of a domestic cassette machine. Grandmaster Flash spent three years practising how to segue all the best breaks and sections of his favourite records on turntables before he went into the clubs and on to the streets to show off the results.[45]

Access to technologies of reproduction and reception such as turntables, scratch mixers, speakers and record collections enabled hip hop as DIY party culture, just as it had informed the performance and production practices of disco (which of course shared many of the spaces and inspired the musical tastes of nascent New York hip hop). The various musical uses put to consumer electronics by musics like hip hop and disco have meant that DJ cultures have been responsible for destabilizing the distinction between production, performance and reception in the realm of musical meaning.[46] They also demonstrated that economics has aesthetic consequences and vice versa. The relationship between technological development and cultural practice is bidirectional: the latter being as likely to drive and regulate the former as the former is the latter. Supposedly outmoded or obsolete vinyl technology has been maintained, in no small part thanks to the continuing popularity of dance musics, for whom turntables and records are irreplaceable components within 'established' modes of production and reception. The death of vinyl, oft-predicted, will at the very least occur over many years, decades after the arrival of its supposed replacement, the compact disc, and the new formats which follow.

Dance music's transformation of the turntable into a musical 'instrument' began in the early 1970s. A few club DJs had begun to use mixers which, by combining the signals of their turntables, enabled them to fade quickly from track to track. In New York, Francis Grasso started to layer different sections of records, and weave together the beginnings and endings of tracks with similar tempos to produce one continuous mix of music.[47] The ability to sequence records – the act of determining the order and the pacing of a set over its several hours for the maximum entertainment of the dance crowd – had always been the most important talent of the successful DJ. By using more than one copy of the same record, or combining music from two different ones, it allowed DJs to extend their means of generating tension, anticipation and pleasure among the dancers. The advent of layering and beat-mixing increased significantly the performative component of DJing, and at the end of the 1970s became the basis for one of the performative kernels of hip hop (along with rapping and break-dancing), cutting and scratching.

Since disco, the techniques of beat-mixing, of DJing as musical performance, have been developed to the extent that DJing is considered an 'art form' in certain discourses around dance culture. There are various skills or criteria in such an evaluation: being able to programme the musical selection, to read and react to the crowd, and to demonstrate an ability in the beat-mixing technique developed by Grasso and those he inspired. Hip hop DJs manipulate vinyl in the most spectacular fashion. A huge array of techniques and tricks are still being developed some twenty years on by scratch virtuosi: hip hop's tradition of competition and display manifests itself in the DMC mixing championships, home to thrilling technical ability. Indeed, there is a danger that this manifestation of hip hop culture sometimes reaches the point at which such technical skill supersedes the musical content; pleasure is replaced by awe at the magisterial expertise of the scratches and the cuts. The excitement generated by the scratches is a function of the visual presence of the DJ: this is in every sense a spectacular activity. The danger is that the programmatic arranging skills, the break and music selections exhibited in the great cut-up records like 'The Adventures of Grandmaster Flash on the Wheels of Steel' or Steinksi's 'History of Hip Hop', are missing: the alchemical skills of hip hop DJs to make staggering new structures out of old records – and its connection to the dance and party cultures (and forms such as disco) is neglected.

In contemporary club cultures beat-mixing has been developed and extended to the point that those listening and dancing to house, and in particular techno, may be hearing two (or three or more) records simultaneously for a large majority of a set. Techno DJs like Jeff Mills construct polyrhythmic plaits out of tracks which are 'minimal' in composition and highly repetitive in structure – by their nature 'incomplete'. These begin to signify when placed not only in series but in parallel by the DJ, who sequences, layers and cuts between them to create a larger musical exposition. Minimal techno tracks only realize their potential when woven into a larger context, when acted on by the DJ, who through a process of mixing and cutting adds verticality to their horizontal linearities. Several strata are accumulated: variable pitch controls enable the synchronization of several records, occasionally augmented by a drum machine or sampler too. This process of layering is accompanied by actively altering the tonality of the music through the equalization controls provided on the mixer. By filtering out a particular frequency range from one record, and replacing it with another, new textures and frictions result, as beats rub against one another in unique patterns of syncopation. Before the signal reaches the speakers it will have been put through a signal processor called a *compressor* which optimizes the amplitude of the music by limiting its overall dynamic range. This component regiments the signals from the several records that might be playing, and in so doing wraps the multiple beats and inflections around the foundation signal, the bass which will squash other sounds as it pulses in and out. The music produced by such techniques is governed by the contradiction between rhythmic regularity and precision, anchored by the kick drum, and the aleatory, unpredictable fashion by which the various other elements combine, constantly twisting and altering.

In the world of consumer hi-fi, decks and DJs we can see slippage between the realms of musical production, performance and reception. The rest of this chapter will present a historical account of some of disco and dance music's other cultural technologies, from twelve-inch singles to the club spaces which destabilized the (privileged) visual sense, and asserted the importance of the aural and the bodily. We assert the importance of these technologies of reception (records, club spaces, sound systems, drugs) for challenging some long-established views on music cultures and their participants, and reconsider the complex relationship between music, the body and the spaces within which they are combined.

The receiving end

Materialist criticism, concerned only with modes of production and considering the record as a copy, severed from the auratic integrity of its source, has consequently paid little attention to its destination, to the meanings that would be conferred on it when and as it is played. It assumes that music is ossified when captured on tape, CD or vinyl, refusing to consider the range of contexts within which recorded sound, the supposed 'mass reproduction of aura',[48] is heard and the implications of these sites of reception for our notions of subjectivity and passivity in the creation of cultural meanings. It disregards the ways in which recorded musics are manipulated and transformed as they are received. The uses of 'commodified' forms are always more varied, and work to open up more spaces within the realm of capital, than analyses which proffer a single view of industrial totality or suggest the notional superiority of resistant 'avant-garde' forms would have us believe.

There are several reasons why the status of reception has been neglected. Popular listeners have been denigrated by the discourses of the élite, considered 'mere' consumers, passive and inert. In the Frankfurt School account of reception, the audience is produced by the material it receives: psychosocially conditioned, incapable of independent thought, the audience for mass cultural products is required to exhibit neither effort nor agency, their musical food being pre-digested, already familiar before being heard. The production of repetition obliterates the moment of reception – listeners are not allowed any kind of indi-viduated response. Whereas Walter Benjamin (inspired by the then new experience of cinema) famously saw mechanical reproduction as potentially posi-tive, neo-Frankfurters writing on music lament the decline of the recital, or the ubiquity of the walkman.[49] They consider music in the era of transmitted and, later, recorded sound as pale and uniform, regretting the removal of the listener from the point of musical emanation, from the vicinity of live performance.

The power of music invisibly to sway the vulnerable or the unsuspecting has also been asserted by those who, after Adorno, criticize pop for failing to resist the pernicious nature of capital, and also – somewhat ironically – by those who fear its effects to inspire revolt, criminality and the loss of virtue. In both arguments music is considered narcotic; either opiate, cushioning the subject from the realization of his/her alienation, or stimulant, spreading violence or civil unrest. Both formulations assume the essential helplessness of the listening subject. Robert Walser describes how the Parents Music Resource Center[50] and its intellectual sponsors (in particular a music professor named Joe Stuessy) used a hypodermic metaphor to conceptualize pop reception:

> [Stuessy] adopts a 'hypodermic model' of musical effects; music's meanings are 'pounded' or 'dumped' into listeners, who are helpless to resist. Young people in particular are thought to be more vulnerable, especially when repetitive listening and headphone use help create 'a direct, unfettered freeway straight into the mind'.[51]

Just as critics of rock have used such discourse to argue for legal powers to censor and impede its distribution and sale, rock's criticism of 'easy-listening' pop forms, and in particular Muzak,[52] has employed quasi-Adornan formulations not far removed (the important difference being that rocker Ted Nugent hasn't attempted to have Muzak banned, although he was reported to have offered to buy the corporation so he could wipe all its tapes[53]). Muzak, an emollient music designed to enhance subconsciously the moods of the offices and shopping malls into which it is piped, is considered by people like Nugent to be a form of mass control technology which numbs the listener in order to promote uniformity and placidity. In the 1980s some of America's right-wing moral majority groups considered rock music to have a similar affective potential, though its results were seen as being very different from that of Muzak: the surrender of virtue and the collapse of civilized society. Their fear of heavy metal and its supposed invocations to Satanism and suicide resulted in several high-profile court cases.[54] As Walser states, groups who use such arguments

> imagine that fans are passive, unable to resist the pernicious images of heavy metal, and thus they themselves commit the sort of dehumanization they ascribe to popular culture ... [their arguments] depend upon denying fans subjectivity or social agency so that they can be cast as victims who can be protected through censorship.[55]

It might seem peculiar that such similarly affective powers should be attributed to popular musics apparently so different in timbre and content. Both the light orchestrations of popular standards and more recent hits produced by General George Owen Squier's Muzak corporation and the music of Judas Priest function in similar ways, according a view of musical reception which characterizes the listener as a mixture of vegetable and victim.

The phrase 'audience reception' implies a mass passivity in the face of popular cultural transmissions: as Thornton points out Adorno's 'mass' was the radio generation.[56] A reunderstanding of the audience as active rather than passive does not mean giving up altogether the term 'reception', but demands that we seriously qualify or complicate it. Much of recent cultural and literary studies has begun to re-evaluate the traditional transmitter–receiver model, which portrays the artist as transmitting a message to a person whose job is to hear, listen and understand. We are having to rethink our preoccupation with the *phatic*, with the communicative function of art. In its place, a more pragmatic model considers the many ways in which music functions in combination with its audience; how it is *used* and *transformed* by those it reaches, rather than how it causes them to behave.

The notion of transformation is important. Neither art, music nor popular culture have ever been consumed or experienced in an entirely linear fashion. They are frequently altered and customized, wrenched as text and product from their supposed, immediate or intended contexts and pressed into service as the generators of new meanings. The existence of criticism, the study of art at institutional levels and the furious debates and disagreements that fuel both these activities, are a testament to this. After a frustrating period of trying to second-guess or fabricate the intentions of long-dead authors, literary studies developed theories of reader response over twenty-five years ago, focussing acutely on the discourses which shape those responses, and the manner of their articulation. If we are to reformulate listening as activity, we must recognize that we are all as listeners guided and informed by a number of learned and adopted musical discourses, each of which possesses distinct histories and aesthetic agendas. Further we do not always follow our instructions; instead exhibiting what David Toop calls *perceptual subjectivity*.[57] As Andrew Goodwin has pointed out, we 'individualise pop through more personal narratives that continue to elude the culture industry'.[58]

Some models of reception also fail to register the modes and locations within which various musics are encountered and interacted with; background or foreground, forming part of our interior space and our wider environment, spilling in from or out into the street, it can be focussed on intently, or distractedly. Both avant-garde and popular musics have engaged with potential variations in the spaces in which musics are heard, and the act of 'listening' itself, suggesting previously neglected combinations of the two. In the 1970s, for example, the pioneers of ambient music (most famously Brian Eno) attempted to reassert the value of unobtrusive sound, of listening without attention to 'backgrounded' music. Ambient, the somewhat more sullen offspring of Muzak, was conceived after Eno was hospitalized in 1975.[59] A friend brought him a record of seventeenth-century harp music and put it on before she left, leaving the volume on very quietly by mistake. Eno tells of how he was fascinated by a listening experience in which he could only just make out the music above the sound of the rain outside, and on recovery he began to work on music functioning as an 'all-round tint to my sonic environment'.[60]

Ambient was theorized as a utilitarian music which worked to effect subtle modulations of lived space, rescinding any representational function; it was no longer aspiring to aesthetic categorization as a lesser form of figurative painting, or as tone poem. This was gaseous sound, music as perfume rather than text or art object:

> Ambient music must be able to accommodate many levels of listening attention without enforcing one in particular; it must be as ignorable as it is interesting.[61]

As Eno describes, his and others' work in this area was spurred on by recent technological developments:

> New sound-shaping and space-making devices appeared on the market weekly (and still do), synthesizers made their clumsy but crucial debut, and people like me just sat at home night after night fiddling around with all this stuff, amazed at what was now possible, immersed in the new sonic worlds we could create.[62]

Such 'spatial' approaches to sound production were not conceived in the 1970s, but much earlier. The development of the recording studio enabled the creation of composite sound-fields which combined the acoustic properties of various actual rooms and chambers, and 'artificial' effects processes, often designed to emulate acoustic environments but usually producing distinctive and previously unheard results. Ambient musics, in common with other forms which had been highly influential on it such as dub reggae, highlighted the spatial processes involved in the creation of recorded musical sound. It reflected a growing interest in exploring the many options granted by emergent studio technologies in constructing sounds and timbres as a primary activity, rather than as a means of presenting a 'good tune' in its best light.

The advent of reproduction and its technologies has also exploded the range of spaces within which music can be heard and the opportunity for meaning presented. The cheapness of the cassette recorder has enabled listeners to assemble their own listening experiences in whatever spaces they choose. Musical space need no longer be sedentary. Portable stereos, from boom-boxes to walkmans, allow listeners to transform the world they inhabit, publicly or privately: to give it a new soundtrack. Iain Chambers, writing about the walkman,[63] describes how the apparent solipsism of headphones is transformed by the ambulant listener. A nomadic listening identity is constituted as the subject actively recreates the landscapes which surround him/her, 'constructing a dialogue with it, leaving a trace in the network'.[64] This act of concentration is not the modernist subject withdrawing into 'head' space, under threat from the urban other, but an extension and confirmation of the body in transit, what Chambers terms a 'diasporic identity'. Technologies such as the walkman enable the listener to transform music in subtle but significant ways. The aleatory also occupies a small space within the world of hi-fi, in the form of CD players which allow random passage through what were once predetermined musical journeys, forcing one to reconsider the previously arranged exposition of song. John Corbett describes the joy of discovering shuffle mode on his CD player, enabling a rejection of the implied listening order of the artist, and letting chance select the music he is to hear.[65]

The potential for small interventions on the part of the listener afforded by some of these technologies forms an adjunct to the contemporary notion that the art work is 'incomplete': cultural products are neither 'finished' when the writer puts down his/her pen, or the recording engineer presses 'Stop' on the tape machine, nor when their efforts are reproduced a thousand times over, shrink-wrapped, priced and shelved. It would, though, be a mistake to see such notions as purely a function of *new* technological manifestations. Brian Eno has critiqued the description of a 'newly interactive' layer of media, such as CD-Rom, not least for its implication that previous cultural forms, such as books or records, have *not* been interactive.[66] Similarly we do not desire all music to move to 'enhanced' formats which require opening-out, to arrive raw or unmixed requiring that we 'reheat' it prior to consumption. Rather we seek to acknowledge our agency as listeners in the creation of popular cultural meanings, and the importance of the various technologies we employ and occupy at these moments of reception.

Empires of the senses

> Music requiring bodily motion on the part of the listener for its complete enjoyment, like much popular dance music, is by that token artistically imperfect. The same might be said of performance.
>
> Edward T. Cone, *Musical Form and Musical Performance*[67]

> They were synaesthetic performances, one sensory perception operating in a context reserved for another, as if dance, sculpture, theatre, and music were all at work at once, and in a time when phonograph was all the rage, there was something here which escaped mechanical reproduction. Intellectuals and journalists talked of 'trance' and the 'sacred,' of erotics and exoticism.[68]
>
> John F. Szwed, on Sun Ra

The complex interrelation of musical forms and zones of reception (as technologies in themselves) vitally informs any history of music.[69] Richard Leppert has described how the institutions of western music have sought to police the body within the spaces of performance and audience response.[70] After the Enlightenment 'high' musical discourse saw the textual realm of the *score* as the most important repository of musical meaning, ideally removed from the realm of the performative or the bodily. Music theory transformed the exigencies and approximations of performed music into science, into clean and exact

132

mathematical abstraction. The age of Reason provoked the regulation of both performers and listeners, and the eventual growth of static concert conditions. Consequently, 'classical' musical reception has at times aspired to contemplative stillness.[71] In such contexts institutional high-art spaces have constituted technologies of reception which work to confirm a particular conception of musical experience. The communal isolation of the concert hall and the conservatory assisted in separating the life of the mind and the palpitations of the vulgar body. High-art musics become ocular, to be watched, to be pondered. This constituted a policing of bodily response, governed by strict rules of stillness and silence. As Leppert notes:

> The etiquette of contemplation is, before anything else, a controlling of the body in time, a working against the body, whether self-imposed or imposed by others (like parents who discipline their squirming children). And it is an etiquette that turns music from an inherently participatory activity into a passive one in which the listener maintains physical stasis by exerting the cultural force of will against the body's desires.[72]

This aesthetic of stillness is premised on a notion of clarity, in which the eradication of noise becomes the primum mobile. The process of listening to music is converted into an optical search for perfect representation, for presence without any kind of rupture or interference.

An epistemology of musical transparency similarly underpins the way headphones and hi-fi equipment are sold and fetishized. This transparency is promoted by a manufacturing industry who promote reproductive fidelity as a virtue within the vocabulary by which they sell amplifiers, CD-players and brands of blank cassette. Manufacturers' marketing practices cling to a notion of 'aura' (long pronounced departed by Walter Benjamin), making fallacious claims about their products based on notions of presence. This discourse states that the latest digital sound format or audiophile amplifier or turntable will bring you as subject closer to the music, so close that you will be able to see the music without interference. As before, the act of listening is transformed into an optical search for clarity. This is a manifestation of ocularcentrism: the privileging of the visual sense in this case over the aural. Buy the CD of the Beatles' Revolver and you will be able see/hear the squeak of Ringo's drum pedal,[73] as if the Beatles' primary aesthetic motivation was merely the transparent reproduction of recorded sound. This discourse clings to a notion of fidelity, of truth to the authentic sound message. Yet there are as many 'true' sounds as there are expensive pieces of hi-fi equipment, and none comprise an objective window allowing metaphysical purchase on the real. Fashions in sound characteristics change; some enthusiasts prefer valves or vinyl for the 'warmth' or 'substance' which they consider it lends to the music, whereas others consider the presence of more high frequency sound permitted by digital technologies such as CD as constituting the 'real'. What Goodwin has called 'the mass reproduction of aura'[74] is still a simulation, a copy without an original referent. Nevertheless, a recent Technics Hi-Fi poster campaign shows an enraptured drum 'n' bass producer, Goldie, resembling an orchestral conductor with arms raised as if wielding a baton. It is accompanied by the slogan: 'The closest you'll get to the sound in his head.' This metaphysical slant on the opacity of the reproductive medium still insists that with Technics equipment the listener will be able to tap directly into the Romantic imagination of the artist.[75]

Of course not all hi-fi technology aspires to this plane: some technologies of reception freely advertise their aesthetic agendas, their emphasis of particular frequencies. Those connected with the reproduction of bass-dependent dance musics and black musics, through such facilities as 'Mega-Bass', give listeners the chance further to accentuate these qualities or to compensate for the fact that the music is not coming out of very large club speakers. Similarly, graphic equalizers, 'surround sound' or other such virtual acoustic treatments on midi hi-fi equipment, provide us with the chance to meddle, to adapt or further distort the already mediated sound contained on the record, CD or tape – to enact small rebuttals of the culturally-attributed passivity of the listener.

When the eradication of any additional noise or distortion becomes the prime concern of the moment of musical reception, one is being urged to listen to what is *not* present rather than what is. As John Corbett points out, noise 'foregrounds the physicality – and potentially the social production'[76] of music – that it is *authored* not *autocthonous*. Dance musics such as hip hop, house or techno have rarely sought to eradicate noise, often choosing instead to privilege lo-fi, rough or distorted sounds (often as indexes of 'authenticity' as we noted above). It is for many producers a defining timbral characteristic. For example, German techno producer Maurizio (Basic Channel, Rhythm and Sound) does not attempt to mask the background noise emitted by the effects processors which he employs: the hum frames the other sounds, strengthening the listener's sense of their materiality. Similarly his engineer, Stefan Betke (recording as Pole) has recently made a record out of an assortment of vinyl clicks and pops, sampled, effected and spatialized. Digital music production has reached the hyper-real stage where the artefacts associated with now 'authentic' analogue technologies, such as records and tape, can be created digitally by means of computer music system 'plug-ins' that add vinyl crackle or simulate tape-saturation.

The necessity of emphasizing materiality, and the body, has been written into recorded dance musics, and the means by which they are experienced and reproduced from the outset. Bass-heavy dance music provokes the recognition that we do not just 'hear' with our ears, but with our entire body. This embodiment is achieved through the experiential characteristics, the kinaesthetic effects of the disco, the club, the dancefloor, and the performative and reproductive technologies employed within them. An examination of spaces of reception in dance cannot reassemble the notional subject, but it can instead extend its scope past the Cartesian dualism between mind and body, inner and outer space. The refusal of specular identity which takes place within certain club spaces does not involve a disappearance of the body (as is implied by the ideologies of high-art spaces) or a prioritization of another sense, but an augmentation and commixture of the sensory and bodily. Music forms part of an assemblage, with the groups of people who come to clubs, raves and concerts, and the spaces in which they are located.

We should remember that such dance musics as house (an abbreviation of 'warehouse') and disco took their names from the spaces in which their development occurred, the zones of reception in which their musical forms and meanings were heard, in which specific attributes were tested, repeated, confirmed or rejected.[77] DJs from Francis Grasso to Larry Levan played a diverse range of music – whatever provoked favourable responses in their crowd – initially a 'disco' record was merely a record that could be successfully played in a disco. So, when in an NME singles review in 1978, Paul Rambali comments that Devo's cover of '(I Can't Get No) Satisfaction' 'would even make a good disco record' he is not saying that Devo sound like Chic.[78] (As time passed and a combination of reportage, critical discussion and mediation canonized certain records as typifying the disco 'movement', the understanding of what constitutes a disco record changed; it becomes one that adhered to each item from a specific stylistic list – 'four to the floor' bass drum rhythm, florid orchestral instrumentation, an extended structure which unfolds the familiar verse-chorus syntax of popular song and so on.)

There was also another technological definition. 'Disco single' became the phrase used, particularly by larger record companies, to refer to the new twelve-inch single format which emerged during the later part of the 1970s. The twelve-inch single as musical technology grew directly out of club space, out of the popularity of the discotheque[79] and the musical practices being created there by the relatively new figure of the DJ. It developed as DJs like Walter Gibbons started to use tape editing to extend dancefloor favourites, lengthening introductions and instrumental sections, allowing the groove to unfold even further beyond the strict remit of the song, which had often been tightly structured with the demands of radio and its three-minute pop ideal in mind. This was the nascent remix, played in clubs from reel-to-reel tape machines or cut on to heavy one-sided discs of acetate, as 'slates' or 'dub plates',[80] to be played until the softer plastic wore beyond acceptable levels of quality. Gibbon's extended mix of Double Exposure's 'Ten Percent' for Salsoul was the first such mix to be released commercially.[81] Club DJs were now influencing the record producers, and many subsequently became record producers – such DJs as Gibbons, Larry Levan and François Kevorkian, and later, Frankie Knuckles and David Morales, were given access to the multitracks of new dance records in order to produce their own dubs and mixes. Figures such as Kevorkian, Morales and Derrick May (originally a house DJ) would later become more renowned as record producers than spinners.

These extended tracks necessitated more vinyl – a seven-inch single would not be able to accommodate them without sacrificing amplitude and sound quality. Although twenty-five minutes of music could be fitted on to one side of an LP, accommodating so much information meant closer, thinner grooves, resulting in a lower ratio of musical signal to noise. Attempting to cram too much sound on a record, at too high an amplitude, forced adjacent grooves dangerously close, and if they touched the needle would jump whenever it reached that point. However, if one used the amount of vinyl traditionally employed for four or five tracks to reproduce just one, one could happily accommodate a ten-minute disco mix while also obtaining a large increase in amplitude. Wider grooves also allowed better reproduction of low frequencies: the bass that was traditionally emphasized by club speakers could be built into the record from the start without any danger of the needle jumping. The reproductive qualities of the new format were in concert with the requirements of the music it carried, and in turn gave that music vital space in which to develop sonically, to extend further into the lower reaches of the frequency spectrum, an opportunity which was eagerly taken up by the dance forms which followed disco, creating and utilizing ever heavier and deeper bass and sub-bass sounds.

Dance musics like disco or house did not seek the harmonious balance of sound, but were predicated on the emphasis of bass and sub-bass, alongside the higher frequencies. Consequently most night clubs and discos do not echo the concert hall and its search for sonic 'transparency'. Their ideal club sound is heavily mediated: treated, compressed and equalized in emphasis of the body. Although clubs like New York's Paradise Garage and London's Ministry of Sound, have been famed for (and promoted on) their fetishization of the aural, other clubs became famous despite the quality of their PA systems. When Factory Records decided to invest the money they had made from New Order's hit single 'Blue Monday' into the renovation of a former Marina yachting showroom in one of the less salubrious areas of central Manchester, the resulting club, the Haçienda, became infamous initially for its 'terrible' sound. In spite of this, it went on to play a formative role in the explosion of the acid house phenomenon in the UK, and became the pre-eminent icon of British dance culture for a heady three and a half years.

The Haçienda in terms of a club space is worth further consideration. The accounts of its conception and execution contained in Jon Savage's tenth anniversary history, The Haçienda Must Be Built, acknowledge the aim of creating an interchangeable zone capable of switching between disco and live-music venues. It was directly inspired by shared spaces of disco and punk within New York clubs like Danceteria and Hurrah's, which enthusiastically played black American funk and dance records, as well as hosting live gigs. However, from the beginning of the project there was a marked bias: designer Ben Kelly placed the dancefloor squarely in the middle of the club, flanked by the steel girders which held the building up and announced by bollards striped (like the girders) with distinctive yellow and black hazard markings. In contrast, the stage was meagre, insufficiently large enough to house the lighting rigs of many acts who would otherwise have chosen to play there. The Haçienda was constructed around absence, a cavernous space which was literally built by the bodies that assembled therein (to the detriment of its acoustics). Its nominal invocation of Ivan Chteglov's situationist,

urbanist manifesto 'Leaving the Twentieth Century' explicitly denied the importance of the specular in any attempt to understand or narrate the club, or the
experiences of its patrons: 'You'll never see the Haçienda. It doesn't exist. *The
Haçienda must be built.*'[82]

This is in contrast to Andy Blackford's evocation of the opulent Studio 54 in
New York in the 1970s, which appeared to emphasize the visual senses.
Blackford's account implies that Studio 54 owed much to the consideration of
space and play in architectural postmodernism, and explicitly invites comparison
with the casino and entertainment complexes beloved of Venturi *et al.* in *Learning
From Las Vegas.*[83] This disco is a bewildering space, shifting and remaking itself as
the evening continues:

> Nothing in Studio 54 is really real. You can't even trust the walls, which
> are built up of endless partitions and backdrops. Pull a lever here, operate
> a pulley there and you can alter the geometry of the place entirely. The
> floor too is not what it seems. It can suddenly divide into sections, like
> an iceberg beneath your feet.
>
> As if all this weren't enough, the total illusion of the environment is
> completed by an extraordinary barrage of images projected onto the
> 'walls', giving an altogether baffling effect of *trompe l'œil*. The special
> effects are nothing if not spectacular. One minute you're in the centre of
> a fake snowstorm – the next you're the hero of a ticker tape welcome –
> the next you're fighting your way through a waist-high sea of coloured
> balloons.[84]

Blackford goes on to describe Howard Stein's club, Xenon, which contained a
light display called the 'MotherShip', created by Douglas Trumbull, Hollywood's
most famous visual effects man, who had just worked on Spielberg's *Close
Encounters.* This spacecraft-shaped lighting rig lowered itself on to the dancefloor in
a brash explosion of neon and laser light. In his description, Blackford uses the
same points of reference as Venturi: 'The whole thing looks like an enormous,
brash piece of American pop art. A sort of *reducto ad gloriam* of Vegas arcade
culture.'[85]

The technological complexity of these clubs was partly an index of opulence
and exclusivity in the battle for the patronage of New York high society but this
extravagance does not wholly serve to amplify the narcissistic disco spectacle
identified in some political critiques of disco – a lightshow for the idle rich to
watch rather than dancing. It is more meaningfully placed within a context of
sensory overload where the disco as space works to defeat the domination of the
visual sense through a surfeit of stimulus akin to noise interference. Synchronized
with the music, in varying degrees of rhythmic density, the result is a synaesthetic
blur. This synaesthetic experience has been a key component of disco since late
1960s nightclubs like New York's Electric Circus, heavily influenced by the extrav-
agant psychedelic lighting effects of the West Coast's rock clubs and happenings.

Rather than apparently privileging the eye or the ear, these clubs and discos attempt to create synaesthetic effects which refuse both the hierarchy of the senses, and the emphasis of any one bodily zone.

Moving from space to space, from dancefloor to dancefloor, radically alters the experience of reception; club spaces are highly disparate, from intimate, condensation-soaked, low-roofed cellar spaces, to larger-scale purpose built dance zones, appropriated warehouses, marquees, aircraft hangers, or fields open to the sky. Obviously hearing a record at home, in a shop, or in the street is vastly different to hearing it in a club, not just because of this potentially various sonic kinaesthetic experience. The aural experience is just one dimension of a synaesthetic combination of space, sound and sight which comprise the dancefloor's affective potential. There is also another vital component which contributes to the realignment of the senses, and certainly qualifies as a technology of dance music reception – drugs. The chemically diachronic experience of dance, as the participants move along axes of euphoria and narcosis, means that any account of dance and cultures needs to consider the chemical technologies of pleasure.

Ecstasy express

It is an indisputable fact that 'drugs' are central to contemporary dance culture.[86] Indeed, since at least the 1960s they have played an important part in most dance-oriented cultures. 'Dance culture' and 'Ecstasy culture' have become virtually synonymous terms in the United Kingdom today. The rise of dance culture in the UK has occurred simultaneously with an exponential rise in the numbers of people who regularly use illegal drugs.[87] The names of artists and records, and the samples and vocals contained within, have alluded sometimes obliquely, sometimes obviously, to the iconography and language of attendant drug cultures. The syntactic structure and timbral qualities of contemporary dance records are directly informed by a wider cultural knowledge of their specific chemical destinations – their potential effects on the pharmacologically altered brain and nervous system.

As Matthew Collin has suggested, 'drugs' can usefully be theorized as a form of technology.[88] This formulation brings certain benefits to the discussion of drugs and their relationship to culture. First, it enables us to examine the axis between the chemical experience and the cultural effects of MDMA and other 'dance drugs' without becoming weighed down by such issues as the morality of prohibition.[89] It also prompts us to consider that the very concept 'drugs' is both arbitrary and culturally specific. Human beings interact with a huge range of organically derived substances in a variety of ways, including many forms of ingestion. Delineating one group of substances and naming them as 'drugs' is, the anthropologist Andrew Sherratt argues, a practice specific to modern European culture.[90] Sherratt suggests that the term is not a useful one, certainly not for the consideration of the status of psychoactive substances in other cultures. Rather, he suggests that 'the study of psychoactive substances is part of the anthropology of consumption'. The excellent work of Sherratt and his colleagues attests that in many cases this is certainly the most productive way to study 'drug' use in European as well as non-European cultures. However, we would like to suggest a complementary approach which can also provide us with useful ways of thinking about the status of 'drugs' in contemporary culture.

As we have considered above, the social and cultural effects of any given technology are almost entirely dependent on the actual uses to which it is put, and this is dependent not on the technology itself but on the socio-cultural context which produces it and in which it is deployed. We can see the type of simplistic discourse on 'drugs' which tends to be circulated by the state and the media as one example of technological determinism – the belief that technologies have a kind of life of their own, an autonomous capacity to effect change without themselves being the results of conscious action. Rather than recognizing this set of chemicals as a number of different technologies with a range of possible uses and effects – some positive, some negative – this discourse tends to reproduce the notion that any kind of contact with any of these substances will inevitably have deleterious effects on a person, area or social group.[91]

The story of 'rave' culture is also often told in terms which reproduce a largely deterministic notion of the effects of 'drugs'; in this case, MDMA. 'E' is often seen as having been *responsible for* 'rave' culture. However, MDMA has been available in the developed world for most of the twentieth century. The fact that it did not become popular as a recreational drug until the late 1980s suggests that it was not the effects of Ecstasy which created contemporary dance culture (in which case, it could have emerged at any time), but that it was the specific historical context of British and American culture at that time which led people to find a specific set of uses for the drug. It is also important to remember that the determinist account also works to exclude the experiences of all those who enjoy the activities of clubbing and dance musics without recourse to drugs.

This is not to deny that technologies themselves have effects on given cultural formations; such musics as trance and house, both typical of the UK and western Europe, would obviously not sound as they do if they were not designed specifically to accentuate the effects of certain drugs, in particular MDMA. Even in this case, however, a particular set of cultural priorities determines the effects of the technology in question, as such musics are always designed in order to accentuate specific effects of MDMA rather than others. Euro-house's drum rolls and big string washes are designed to accentuate its celebratory, ecstatic, communal effects much more than its hypnotic, introspective ones, for instance.

The observation that 'drugs', like any technology, only have meanings and effects in particular given contexts leads us to think about the ways in which 'drugs' relate to those contexts. A much remarked on phenomenon of recent years has been the apparent 'normalization' of drug use among young people, particularly in the UK and the States. This term designates the extent to which 'drug' use has gone from being a marginal activity with all kinds of implicit meanings derived from its marginal status – rebellion, oppositionality, militant apathy – to

139

being an unremarkable feature of the everyday life of many people. Drug use has apparently become 'normal' for young people today. What the simple concept of 'normalization' does not take into account is the extent to which this process is one of close interaction between specific 'drugs' and specific cultural contexts; only particular types of 'drug' use become 'normalized' and relatively specific meanings are still attached to those uses, even if those meanings have changed ('drugs' may now simply equate with 'leisure'). This process can be better understood in terms of the notion of the 'enculturation' of technologies.[92] Although this term was originally deployed to refer to the domestication of technologies like television, it can usefully be applied to 'drugs' in so far as it can designate the extent to which drug use becomes normalized *as part of a culture*. Music, fashion, club spaces, advertising imagery, ritualistic forms of consumption (of drugs and associated substances – gum, soft drinks, even Vicks Vapo-rub) – constitute a coherent formation which delimits and defines the range of meanings and effects which the particular technology ('drugs') can have.

As this chapter has pointed out, the enculturation of a whole range of technologies – from vinyl discs to digital sequencers to MDMA, LSD and amphetamines – has been one of the key processes according to which contemporary dance culture has been constituted. Due to space limitations, we have only been able to hint at the detailed histories and subtleties of these technologies of production and reception, but we are convinced of the importance of their examination and discussion, both for the understanding of pop practice and as ammunition in hard-fought battles over activity and agency in the realm of cultural meanings and values. There remains great deal of work to be done on this topic.

Notes

1 Michael Chanan, *Musica Practica: The Social Practice of Western Music from Gregorian Chant to Postmodernism* (London, Verso, 1994), p. 166.

2 In the introduction to her anthropological study of IRCAM (Institut de Recherche et Co-ordination Acoustique/Musique, housed in the Pompidou Centre, Paris), Georgina Born criticizes what she terms 'instrumentalist' accounts of the relation between aesthetics and technology. She states that: 'Instrumentalist views are common in postmodern cultural studies and popular music theory, in which new music technologies are seen as heralding new progressive forms of popular music: punk, rap, hip hop and so on', *Rationalising Culture: IRCAM, Boulez and the Institutionalisation of the Musical Avant-Garde* (Berkeley, University of California Press, 1995), p. 341 (note). Similarly, Andrew Goodwin's essay, 'Sample and Hold: Towards an Aesthetic of Digital Reproduction' (*Critical Quarterly*, vol. 30, no. 3, Autumn 1988) warns against attempting sweeping prognoses of radical new musical activity. While agreeing that caution must be exhibited before connecting 'new technologies' and 'radical' musical practice, this chapter risks accusations of 'instrumentalism' by suggesting that there is a complex interdependence between the technologies employed in dance musics, and the formal characteristics/accompanying aesthetic formulations; and that it is useful to consider these side by side, if not simply as cause and effect.

3 They declare themselves 'wary, on the one hand, of the disempowering habit of demo-
   nizing technology as a satanic mill of domination, and weary, on the other, of
   postmodernist celebrations of the technological sublime', Constance Penley and
   Andrew Ross (eds), *Technoculture* (Minneapolis, University of Minnesota Press, 1991),
   p. xii.

4 'There is no determinism anywhere, if by determinism we signify a one-to-one corre-
   spondence between the causal agent and its effects; rather technology permeates',
   Michael Menser and Stanley Aronowitz, 'On Cultural Studies, Science and Technology',
   in Stanley Aronowitz *et al.* (eds), *Technoscience and Cyberculture* (London, Routledge, 1996),
   p. 8.

5 Both Alan Durant ('Improvisation in the Political Economy of Music', in Christopher
   Norris (ed.), *Music and the Politics of Culture*, London, Lawrence & Wishart, 1989) and
   Simon Frith (*Performing Rites*, Oxford, Oxford University Press, 1996) examine the separation of the acts of composition, performance and reception (and the implicit
   hierarchy which places them in that order) in western musical ideology.

6 'A New Day for Music – Digital Technologies in Contemporary Music Making', in
   Philip Hayward (ed.), *Culture, Technology and Creativity in the Late Twentieth Century* (London,
   John Libbey, 1994), p. 178.

7 For example, this letter to *Making Music* magazine: 'In reply to that cretin who started the
   debate on scratch/sample/hip-hop/trash, it may well be the most exciting thing since
   punk, but can we really call it real music played by real musicians? It may also be what
   the 1980's is remembered for, but that is not all that happened. Great guitar, drums,
   vocal, bass (and even keyboard) gods emerged from nothingness, instead of some idiot
   being able to press a couple of buttons', 'The Post', *Making Music*, no. 30, September
   1988, p.11.

8 Nelson George bemoans the exactitude of Euro-disco in *The Death of Rhythm and Blues*
   (London, Omnibus, 1989), p. 154.

9 Fred Goodman, *The Mansion on the Hill: Dylan, Young, Springsteen and the Head on Collision of Rock and
   Commerce* (London, Jonathan Cape, 1997), pp. 8–9.

10 Michael Chanan does discuss musicians like the pianist Glenn Gould who became
   primarily concerned with recording rather than recital. See *Repeated Takes: A Short History of
   Recording and its Effects on Music* (London, Verso, 1995), pp. 131–3.

11 Tricia Rose, *Black Noise: Rap Music and Black Culture in Contemporary America* (Hanover, Wesleyan
   University Press, 1994), p. 8.

12 The edict has since been quietly dropped: currently some acts sing live, others mime,
   and the distinction does not always trace lines between the more or less 'authentic'.

13 Steven Pile and Nigel Thrift, *Mapping the Subject: Geographies of Social Transformation* (London,
   Routledge, 1995), p. 7.

14 Donna J. Haraway, 'A Manifesto For Cyborgs: Science, Technology and Socialist-
   Feminism in the late Twentieth Century', in *Simians, Cyborgs and Women: The Reinvention of
   Nature* (New York, Routledge, 1991), p. 150.

15 Chanan, *Musica Practica*, pp. 14–15. Chanan admits that 'the process is not entirely negative', alluding to the production of 'new ways for music to be heard' and for the
   listener 'totally new ways of using it'.

16 Walter Benjamin, 'The Work of Art in the Age of Mechanical Reproduction', in Hannah
   Arendt (ed.), *Illuminations* (London, Fontana, 1992).

17 'I Am the Dub Organiser and Not the Dub Miser', *Mixmag*, vol. 2 no. 70, March 1997,
   p. 96.

18 See Simon Schaffer, 'Babbage's Dancer and the Impresarios of Mechanism', in Francis
   Spufford and Jenny Uglow (eds), *Cultural Babbage: Time, Technology and Invention* (London,
   Faber & Faber, 1996), p. 69.

19 Gilles Deleuze and Felix Guattari, *A Thousand Plateaus, Capitalism and Schizophrenia*, trans. Brian Massumi (London, Athlone, 1988), p. 3.

20 *Sound on Sound*, vol. 12, no. 6, April 1997, pp. 68–76.

21 See Jon Savage, *England's Dreaming: Sex Pistols and Punk Rock* (London, Faber & Faber, 1991), pp. 279–81.

22 Jacques Attali, *Noise: The Political Economy of Music*, trans. Brian Massumi (Manchester, Manchester University Press, 1985), pp. 135–6.

23 In her afterword to *Noise*, ibid., p. 156.

24 See David Toop, *Ocean of Sound: Aether Talk, Ambient Sound and Imaginary Worlds* (London, Serpent's Tail, 1995), pp. 208–13.

25 'Our technology is becoming more and more like magic – with a class of people who know the incredibly complex spells and incantations needed to get the stuff to work, but almost none of whom can get in there to fix it', 'Black to the Future: Interviews with Samuel R. Delaney, Greg Tate, and Tricia Rose', in Mark Dery, *Flame Wars: The Discourse of Cyberculture* (Durham, Duke University Press, 1994), p. 192.

26 David Buxton, 'Rock Music, the Star System and the Rise of Consumerism', in Simon Frith and Andrew Goodwin (eds), *On Record: Rock, Pop and the Written Word* (London, Routledge, 1990), p. 437. Buxton's comment also fails to anticipate how tenaciously a pop industry would cling to the face, and the creation of the star, in order to promote and present the product. Synth-pop produced some of the 1980s most recognizable images and personalities: Chris Lowe, for example, the Pet Shop Boy who sulkily prodded an expensive keyboard with one finger in a pastiche of the rock 'n' roll misfit.

27 Kraftwerk have been celebrated in the pop music press and by the musicians whom they inspired (particularly the electro and techno musicians of Detroit who created a complex dystopian politics of technology adapted and inspired sonically and politically by the Dusseldorfers' blueprint), but remain the object of but few passing comments within academic treatments of popular music culture. Tricia Rose acknowledges Kraftwerk's influence on hip hop via 'Planet Rock' and briefly discusses (with Mark Dery) black music culture's engagement with music technologies within a post-industrial urban context, in Dery, *Flame Wars*, pp. 212–14.

   For further reference, David Toop's updated history of rap's first decade, *Rap Attack 2: African Rap to Global Hip Hop* (London, Serpent's Tail, 1991), provides a short account of hip hop's encounter with and influence by Kraftwerk. See, also, Pascal Bussy's biography, *Kraftwerk: Man, Machine and Music* (Wembley, S.A.F., 1993).

28 See Spufford and Uglow, *Cultural Babbage*, and Charles Michael Carroll, *The Great Chess Automaton* (London, Constable, 1975).

29 Lester Bangs, 'Kraftwerkfeature', in Kureishi and Savage (eds), *The Faber Book of Pop* (London, Faber & Faber, 1995), p. 484.

30 Bussy, *Kraftwerk*, p. 63.

31 John F. Szwed, *Space is the Place: The Life and Times of Sun Ra* (Edinburgh, Payback Press, 1997), p. 277.

32 Brian Eno, *A Year With Swollen Appendices* (London, Faber & Faber, 1996), p. 94.

33 Andrew Goodwin, 'Sample and Hold: Towards an Aesthetics of Digital Reproduction', *Critical Quarterly* vol. 30, no. 3, Autumn 1988.

34 *Running with the Devil: Power, Gender and Madness in Heavy Metal Music* (Hanover, Wesleyan University Press, 1993), p. 29. The full quote reads: 'Like genres and discourses, musical meanings are contingent but never arbitrary.'

35 Mark Dery asks Tricia Rose about why hip-hoppers like the 'calculatedly funkless' Kraftwerk. Dery, *Flame Wars*, p. 212.

36 Nelson George, *The Death of Rythm and Blues* (London, Omnibus, 1989), p. 154.

37 Ibid.

38 Anthony Haden-Guest, *The Last Party* (New York, William Morrow, 1997), pp. 152–3.

39 See Andrew Goodwin, 'Drumming and Memory: Scholarship, Technology and Music-making', in Swiss et al. (eds), *Mapping the Beat: Popular Music and Contemporary Theory* (Oxford, Blackwell, 1998), pp. 121–36.

40 Chambers Dictionary gives a definition of 'funky' as meaning 'with a strong, musty or bad smell'. For a hilarious explanation of the term's vernacular history, listen to Redd Foxx, 'Funky … Or How Time Can Change the Meaning of a Word', on *Atlantic Grooves*, EastWest Records, 1994.

41 Chris Kempster (ed.), *History of House* (London, Sanctuary, 1997), p. 157.

42 Ibid., p. 166.

43 Toop, *Oceans of Sound*, p. 38.

44 See Rose, *Black Noise*, p. 74.

45 'The major things black art has to have are these: it must have the ability to use found objects, the appearance of using found things, and it must look effortless. It must look cool and easy. If it makes you sweat, you haven't done the work. You shouldn't be able to see the seams and stitches', Toni Morrison, quoted in Paul Gilroy, *The Black Atlantic: Modernity and Double Consciousness* (London, Verso, 1993), p. 78.

46 According to David Toop, disco was one of the forces 'chipping away at the heirarchical, separated roles of producers and consumers … early disco DJs had also eroded fixed definitions of performance, performer and audience', Toop, *Oceans of Sound*, p. 41.

47 For a short biography of Francis Grasso and his tenure at the New York disco The Sanctuary, see Albert Goldman, *Disco* (New York, Hawthorn, 1978), pp. 114–16.

48 Goodwin, 'Sample and Hold', p. 35.

49 Chanan, *Musica Practica*, p. 30.

50 An American political lobbying group set up by Tipper Gore to campaign against the pernicious effects of pop music, which focussed on the lyrical content of rock and rap alike.

51 Robert Walser, *Running With the Devil*, p. 141.

52 See Joseph Lanza, *Elevator Music: A Surreal History of Muzak, Easy-Listening and Other Moodsong* (London, Quartet, 1995).

53 Ibid., p. 203.

54 See Walser, *Running With the Devil*, pp. 145–51.

55 Ibid., p. 144.

56 Sarah Thornton, *Club Cultures: Music, Media and Subcultural Capital* (Cambridge, Polity, 1995), p. 109.

57 Toop, *Ocean of Sound*, p. 99.

58 Goodwin, 'Drumming and Memory', p. 132.

59 Eno, *A Year with Swollen Appendices*, pp. 295–6.

60 Ibid.

61 Ibid.

62 Ibid., p. 294.

63 'The Aural Walk', in Iain Chambers, *Migrancy, Culture, Identity* (London, Routledge, 1994).

64 Ibid., p. 50.

65 'In place of this sequential logic, shuffle offers a random number generator, an exciting turn of events. Now a disc can renew itself virtually every time it's played, putting together unforeseeable combinations, segues, connections, and leaps of faith', John Corbett, *Extended Play: Sounding off from John Cage to Dr. Funkenstein* (Durham, Duke University Press, 1994), p. 1.

66 See 'Interview With Garrick Webster for PC Format', and 'CD-Roms', pp. 308–9, in Brian Eno, *A Year with Swollen Appendices*, pp. 345–6.

67 Cone, *Musical Form and Musical Performance* (New York, W. W. Norton, 1968), p. 17.

68 Szwed, *Space is the Place*, p. 288.

69 Chanan, *Musica Practica*, p. 49.

70 Richard Leppert, *The Sight of Sound: Musical Representation and the History of the Body* (Berkeley, University of California Press, 1993).

71 Heroes of the avant-garde from Luigi Rossolo to John Cage have worked to short-circuit this scheme by various strategies. Rossolo allowed the noise of urban industrial society to intrude, attempting to reproduce its characteristic noises by means of bizarre new instruments, such as the 'crackler' and the 'burster' (see Barclay Brown's introduction to his own translation of Rossolo's *The Art of Noises*, New York, Pendragon Press, 1986). Cage, of course, turned a mirror on the ocular realm of the concert hall, by putting absence at its heart with his silent piece for piano 4'33".

72 Ibid., pp. 24–5.

73 To use Goodwin's example in 'Sample and Hold', p. 46.

74 Ibid., p. 35.

75 The supposedly jarring effect of seeing a black dance producer in a pose more familiar with the conductor Georg Solti is entirely in accordance with the sales pitch of a music industry which still trades on the potency of the auteur–genius. Goldie has been marketed by his label London Records as the emergent form's first star: this campaign also coincided with the release of an hour-long orchestral work ('Mother') as part of his second album, *Saturnz Return* (London Records, 1998).

76 'Free, Single and Disengaged: Listening Pleasure and the Popular Musical Object', in Corbett, *Extended Play*, p. 41. Corbett dicusses autonomy in relation to the erasure of the physicality of music/the body in music, but does not consider experience or significance of the receiving body.

77 In the case of house music the name does not mean it was developed in the domecile, but refers specifically to the Warehouse, the Chicago club in which, under the residence of DJ Frankie Knuckles, this genre began to emerge. Similarly 'garage', a New York-based genre of house, featuring soul/gospel vocals, was named after one of New York's legendary dance clubs the Paradise Garage. See Kempster, *History of House*; and Matthew Collin, with contributions by John Godfrey, *Altered State: The Story of Ecstasy Culture and Acid House* (London, Serpent's Tail, 1997).

78 NME, 8 April 1978, p. 29.

79 The term is a French neologism conflating the words 'disc' and 'bibliotheque'. See Goldman, *Disco*, p. 23.

80 The term 'slates' refers to the brittle and heavy materials originally used to make early recorded discs – which were actually made of a vulcanised rubber called ebonite and later shellac rather than slate, but were similarly fragile and prone to breakage. For a neat history of the recorded disc and its material progress from ebonite, through to vinyl, see Michael Chanan, *Repeated Takes*, (London, Verso, 1995) pp. 28–30. 'Dub plates' alludes to reggae culture and the practice of producers recording unique one-off mixes, called 'dubs', of existing tracks, with certain parts muted and new equalization and effects added, which would be cut on to acetates for specific DJs to use.

81 Collin, *Altered State*, p. 13.

82 Quoted in Jon Savage (ed.), *The Haçienda Must Be Built*, (London, International Music Publications, 1992), p. 16.

83 Robert Venturi *et al.*, *Learning From Las Vegas*, (Cambridge, Mass., M.I.T. Press), 1977.

84 Andy Blackford, *Disco Dancing Tonight* (London, Octopus Press, 1979), p. 13.

85 Ibid., p. 16.

86 See Mary Anna Wright, 'The Great British Ecstasy Revolution', in George McKay (ed.), *DIY Culture* (London, Verso, 1998).

87 Parliamentary Office of Science and Technology, Report Summary 79, May 1996.

88 'The Technologies of Pleasure', Collin, *Altered State*, pp. 10–44.

89 For the record we do not regard this as a matter over which there can be any serious debate. None of the arguments usually put forward in favour of drug prohibition

possesses any great degree of logical consistency. Taking drugs can harm or even kill people, but alcohol and tobacco consumption and motor car use are all clearly responsible for more death, injury, illness and anti-social behaviour than are the use of MDMA, amphetamines, psychedelics and cannabis combined, *even in proportion to their use*. Drinking, smoking and driving are not illegal, and those who argue in favour of drug prohibition might be expected to turn their attention to them if they want to ban those things which can do harm; but, of course, they don't.

Despite the fact that a few commentators on both the left and the right have questioned the right of the state to tell citizens what they can and can not put into their own bodies, much of British media and most of the executive and legislature seem unwilling and/or incapable of engaging in any kind of sensible consideration of the question. The New Labour government has categorically ruled out a Royal Commission into drug reclassification, decriminalization or legalization. Safe in the knowledge that it will not need to do so in the foreseeable future, 'anti-drugs' discourse rarely even attempts to legitimate itself in objective terms, almost always falling into rhetoric about the social fabric which prohibition is presumed to protect.

90 See Jordan Goodman *et al.* (eds), *Consuming Habits: Drugs in History and Anthropology* (London, Routledge, 1995).

91 At the time of writing (1998), the most recent publicity campaign to do with 'drugs' uses a poster bearing the legend '40 per cent of children will use drugs', alongside a disturbing photograph of a dirty hypodermic needle. The explicit message is that those people who use any prohibited substance are likely to end up using intravenous drugs under dangerously unsanitary conditions. Statistically, this is not the case; the vast bulk who make up the '40 per cent' will only ever use 'drugs' which are less harmful than alcohol.

92 Roger Silverstone and Eric Hirsch, *Consuming Technologies* (London, Routledge, 1992).

6

NO MUSIC, NO DANCING

Capitalist modernity and the legacy of Puritanism

> Drug and club money is not a fuckin luxury. It's a fuckin essential....
> Because we are social, collective fucking animals and we need to be
> together and have a good time. It's a basic state of being alive. A basic
> fuckin right. These Government cunts, because they're power junkies, they
> are just incapable of having a good fuckin time so they want everybody
> else tae feel guilty, tae stay in wee boxes and devote their worthless lives
> tae rearing the next generation of factiry fodeer or sodgers or dole moles
> for the state.
>
> Lloyd, in Irvine Welsh, *Ecstasy*[1]

Puritan modernity

The notion of the 'subject' as a coherent category of human experience is
normally identified as emerging as one of the central aspects of modernity itself,
at the end of the Renaissance. We can understand the 'subject of modernity' as an
effect of a specific interaction between different discourses with different historical time-spans; in particular it is the interaction of the long discourse of
phallogocentric metaphysics with the bourgeois discourse of possessive individualism which results in the creation of the modern subject. By the same token, it is
institutions motivated by a commitment to metaphysical ideals on the one hand,
and to bourgeois hegemony – the rule of the capitalist classes – on the other,
which have been most central in enforcing this model of subjectivity. Perhaps no
set of institutions has been so committed to these conjoined projects as those
which are responsible for the dissemination of music discourse since the start of
the nineteenth century. 'Classical' music discourse as we know it today, is still
predominantly bourgeois, metaphysical discourse, predicated on and concerned to
promote the bourgeois-modern subject. Popular music discourses, with their
mobilizations of Romantic aesthetics and their obsessional star-systems, likewise
tend to replicate and perpetuate the individualist and phallogocentric terms of
these wider discourses. What is particularly interesting from our point of view,
therefore, is the extent to which rave and post-rave dance cultures can be seen to
have posed a threat to this model of subjectivity.

We have already looked in some depth at the ways in which dance music and its attendant cultures disrupts the terms of phallogocentric discourse. In order to understand how it has a similar effect on specifically bourgeois discourse, we need to understand a little more about the precise forms which that discourse has taken. One of the best formulations of what is perhaps the principal organizing discourse of bourgeois thought since the seventeenth century remains that offered by the political philosopher C.B. MacPherson. MacPherson termed this strand of thought 'possessive individualism', and identified it as the common theme of a number of the central thinkers of the early modern period. In *The Political Theory of Possessive Individualism*, MacPherson sums up the statements which comprise this discourse as follows:

(i)   What makes a man free is freedom from dependence on the wills of others.

(ii) Freedom from dependence on others means freedom from any relation with others except those relations which the individual enters voluntarily with a view to his own interests.

(iii) The individual is essentially the proprietor of his own person and capacities, for which he owes nothing to society....

(iv) Although the individual cannot alienate the whole of his property in his own person, he may alienate his capacity to labour.

(v)   Human society consists of a series of market relations....

(vi) Since freedom from the wills of others is what makes a man human, each individual's freedom can rightfully be limited only by such obligations and rules as are necessary to secure the same freedoms for others.

(vii) Political society is a contrivance for the protection of the individual's property in his person and goods and (therefore) for the maintenance of orderly relations of exchange between individuals regarded as proprietors of themselves.[2]

This is a philosophy which emerges in the pages of texts by thinkers from Bacon and Hobbes onwards. However, it also becomes the common sense of western cultures by the beginning of the nineteenth century, informing debate and discussion in the fields of politics, culture, social science, and so forth, as well as everyday informal discussion of these and similar issues. The notions of the autonomous individual and the sanctity of property remain central to many such discussions today. Clearly, these are notions which are central to the project of capitalism. The word 'capitalism' in its most straightforward and uncontroversial definition means simply the private ownership of wealth and its deployment for further profit. Throughout its history, it has been a prerequisite for the extension of capitalist social relations that most or all of this discourse inform the arrangements according to which a society is governed. The struggle of the capitalist classes against feudalism and the absolutist state of the classical period took the form of an assertion of the rights of the individual against the ancient privileges of the traditional ruling élites – rights which manifested themselves above all as the ability to freely engage in economic activity. In the latter part of the twentieth century, their struggle against forms of socialism (most typically in Britain under Thatcher's Conservative government) has taken the form of a dogmatic insistence on the superiority of market relations over any other means of generating and distributing wealth and power. Throughout this period, we can see possessive individualism as one of the central modes of bourgeois discourse.

However, possessive individualism did not enter into the common sense of the emergent, early modern bourgeoisie in the form of a carefully worked out political philosophy and economic theory. The former took at least a century to evolve, the latter two centuries. The earliest forms of possessive individualism, it has been argued, appeared not as ideas about property or politics, but about religion. The Reformation of the sixteenth century, which found the greatest support among the proto-capitalist classes, instituted a form of religion which, in absolute contrast to medieval Catholicism, stresses the importance of an individual's personal relationship to God. Rather than participation in the collective ritual of Mass and communion through the mediation of a priest, most forms of Protestantism regard private prayer as the privileged medium of that relationship. The Protestant Church of whatever denomination is usually regarded far more as a human construction for the purpose of enabling relationships between God and individuals to develop than is the Catholic Church, whose believers see it as an institution with specific and uniquely divine authority. The development of printing and the first widespread circulation of copies of the Bible in the vernacular languages of northern Europe enabled a direct relationship to develop between the scriptures and believers, who could for the first time read the word of God for themselves, forming their own opinions as to its correct interpretation, thus displacing the authority of Latin and the Church. In Protestantism, then, we see the emergence of several of the key terms of possessive individualism, particularly its model of the subject as an irreducible individual, the proprietor of its own capacities (even spiritual ones) entering into discrete, almost contractual relationships with others (even God).

Various writers have commented on the centrality of Protestantism to the development of early capitalism, although they have not always agreed on the nature of the relationship between them. Max Weber famously argued that the 'Protestant ethic' actually helped to create the conditions for the development of capitalism.[3] Weber characterized this ethic principally in terms of its asceticism and the belief in individual dedication to a particular 'calling' in life. When combined, these two beliefs encourage hard work on the one hand, and on the other a conviction that the fruits of that labour are not simply to be enjoyed. The result is that wealth is acquired but not spent, so it is invested and saved, hence capitalist accumulation begins. More Marxist-oriented writers (for example, R.H. Tawney) have argued instead that Protestantism took the forms it did *because* it was the religion of the capitalist classes, seeing its values as an expression of their way of life and their consequent world view. According to this view, early Protestantism was an *effect* of capitalism rather than a cause. Put another way, Protestantism can be understood in Marxist terms as a manifestation of latent class-consciousness on the part of the emergent bourgeoisie – that is, an expression in cultural-political-philosophical terms of their underlying economic interests.

We would argue that this is a false dichotomy. It is not possible simply to ascribe causality to economic, political or cultural factors in a case such as this. The fact is that early Protestantism as a religio-cultural project and early capitalism as a politico-economic one are more or less indistinguishable, at least in north-western Europe. Central to both of them – binding them together – is the emergent discourse of possessive individualism. More important to understand for our purposes here is the precise form which early Protestantism took under these conditions, conditions which must also be understood as including its articulation with the older discourses of phallogocentric metaphysics. That form had a name which has resonated with very specific connotations from Shakespeare's time until the present day: Puritanism.

Puritanism, a term designating a desire to purify the Church of Catholic elements, was the name given to the radical Protestantism which was most adhered to by the emergent middle classes of early modern England. Puritanism did not just want to purify the Church. At its most radical moments it sought to use the relatively new machinery of the state to enforce on the populace as a whole its beliefs as to the best way to live. In this way it can perhaps be seen as the first complete *modernizing project* to be carried out in Britain; a coherent attempt to reshape and reorder, not just the political system (it was the Puritans who led the English revolution which resulted in the short-term establishment of a republic and the long-term ascendancy of the House of Commons within the British state[4]), not just economic practices and relationships, but the everyday life of people of all classes. From the moment of the Reformation in the 1530s and 1540s, an attempt was made to clamp down on traditional popular festivities, a project which eventually had a considerable degree of long-term success, as traditional holidays gradually disappeared[5] and a culture which privileged work above all other modes of experience and which regarded sensuous pleasure as suspect in itself became and remained hegemonic within British society. This is the history of the suppression of 'carnival' practices detailed by Stallybrass and White in their book, *The Politics and Poetics of Transgression*.[6] Although self-declared radical Protestants only ever held state power in England for a brief period (during the 1650s), Puritan ideology has a long history of influence on British political culture life. It remains a testament to its success that the Lords Day Observance Act of 1780 – only the last in a 250-year history of such measures – still technically prohibits the selling of tickets for dancing on a Sunday in the UK.[7] In the twentieth century, the introduction of licensing legislation to control the sale and distribution of alcohol, the series of laws and the vast amounts of public money spent trying to enforce the prohibition of other intoxicants, the increasing amount of legislation

aimed at containing and prohibiting rave culture, and even the consistent principle informing all welfare provision – that those who can work must do, even if
the only work on offer is demeaning and exploitative – are all manifestations of
this tradition.

We can see from this history that among the main priorities of puritanical
discourse have been a hostility to physical pleasure, intoxication, unregulated
social gathering, music and dancing. Puritanism can thus be understood as an
intersection of numerous discourses and practices, and by the same token as a
point at which those same discourses and practices modify each other in very
precise ways. Phallogocentric metaphysics' belief in the rationally self-present
subject converges with possessive individualism to produce a notion of the
human subject as defined radically in terms of *self-control*, and hence a particular
hostility to intoxicated and ecstatic states develops. That individualism leads this
discourse on the human subject to be particularly hostile to forms of *social* pleasure. Those developing techniques of rationalization and governance which are
often seen as typical of modernity itself, are used for the purpose of enforcing this
notion of human subjectivity. The term 'Puritan' may date back to the sixteenth
century, but this cluster of phenomena is still very much part of the dominant
culture in Britain today,[8] as various pieces of legislation have demonstrated;
precisely those pieces of legislation which have been aimed at dance culture and
its participants.

To a certain extent anti-dance culture legislation has been an extension of
existing laws to cover new situations. The 1990 legislation aimed at clamping
down on commercial raves[9] was in fact an extension of existing British licensing
laws, simply increasing the penalty for breaking them with regard to the holding
of unlicensed pay parties. The 1997 Public Entertainments Licences (Drug Misuse)
Bill, introduced by Conservative MP Barry Legge,[10] and which grants the police
new powers to shut down licensed establishments where they think that illegal
drugs may be being misused (i.e., any club remotely connected to post-acid house
dance culture), is an extension of the principle that any practice encouraging or
enabling the consumption of illegal drugs should be prohibited (it is technically
illegal to allow someone to smoke cannabis in your own home). But one piece of
legislation was not a simple extension of existing legal principles but a direct
attack on rave culture in its most self-consciously political manifestations: The
1994 Criminal Justice and Public Order Act.

The Criminal Justice Act

The 1994 Criminal Justice and Public Order Act was a wide-ranging, composite
piece of legislation, which covered many areas of the law. But a large part of it was
explicitly aimed at suppressing the activities of certain strands of alternative
culture. The main targets of this draconian piece of legislation were squatting,
direct action protest involving the occupation of land, hunt sabotage and outdoor
free parties. In particular, it aimed to stop the unlicensed dance parties which had

become a feature of weekend life for many people in both rural and urban areas. Attendance at these parties was often free of charge; music and other services were provided by dedicated crews of sound engineers, DJs (who usually played hard, fast techno tracks, quite distinct from the smooth, gospel-influenced 'garage' music being played in most clubs at the time), van drivers, phone operators, and so forth, who would chose the location, organize the party, and distribute information as to its time and place through a variety of informal channels. The sections of the 1994 Criminal Justice and Public Order pertaining to raves constituted one of the most direct interventions in popular culture by a British government in the twentieth century. The relevant sections of the Act are as follows:

Criminal Justice And Public Order Act 1994
Part V
Public Order: Collective Trespass or Nuisance on Land
Powers in relation to raves
63. (1) This section applies to a gathering on land in the open air of 100
or more persons (whether or not trespassers) at which amplified music
is played during the night (with or without intermissions) and is such
as, by reason of its loudness and duration and the time at which it is
played, is likely to cause serious distress to the inhabitants of the locality;
and for this purpose –
(a) such a gathering continues during intermissions in the music and, where
     the gathering extends over several days, throughout the period during
     which amplified music is played at night (with or without intermis-
     sions); and
(b) 'music' includes sounds wholly or predominantly characterised by the
     emission of a succession of repetitive beats.
(2) If, as respects any land in the open air, a police officer of at least the rank
of superintendent reasonably believes that –
(a) two or more persons are making preparations for the holding there of a
     gathering to which this section applies,
(b) ten or more persons are waiting for such a gathering to begin there, or
(c) ten or more persons are attending such a gathering which is in progress,
he may give a direction that those persons and any other persons who come
to prepare or wait for or to attend the gathering are to leave the land and
remove any vehicles or other property which they have with them on the
land.

This Act was passed by Parliament without significant opposition from any of the major political parties. It is perhaps this fact which requires the most explanation. It easy to see why John Major's Conservative government passed the legislation. His party was trailing the Opposition Labour Party in the opinion polls, had suffered severe blows to its political and economic credibility, and was under pressure from its own supporters to reinvigorate the ideological project inherited from the previous prime minister, Margaret Thatcher. Central to Thatcher's idea had been an overt hostility to 'minorities' (ethnic, sexual, or otherwise) who appeared to question the normative values of 'English' culture, combined with an authoritarian rhetoric of 'law and order'.[11] At about the time of the introduction of the Act, the Labour Party had recently made the historic step of taking on board much of the social authoritarianism associated with Thatcherite conservatism, and this in part explains its support. There are other very basic reasons as to why the Government should have been keen to repress rave culture, in particular its non-commercial elements. The UK's brewing industry, which has traditionally been a major donor to the Conservative Party, was undoubtedly worried about the reported drop in alcohol consumption associated with the rise in popularity and availability of dance drugs.[12] Free parties rarely made a profit for anyone, and as such posed a possible threat to most of the commercial leisure industries. But these reasons are not sufficient to explain why the legislation against these gatherings took precisely the form it did, and why it received so little formal opposition. We would argue that we can only really understand the lack of opposition to the 1994 Act if we consider the Act itself as part of a long history of the repression of social pleasure and the pleasures of the body.

The opposition to dancing in intoxicated crowds makes is appearance alongside the invention of the modern subject; it is central to the particular way in which the discourses of metaphysics and possessive individualism were mutually articulated during the early phase of north European capitalism. The very idea that human beings are hermetically sealed units, irreducible and unitary individuals, rational agents, is challenged by the ecstasy and collectivity of the dance. As Paul Spencer writes of dancers the world over, 'In their *ecstasy* they literally *stand outside*'.[13] Standing outside of oneself, especially when that means exposing one's individuality to the being of others, is what that metaphysics of the subject which has dominated European culture at least since the seventeenth century simply cannot stand.

Of course, there was another key reason as to why there was such widespread support from the political establishment for the 1994 Criminal Justice Act. Rave culture was associated with recreational 'drug' use, and was seen by many as a legitimate target for the implementation of draconian laws. The fact that such a bizarre prejudice can continue to inform British public legislation at the end of the twentieth century is further evidence of the continued influence of Puritanism on British political discourse, as we shall see.

Puritanism and prohibition

By 1997, many voices in the media were arguing that the Government's 'war on drugs' was clearly lost, and that the only logical response to the increasing normalization of 'drug' use among many sections of the population was a relaxation of prohibition. During that year and the early part of 1998, hardly a week went by without some public figure or major media outlet calling for a public debate on the legal status of substances ranging from cannabis to heroin. At the same time as the New Labour government appointed Keith Hallewell as its 'Drugs Tsar' (a term borrowed from George Bush's administration), the *Independent on Sunday* newspaper ran a highly-publicized campaign for the decriminalization of cannabis. The BBC screened an inconclusive evening of debate on the subject in May 1998, following the publication of a Government White Paper indicating little real change in direction for a policy agenda still driven by the assumption that 'drugs' – an effectively homogenous, undifferentiated category of experience – were an evil in and of themselves. The White Paper included measures which could lead to anyone convicted of possessing cannabis to be forced to accept treatment for their social disorder. The distance between British youth and the Government – with its unwavering commitment to prohibition – was vividly illustrated when, in December 1997, the son of the Home Secretary Jack Straw, was cautioned by police for supplying cannabis to a newspaper reporter.

Several issues are raised by the debate around drugs. First, drug prohibition results in thousands of people being imprisoned for drug-related offences. Over 10 per cent of the UK's prison population has been incarcerated for breaking laws relating to drug prohibition.[14] Incarceration can be seen as a form of violence, and the infliction of such violence on people surely requires justification. Second, the cost to the state of imprisoning so many people and of devoting police resources to the enforcement of prohibition is enormous, as is the loss of potential tax revenue caused by the illegal status of substances no less harmful than alcohol and tobacco. Those resources could be used for purposes the value of which would be far less controversial than drug prohibition. Third, many professionals working to prevent the various forms of harm which drug use can undoubtedly cause, agree that the chief cause of that harm is precisely the illegality of those drugs. Without proper legal regulation, participation in the drugs market is a hit-and-miss affair; with no quality controls, impurity and, in some cases, over-purity is always a danger for the user. Violence and crime attend any market which functions only outside the law; if the drugs market was regulated, then it could be a safe and peaceful place. Illegality keeps the price of drugs artificially high, forcing users and addicts into crime in order to pay for them. Finally, and perhaps most importantly, drug prohibition is a legal discourse which has its roots in nothing more substantial than a set of racist and sexist prejudices which most people would today consider abhorrent.

If drugs, as we suggested in the previous chapter, are merely one technology among many others which characterize modern life (many of which – cars, for example – might be considered far more dangerous), why is it that the state and the powerful cultural institutions that be are still so hostile to recreational drug use? This question can be answered by considering the discourse of drug prohibition as articulated at the intersection of several different histories. An interesting starting point is the history of drug prohibition in the UK. Andrew Sherratt writes:

153

Even powerful alkaloids such as morphine … were widely sold in advanced countries in the later nineteenth century, both in commercial preparations as patent medicines and in pure form for personal use as narcotics. While opiate preparations such as laudanum were displaced in everyday use by analgesics such as aspirin, changes in recreational or hedonistic use owed more to social conventions. It was the increasing social tensions and consequent imposition of discipline (aimed initially at munitions workers) at the time of the First World War and its after-math, that produced first the UK licensing laws and then the Dangerous Drugs Act (1924).[15]

Sherratt is right to draw a parallel between the implementation of licensing laws and drug prohibition. Indeed, this was the same historical moment at which the US Federal Government implemented a nationwide prohibition on alcohol which lasted throughout the 1920s. Clearly, while specific groups (for example, British munitions workers) may have become localized sites of anxiety at particular times, there was in general a significant shift in attitudes across the developed world in favour of the regulation and – where at all possible – the prohibition of the consumption of intoxicants. It is worth bearing in mind that it was not only the agents of the state who supported this view; Keir Hardie, the first Labour member of the British parliament, stood for election on a prohibitionist platform.

There are a number of reasons as to why this shift occurred when it did, and one way of understanding them is to consider the details of how it came about; what forms did this historic shift in attitude take? This moment is charted in fasci-nating detail by Marek Kohn in his book, *Dope Girls*. Kohn clearly demonstrates that drug prohibition was enforced both legally and culturally in Britain largely in response to the set of social and cultural crises which occurred at this time, of which the Great War was only a part. Kohn maps the history of the first moral panics around 'drug' use in Britain, outlining the ways in which 'in Britain the detection of a drug underground provided a way of speaking simultaneously about women, race, sex, and the nation's place in the world'.[16]

In simple terms, the First World War was a key crisis in the history of imperi-alism, marking the beginning of the end of Britain's place of international pre-eminence. It was also during this era that the relative continuity of imperial administrative structures on the one hand, and the damage which imperialism had done to the economic infrastructure of many parts of the world on the other, began to bring large numbers of non-white immigrants to Europe. Increasing anxiety about imperial white identity encouraged the emergence into mainstream political discourse of eugenics – a set of ideas and policies predicated on notions of racial superiority and of the need to protect the European 'races' from 'degener-ation' or miscegenation. The earliest arguments in favour of drug prohibition focussed on 'drugs' precisely as potential causes of these two racial catastrophes. It is worth reflecting that in this sense, prohibition has its roots in the same moment and the same set of fears and ideas as fascism. At the same time, while it marked the beginning of its emergent international hegemony, this moment was critical in the history of American national identity, as it was during this period that America ended its century-long westward expansion, and began to question its historic open-door immigration policy. In both cases, for various related reasons, the stability of Anglo-Saxon identity was perceived as being under threat. One response was to identify 'drugs' as a part of this threat and to try to ban them. As Kohn shows, the first anti-drug legislation to be passed in the UK was done so more than anything in response to a generalized fear that access to cocaine encouraged young white women to mix and have sex with black and 'oriental' men.

It is crucial to be clear about the intellectual and ideological context in which the British government, along with many other western governments, gave in to pressure from America to enact legislation prohibiting the use of various chemicals for the purpose of deliberate self-intoxication. It was at this time perfectly respectable – indeed, normal – for public figures and legislators to take the view that the non-white races were inferior to whites, and that women were congenitally inferior to men in terms of intellect, will-power and rationality. Cocaine, opiates and cannabis were all banned not because of any serious concern for public heath, but because they were associated with the cultures of non-white immigrant communities and of groups of young women enjoying unprecedented (for at least a century) degrees of social, economic and sexual independence. The discourse of prohibition as it was mobilized at this time was entirely predicated on a belief in female and non-white inferiority. While it may no longer be acceptable within public discourse to argue that women and non-whites are self-evidently inferior to white men, the terms in which that inferiority was defined seventy-five years ago remain central to dominant discourses today. Women and non-whites were regarded as less rational, less in control of themselves, less capable of hard work than white men. In other words, they were less capable of achieving the status of the bourgeois, Puritan, modern subject than white men. Anti-drugs discourse has been and remains largely couched in such Puritan terms. The idea of engaging in any form of activity purely for pleasure's sake is considered suspect within the terms of that discourse; to engage in an activity which – however temporarily – decreases one's capacity for reason, and to do so for purely hedonistic purposes, in this view could hardly be more reprehensible. Indeed, drug experiences can be seen to challenge some of the most basic terms according to which any metaphysics of the subject must be constituted. The distinction between the body and the mind/soul is radically problematized by the experience of having one's mental condition dramatically altered by the ingestion of specific material substances (including alcohol). It is notable that it is still illegal in the UK to advertise alcohol on the basis that it can get you drunk; flavour and quality are the only reasons for which we are supposed to decide to consume it.

The fact that the anti-drugs discourse is still tied to the continuing hegemony of forms of Puritanism is illustrated by contemporary arguments against ending drug prohibition. Using drugs, it is argued, saps the user's will to achieve, and above all their will to work. Hence the ludicrous concept of 'anti-motivational syndrome',[17] a medicalized term for extreme laziness still cited in government documents as a worrying effect of cannabis use. Perhaps, one wonders, laws ought also to be passed against jobs which are under-stimulating. Indeed, perhaps work itself – which tends to make people tired, and therefore less motivated as the day goes by – ought to be banned. On these grounds, there is about as much logic to banning work as there is cannabis, except for the fact that cannabis is considered by users to be pleasurable. The fact that it is considered legitimate to put people in prison for possession of a substance because that substance might give people pleasure while making them lazy is an indicator of how powerfully the Puritan discourse today still defines the terms of political, juridical and even medical discourse.

Whatever forms it has taken, dance culture has almost always been resistant to the cultural-political domination of Puritanism; a culture of collective hedonism could hardly be anything else. Rave and its descendants have always been both explicitly social-ist formations, manifesting a utopian politics of community wherein being together was the central, and in certain senses the only point of being there at all, and hedonistic ones, explicitly committed to the pursuit of plea-sure. As we will see in the next chapter, however, anti-Puritanism has not always necessarily equated with progressive politics.

Notes

1 Irvine Welsh, *Ecstasy* (Vintage, London, 1997), p. 213.
2 C.B. MacPherson, *The Political Theory of Possessive Individualism* (Oxford, Clarendon Press, 1964).
3 Max Weber, *The Protestant Ethic and the Spirit of Capitalism*, trans. Talcott Parsons (London, Unwin, 1930).
4 See Christopher Hill, *The Century of Revolution 1603–1714* (London, Routledge, 1980).
5 See David Underdown, *Revel, Riot and Rebellion* (Oxford, Oxford Uuniversity Press, 1985), pp. 44–73, 239–71.
6 Stallybrass and White, *The Politics and Poetics of Transgression* (London, Methuen, 1986).
7 This law may shortly be changed.
8 It is interesting to note that 'Puritanism' was a term used to describe a particular cluster of attitudes in a report by the Rowntree Foundation (November 1997; http://www.jrf.org.uk/jrf.html): 'Few young people hold a strongly "puritanical" outlook, for instance believing "strict discipline is in a child's best interest", "criminals should be punished with the maximum prison sentences" and "people who dislike hard work have weak characters".'
9 See, Matthew Collin, with contributions by John Godfrey, *Altered State: The Story of Ecstasy Culture and Acid House* (London, Serpent's Tail, 1997), p. 111.
10 See Tash Lodge's website: http://ourworld.compuserve.com/homepages/tash_lodge/main.htm.
11 See Stuart Hall, *The Hard Road to Renewal* (London, Verso, 1988), p. 55.
12 See M. Collin, *Altered State: The Story of Ecstasy Culture and Acid House* (London, Serpent's Tail, 1997), pp. 273–6.
13 Spencer, *Society and the Dance* (Cambridge, Cambridge University Press, 1985), p. 28.
14 HMSO Prison Statistics England and Wales (HMSO, 1995).

15 J. Goodman, P. E. Lovejoy and A. Sherratt (eds), *Consuming Habits: Deconstructing Drugs in History and Anthropology* (London, Routledge, 1995), p. 5.

16 Marek Kohn, *Dope Girls* (London, Lawrence & Wishart, 1992), p. 4.

17 Parliamentary Office of Science and Technology, 'Common Illegal Drugs and their Effects' (HMSO, May 1996).

7

THE POLITICS OF POPULAR CULTURE

I think I'll stick to drugs to get me through the long, dark night of late capitalism.

Irvine Welsh, *The Acid House*[1]

In the previous chapter we examined the historical roots and discursive terms of the cultural and legal regulation of dance culture. In this chapter we will consider ways of understanding the politics of dance culture itself. Much of the argument of the preceding chapters has focussed on the implicit radicalism of the experiences which are central to contemporary dance culture. However, we should make clear that we consider those experiences to be 'radical' only in the particular cultural contexts in which they occur. Even when we are considering large-scale phenomena like phallogocentrism or capitalism, it is important to bear in mind that such discursive formations do not constitute immutable realities but specific historical contexts, and it is only in relation to these contexts that dance culture can be said to be in any sense subversive. Like all politics, the politics of dance cultures is relational and context-specific, a matter of the relationships between different groups and formations, rather than something inherent in its very nature.

In recent years, the most influential way of discussing the politics of cultural forms has probably been that developed by British cultural theorists in the 1970s. The researchers at the Birmingham Centre for Contemporary Cultural Studies and the critic and theorist Raymond Williams developed a vocabulary for discussing the politics of culture which drew heavily on the work of the pre-war Italian communist, Antonio Gramsci. This vocabulary is largely concerned with describing the extent to which a given cultural formation can be said to serve the perpetuation of ruling class hegemony, or to oppose that hegemony. One of the most important terms in this vocabulary is 'incorporation'.[2] Incorporation is the process according to which a group, subculture or discursive formation which at one time existed outside of and/or in opposition to hegemonic culture, the dominant discursive formation, gets taken over by that culture, becoming neutralized as it becomes a part of that which it previously opposed. As Sarah Thornton has pointed out, this vocabulary has a precise analogue in the ways in which such issues are discussed *within* dance culture itself. 'Underground' music and culture are frequently discussed as if they existed somehow outside of, in opposition to, and untainted by, the forces of capitalism and the institutions which regulate public culture (in particular media institutions). To become part of the 'mainstream', to 'sell out', is to lose that status by becoming a part of the dominant culture; in other words, to be incorporated.[3]

Thornton demonstrates conclusively the *naïveté* and insupportability of the rigid distinction between 'underground' and 'mainstream' cultures. She develops Pierre Bourdieu's notion of 'cultural capital' to produce a model which sees not oppositionality, but élitism and exclusivity, as the key motivations for most youth culture. According to Thornton, participants in youth cultures are largely concerned with carving out cultural spaces (for example, the 'underground') distinct from parent cultures and with delineating hierarchies and distinctions *within* the space of youth culture which do not follow the parameters of those stratifying wider society, but which none the less serve a stratifying purpose. If class is still the primary category of social distinction in adult society, then 'youth culture' tries to constitute itself as a space in which 'hipness' and 'fashionability' are alternative markers of cultural distinction, markers which supposedly operate along axes not determined by the conventional stratifications of race, class and gender (but may well reproduce those stratifications as often as they work against them). Thornton gives the name 'subcultural capital' to the accumulated sets of shared terms, values and knowledges according to which subcultural groups distinguish themselves from outsiders.

Thornton offers a way of understanding the mechanics of youth culture which has devastating implications for received notions, both within youth culture itself and in certain strands of sociology and cultural studies. Conventional accounts shared by both subcultural participants and sociologists of subculture have tended to present youth subcultures as inherently oppositional, resisting the dominant bourgeois culture and bravely defending their autonomy from the encroachment of hegemonic 'mainstream' culture which – usually via the agency of the capitalist media – seeks to 'incorporate' them back into itself. Thornton demolishes this model, demonstrating that far from being concerned with opposing the dominant culture of the parent society, youth cultures are largely concerned with establishing hierarchies and distinctions among and between young people themselves. Thornton's model therefore exposes the élitism which defines much of 'youth culture', and in particular dance culture. In addition, she demonstrates the extent to which subcultural groups exist in a symbiotic relationship with the very 'mainstream' media they usually claim to wish to remain autonomous from. If punk had not got the attention of the national media, then its spectacular antics would have had minimal impact. If the tabloid newspaper the *Sun* had not proclaimed it so, then no-one would ever have thought that acid house was subversive.

However, Thornton's model does have weaknesses. In particular, it tends to imply that all cultural practices are equally apolitical; however 'radical' a group may consider their particular practice to be, in truth they are merely trying to accumulate subcultural capital at the expense of the unhip. In fact, for all of its rootedness in orthodox sociology, Thornton's argument is remarkably non-contextual. It pays little attention to the specific content of given cultures and given moments, and therefore refuses any distinction at all between the 'opposi-tional', the 'alternative' and the 'hegemonic'. This is also a mistake. What is needed is not a model of culture which simply refuses to read it politically, nor a return to the simplistically Marxist-derived models which merely demand to know whether a phenomenon like 'dance culture' is 'really' radical, really opposed to capitalism. Instead, we would propose a model informed by the post-Marxist political theory of Ernesto Laclau and Chantal Mouffe. According to such a model, we need far more precise accounts of the power relationships existing within and between cultural formations, dominant and non-dominant, accounts which recognize that there is no single locus of power in society, but rather a multiplicity of points at which power is condensed and dispersed. There is thus no single, overarching dominant discursive formation to which cultural forms can be considered 'oppo-sitional' or not. There is, as Thornton points out, no 'mainstream'. Rather there are a range of complex relationships between different formations.

An important implication of this model is that the category of 'incorporation' becomes redundant. There is no single dominant formation which can 'swallow up' smaller ones whole. Rather, the field of cultural relations is to be thought as operating according to the logic of what Laclau and Mouffe call 'articulation'. As they put it, 'any practice establishing a relation among elements such that their identity is modified as a result of the articulatory practice'.[4] The concept of 'artic-ulation' – derived from Laclau's and Mouffe's complex reworking of the ideas of Gramsci – is useful because it allows us to discuss relationships between different formations and elements in a more differentiated way than by simply referring to formations 'opposing', 'determining' or 'incorporating' each other.[5] The most important effect of such an approach is to enable us to see the extent to which 'dominant' and 'non-dominant' cultures and formations interact with each other, not simply 'winning' or 'losing' their mutual struggles, but negotiating complex and usually ambivalent outcomes. (It is worth reflecting that this is arguably an approach which is closer to the spirit of Gramsci's writings than one deploying a simple notion of 'incorporation', which was in turn always a more complex notion than it has often been treated as.) The question would therefore not be how likely dance culture is to bring down capitalism or patriarchy, but at what precise points it succeeds or fails in negotiating new spaces. In particular, it is not a simple question of dance culture being 'for' or 'against' the dominant culture, but of how far its articulations with other discourses and cultures (dominant or otherwise) result in *democratizations* of the cultural field, how far they successfully break down existing concentrations of power, and how far they fail to do so.

In this regard, we agree wholeheartedly with much of Thornton's critique of the pretensions of dance culture ideologists. In particular, the notion of a cultural 'underground' which is politically radical simply by virtue of being 'under-ground' is nonsense. At certain times, in certain places, cultures may wish to keep themselves 'underground' in order to preserve their capacity to constitute democratic spaces. Club promoters and free party organizers frequently refer to the need to exclude those who do not subscribe to their progressive values; for instance, groups of men who are likely to get drunk and harass women and other men in a perpetuation of forms of behaviour which people come to those spaces to get away from.[6] Even this argument is problematic, however, for how are those men ever going to learn to act differently if they are excluded from your club or party?[7] By only allowing people with the same values to mix with one another, are you not preventing those values from spreading? Whatever the possible outcome of such ruminations, it is almost certainly more common for 'underground' discourse to be mobilized simply in order to preserve the élite status of those mobilizing it, a localized deployment of power/knowledge on the part of groups more concerned with shoring-up their collective egos with subcultural capital than dissolving their individual ones in the ecstasy of dance. In addition, the deliberate self-marginalization of those who aspire to 'underground' status is at once élitist and politically defeatist. The only reason for staying underground is that in relation to dominant structures of power, you are weak. To celebrate that weakness rather than to try to overcome it is to concede social authority to those dominant discourses. It is, in fact, to *choose* to remain in a subordinate position and to condemn others to a similar position. While we do not believe that it is reasonable to expect formations like 'dance culture' to somehow transform themselves into movements for the wholesale transformation of society, it might not be unreasonable to hope that its participants would have more sense than to actively celebrate their own oppression, which is what the celebration of 'underground' status often amounts to.

This approach to the politics of culture also enables us to understand the problems associated with speaking in terms of a single, homogenous, 'dominant culture'. If such a thing exists, then it is the result of specific, historically contingent articulations between different discursive formations. If 'bourgeois modernity' can be conceived in terms of the mutual articulation of bourgeois and patriarchal discourses with the terms and priorities of the metaphysical tradition, then it must also be possible to conceive of that particular cluster of terms and elements becoming disarticulated. Indeed, it may be that certain aspects of dance culture are exemplary of just such a process. It might be, as we suggested in Chapter 6, that many of the aspects of dance culture which seem to refuse the terms of metaphysical discourse are at the same time fully in tune with the needs of contemporary capitalism. The development of an advanced commodity culture and an information economy might require of its subjects just those qualities of hedonism and fluidity which seem to characterize much of contemporary dance culture. It is the development of capitalism which has made available all of the technologies which are the medium of dance culture. This does not mean that those things are 'bad'. Many aspects of capitalism can be seen as bad; but it can at times also be a liberating and democratizing force. We would not in any way wish to endorse a right-wing political perspective. We are not advocating some form of anarcho-capitalism. In comparison to alternative forms of social organization, capitalism is usually disastrous in its effects. At certain times and in certain ways, however, such as in its capacity to circulate new technologies, making them available to an ever-expanding public, in the sheer power of demand in a relatively open market place to break down and render effectively useless legal restrictions on all forms of activity from broadcasting (Kiss FM, the most popular of the London pirate radio stations, eventually gained a license despite initial resistance from the authorities and continues to be the main outlet for dance music broadcasting in the UK: a fine example of the market overcoming the state) to the circulation of prohibited 'drugs', it can be seen to have its democratizing uses.

There is one particular problem with the notion of rave as offering a radical challenge to the dominant culture, which should be considered here. Notions like 'freedom', 'democracy', 'emancipation' and 'progress' are themselves products of that culture; to step completely outside of it might be to make oneself unable to speak of them. What if the ecstasy, the liberatory jouissance to which rave grants us access, is nothing but an empty space from which no political position as such can possibly be articulated? Ecstatic dancing, we have suggested, can be a tremendously liberating experience. Liberation is not the same thing as transformation, however. Escape – especially if only temporary – is not the same thing as political change. The experience of rave may offer a temporary escape route from the strictures of bourgeois Puritanism, of phallogocentric subjectivity, of rationalist modernity. But when we get back from the party, have we just left all those structures as intact as they were before?

There are good reasons for believing this to be the case. Many commentators have pointed out that 'carnival' was not a revolutionary practice, but a well-regulated social safety-valve which allowed the downtrodden lower classes to enjoy themselves and experience a temporary liberation from the grind of their daily lives and the strictures of social convention, while posing no threat to the social order. On the other hand, Stallybrass and White (1986) point out that carnival has often been the occasion for the initiation of more serious political agitation; the playful irreverence of carnival can easily shade into a more serious challenge to authority. The hostility to carnivalesque practices which has been a consistent part of bourgeois culture emerged with the growth of democratic discourse which, while it was central to bourgeois political discourse, always presented it with the danger that democratic ideas might be adopted – and ultimately enforced – by the lower orders themselves. Modernity has been described as a process of dislocation, a process whereby established structures and received ideas become de-sedimented or 're-activated' – deconstructed, made to seem historically contingent rather than eternally immutable – such that people and groups, in experiencing social change, come to believe in the possibility of still further change.[8] Arguably, carnival as such belongs to a pre-modern moment, a moment when there seemed to be no possibility of such real change, when the only response available to continued oppression was temporary festivity. We could trace a history of popular politics in which the carnivalesque and the genuinely political coexist for much of the seven-

162

teenth, eighteenth and early nineteenth centuries, with the parodic, ecstatic features becoming increasingly marginal as real democratic change becomes possible. This history would begin with pre-modern carnival, the simple safety-valve channelling discontent into ecstasy and frivolity and offering no challenge to the prevailing social order; it would end with the emergence of socialism, the development of mass democracy, the socialist revolutions of the twentieth century, the building of the welfare state. Along the way the various forms of popular political engagement charted by such historians as E.P. Thompson[9], could be seen as combining elements of the carnivalesque and of the political.

Such a history would fit neatly into the narrative of modernity offered by the philosopher Jurgen Habermas. For Habermas, modernity is a coherent project, and a fundamentally benign one; its goal is the emancipation of humankind through the achievement of rational and wholly democratic modes of communication and decision-making. Habermas has criticized exponents of 'post-modern' and anti-Enlightenment thinking for rejecting this project, for seeing its failures as evidence of the irredeemability, and above all for failing to understand that it is a project which is still radically *incomplete*. For Habermas, to simply abandon the project before it has been completed is a grave error, a retreat from the horizon of human possibility with potentially dire consequences. Habermas sees almost any turn away from the rational ideal of modernity as such a retreat.[10] The idea of rave as a return to carnival can easily be understood in these terms, as a turning away from the possibility of real political engagement, democratic struggle, and progress for society as a whole; a retreat from modernity which embraces techniques typical of an era in which real democratic change was not a possibility.

There might be a severe danger of dance culture simply serving as a social safety-valve, a distraction and consolation for a generation for whom prospects for secure jobs, rising standards of living and opportunities for democratic control over their own lives all look bleak. This is precisely the problem with the model of the rave as a version of Hakim Bey's 'Temporary Autonomous Zone'.[11] The TAZ is a fully 'spatialized' political tactic, so concerned with carving out 'autonomous space' that it always ends up leaving the big power structures in place, as a carnival can do, as a rave can do. However, we do not give much credence to the idea that dance culture is simply a distraction for the oppressed masses. Apart from anything else, we do not actually believe that people suffering serious oppression are stupid enough to be 'bought off' with an 'E' and a house beat; if many young people are more interested in the latter than in conventional politics, this is probably because of a realistic assessment on their part of the lack of scope for political intervention at the present time. On the other hand, as we have pointed out, there are many ways in which contemporary dance music and culture do themselves challenge hegemonic ideas and experiences on profound levels. Indeed, it is precisely the same set of experiences which dance culture offers us access to which can be understood as radically transgressive or as dangerous escapism. What this observation demonstrates is that the politics of 'rave' cannot be understood in terms of an abstract analysis of those experiences.

Only by taking into account the specific contexts in which those experiences occur can we really hope to understand their actual implications and effects.

Rock and the politics of representation

The question is, then, is rave nothing more than the re-emergence of an archaic resistance to the culture of modernity? Certainly many of those people involved with rave culture who have a specific commitment to paganism seem to believe so. Is it, as our line of argument thus far might seem to suggest, a kind of essential deconstruction, an inevitable and perpetual symptom of the socio-political text of modernity deconstructing itself?

Of course not. To understand the reasons for rave culture's emergence and the nature of the opposition to it, we need to look at the specific historical circumstances that surround it. 1988 was a crucial moment for British youth culture. It is not accidental that British acid house was born in the same year that welfare entitlement was abolished for 16 to 18 year olds. The alienation of an entire generation from mainstream political culture seemed to be summed up by this discriminatory piece of legislation. 1988 was also a crucial year for music culture; in particular, for rock. Between 1988 and the moment in the mid-1970s when punk took hold of one part of the collective imagination and disco took hold of the other, a fairly consistent set of attitudes had remained in place (despite the many mutations they went through). Looking at a copy of the NME from early 1976, we can see in place a fairly coherent politico-aesthetic agenda, but one which seems very alien to what we have come to expect from the 'indie' music press. Theirs was a critical discourse which valorized musical virtuosity over spontaneity, and American blues forms over more characteristically British kinds of rock music. Lacking in any obvious political agenda, it evidently had yet to encounter the shock of feminism or the radical critique of musical values which punk would instigate. In contrast, eighteen months later in the same magazine, we see firmly in place a set of terms and values which dominated British rock journalism up until very recently, and to some extent still do. If we look at the history of British rock culture through that time, of the artists who were hegemonic within this particular strand of British youth culture between 1976 and 1988 (despite the attempts by various critical practitioners, from post-punks like The Fall to new pop theorists such as Paul Morley, to break that hegemony), we can see a fairly consistent thread running right through from The Sex Pistols to The Smiths. Despite very different aesthetic agendas, a number of crucial equivalences and assumptions remained unchallenged. The supreme good, according to this discourse, was authenticity; artists must speak the truth of their (and others') situations. Authenticity was guaranteed by the presence of a specific type of instrumentation (rhythm guitar, bass, drums, voice) and the refusal to deploy this instrumentation in displays of excessive virtuosity (which might attract attention away from the singing voice). The singer was the focus, and it is crucial that he (it was always he) should be authentic and *sincere*, because his fundamental role was to *represent* the culture from which he comes. In speaking the truth of his situation he must speak the truth of his audience's situation. Be it the first wave of anger at the realization that the welfare state settlement was crumbling in 1977, or the sense of resignation as the Thatcher government rolled into its second and third terms, the singer (this could be Johnny Rotten, Ian Curtis, Morrissey or a dozen others) should say what his audience feels.

A number of imperatives were implicit in this particular set of terms and values. Obviously, the phonologocentric ideal of the pure voice, of the *logos* as the site of truth, can be seen at work here. At the same time, there is an attempt to make this ideal coincide with a politics of representation. However little bands like The Smiths may have advertised, or even been aware of, their politicality, implicit in everything they did – indeed, in the fact that they did anything at all – was a faith in such a politics. Faced with the hegemony of Thatcherite individualism, this discourse appealed to a notion of political community not at all unlike the one which Thatcherism was in the process of displacing, the one which had characterized the era of post-war security, whose passing everyone from the Pistols to The Smiths mourned. When The Sex Pistols screamed about not having a future, what was the point of this outburst, so directly addressed to those in authority, if it was not ultimately an *appeal* to The Nation (who they must, at some level, have assumed to be listening) not to forget them? A protest – and this is what, in various forms, the whole dominant strand of English rock culture during this period amounted to – always carries with it the implication that the protester and their audience share a set of values according to which the justice of the protest can be judged. However nihilistic they may have seemed at the time, not even Joy Division (or their disinherited children, the Goths) can really be located outside of this discourse of protest. For just what is the point in complaining about how alienated you are, how poor you are, how bored you are, unless you believe that someone out there might be listening and that they might actually do something about it? As agents of protest, the singers and songwriters were therefore to be the politico-cultural *representatives* of their audience. In culture, as in parliament, we all had our chosen representatives, whose sincerity and realism could comfort us, assuring us that we were not alone, and whose eloquence would doubtless, someday, bring the misery to an end.

It is true to say that the logic of representation is always ambiguous. Ernesto Laclau elucidates the nature of this ambiguity in *New Reflections on the Revolution of Our Time*:

> If the representative and the represented constitute the same and single will, the 're' of representation disappears since the same will is present in two different places. Representation can therefore only take place to the extent that the transparency entailed by the concept is never achieved.[12]

We can perhaps understand the dominant tendency in British rock discourse during the period 1976–88 as one of trying to erase this constitutive distance in the relationship between representative and represented. The voice, the *logos* as truth, was the ideal point at which this transparency would be achieved in the constitution of a hypostatic communion in which we would all be the same, speaking with one voice, feeling the same thing. Did we not see something of this in the spectacle of fans during the 1980s not just adopting a specific *style* but dressing up to resemble their idols as precisely as possible? The armies of Morrissey look-a-likes who roamed British provincial streets in the mid-1980s were only the most obvious example.[13] There are many other, less extreme examples of this logic, and the underlying faith in traditional forms of representative politics that went with it, governing the pop music discourses of this period. This was the moment of movements like Rock Against Racism and Red Wedge, both governed by the notion that music could and should 'speak out' on the issues of the day, and that this could have some effect.

In 1988, a number of things happened in music. The emergence of acid house marked for the first time the birth of a popular music which did not focus solely on the singing voice. (It should be borne in mind that the transformation of jazz from a popular to an 'intellectual' music coincided with the decline in importance of the song form to jazz composition.) Given the significance of the voice in the discourses of western culture, the importance of this development can hardly be overestimated. While northern soul and disco had shifted the consumption of music away from the concert on to the dancefloor, they had at the same time (and indissociably) retained the singing voice as a central point of musical identification and representation, and a notion of dance as a mode of competitive performance. The emergence of rave displaced those terms and left in their place a radical deconstruction of the status of audience, artist, music and dance. Making no claim to musical integrity, acid house offered pleasure – as much as possible – *entirely* for pleasure's sake; where even disco had sometimes promised that a successful performance on the dancefloor would be rewarded one way or another at the end of an evening, acid house (which had more or less been detached from its origins on the Chicago gay scene by the time it reached the UK) offered only itself. Several commentators have referred to acid house as operating according to an aesthetic of *disappearance*, a refusal of representation and consequently a refusal of identity. What bound together acid house's participants was not a shared social habitus but a shared desire to organize a particular type of experience, an experience which was almost contentless by virtue of its absolute transience, its celebration of and confinement to the pure possibility of the here and the now. On the other hand, the discursive contexts which early acid house culture constructed *around* this experience did imbue it with particular political meanings. The loose, asexual clothing typical of acid house dancers constituted an active refusal of the highly sexualized discourses of style culture, with all of their perceived closeness to Thatcherism. The desexualization of the dancefloor which proved liberating for so many – women in particular – was encoded in these dress styles. The simple fact that acid house was about a set of experiences which dominant discourses remained resolutely opposed to meant that those discourses and their key terms – possessive individualism, the work ethic – were being implicitly resisted. However, even later when large parts of 'rave' culture became explicitly politicized, it was still this valorization of the moment which was its organizing logic and that of the various political movements which came to be associated with it.

After the future

For a while, the politics of dancing shifted from moving ahead to holding onto the small freedoms of pleasure.

Barry Walters, *Village Voice*[14]

The 1994 Criminal Justice and Public Order Act served to highlight the connections between rave culture (specifically the free rave movement) and the resurgence of direct-action politics in the mid-1990s. A particular if ambiguous logic can be said to underlie all of these related politico-cultural developments. In one sense, these developments might be said to take part in 'radical democracy's' abandonment of revolutionary politics (predicated as it is on a historical teleology and a simplistic model of power) for a politics concerned with 'the multiplication of public spaces',[15] but they were also always in danger of collapsing into a radical *spatialization* of politics; a search for immediacy and an abandonment of any real orientation to the future. Where the politics of representation had been about speaking vicariously – through a singer, through an MP – the new politics of the present was about trying to make something happen *now*. Get a house *now* (by squatting), stop the road being built *now*, dance *now*, rush your little head off *now*. The *future*, as an abstract point to be waited on and hoped for, had no purchase here; this was a politics which occurred in space – the space of raves, of squats, of roads – but which did not have time to occupy itself with time. We heard this in the music, too. Techno, trance, jungle and garage are all musics about creating a pleasurable moment rather than telling a story. They are not, like rock songs, about creating a space for fantasy, for identification or catharsis. They are not to make us feel that we are like (or different from) the performer, or to give us hope, or to make us angry. They are to be *used* rather than to be *understood*. They are about collapsing the future into the present. One of the most vivid illustrations of this phenomenon lies in the fact that the core group who made up the 'crusty' culture, which was central to the development of the free rave movement, was in fact drawn from the remnants of the anarcho-punk culture of the 1980s. A culture whose politics and aesthetics were more radically determined by an anti-hedonist revolutionary fatalism (until the revolution, the only legitimate form of music would be a painful, noisy, repetitive background to didactic political slogan-making) than any other gave way to one centred on immediate sensory pleasure almost overnight.[16]

Dance culture's spatialization of politics and culture has never been absolute, however, always occurring within the horizon of a radical openness to the future, to futurity itself. The explicit utopianism of so many house anthems, especially those with their origins in gay black America, seems to bespeak a persistent longing for – and belief in the possibility of – a future better than the present. At the same time, these songs are always literally utopian – dreams of a perfect future which could never be realized in actuality; utopia means literally 'no place'. Perhaps the underlying desire of dance cultures is always to try to erase the distance between an unattainable perfection – a future without place, a time without space – and the pure spatiality of the present. A radical openness to the possibilities – social, political, emotional, technological – of the future becomes a demand for all waiting and striving to cease in the attainment of a perfect, if temporary, now. This ambiguous logic is always open to multiple inflections. Futurism can override the demand for present pleasure as in the work of so many dance music producers drawn towards electronic avant-gardism. The achievement of ecstatic perfection in the present can blind us to the fact that in actuality, the 'Promised Land' is still a long way out of reach. At its most effective, however, this logic can be realized as a radical openness to the future underscored by an insistence on expanding the frontiers of present possibility as soon as possible, if not sooner. In the UK in 1988, and since, such a demand seemed to many to entail an almost complete abandonment of established modes of political and cultural engagement.

In many ways this was a realistic and fairly effective response to the political and cultural situation of the past decade. A consideration of the other things that happened in 1988 can certainly give rise to such a reading. This was the moment when the Labour Party Policy Review first signalled to the world that the British labour movement was abandoning any vision of a future that would be radically different from the present. At the same time, this moment marked a profound break in the critical discourses of British rock culture itself. With the departure of The Smiths, the search for a band to take their place quickly came to be couched in terms of a need to *maintain a tradition*. Whereas even The Smiths (who, in remaining the hegemonic artists of British rock culture for five years, had served as an unprecedented point of consolidation and sedimentation for a particular set of values) had initially been legitimated in terms of their originality, the first wave of bands (the Manchester 'baggy' bands) to be heavily promoted as their successors were not only discussed in terms of the authenticity and sincerity with which they represented a unique and historically specific present, but were fêted for their skill at reworking glorious moments from rock's past. The Stone Roses were the first (but not the last) band whom the music press could identify as self-conscious traditionalists without that automatically consigning them to irrelevance.[17] Rock culture had begun the turn to explicit conservatism which would find its full manifestation in the moment of Britpop.

Thus, from one perspective, what began to happen in the most radical areas of popular culture in 1988 – and has continued since – was the only thing left that could happen. That is, that the radical youth stopped waiting for things to improve, and started to try to make life bearable for themselves. They had given the mainstream political culture (or its revolutionary doubles), and the Labour Party which belonged to it, a decade to regroup. They had gone out and voted for it, they had joined the Young Socialists and CND, marched, stayed at peace camps, they had bought Billy Bragg records (or hand-pressed Crass albums), and it had got them nowhere. Their voices were not being heard. If life was not going to be made bearable by the welfare state, if the crying of voices was not going to make their lives worth living, then it would have to be made bearable by means which the poor and disenfranchised had always used: drugs, dancing and sporadic physical resistance.

Rave music and direct-action politics therefore threatened an entire set of values which underpinned not just the culture of the home counties, but of the Labour Party and the *Melody Maker* as well, and the reaction to this threat came from a number of not unrelated areas. The post-1988 generation's abstention from a certain political culture involved a wholesale rejection of that metaphysics which underpinned it, that same metaphysics which had guaranteed the authenticity and representativeness of the rock voice, so at the same moment traditional politics *and* rock culture began to lose their youth constituency. The agents of British rock culture – principally the 'indie' press and BBC Radio 1 – responded by lending their vigorous support to a movement which seemed to them to offer to win it back: Britpop.

Britpop was a music discourse which emerged around 1993 and came to dominate large sections of the media for about three years. It was a set of bands, their musical products, a set of critical discourses which provided preferred understandings of the significance of the bands and their music, and a set of media practices which privileged that music and those critical discourses. In naming itself as it did, in claiming to represent British pop as such, it aimed to some extent to define and delimit both British identity and the whole field of popular music. The bands in question all played music which self-consciously referenced a retroactively-imagined tradition of British white guitar pop, from the Beatles, The Rolling Stones, The Kinks, The Who and The Small Faces in the 1960s through to The Smiths and The Stone Roses in the 1980s. A particular notion of British cultural identity was therefore mobilized to which 'classic' guitar pop played by young white men on conventional rock instruments was central. This was effected through the articulation of some very specific 'chains of equivalence', both synchronically (guitar pop = Britishness = white masculinity) and diachronically (The Beatles–The Kinks–The Smiths–Blur/Oasis) in order both to articulate a coherent sense of 'Britishness' in the present and to define a number of moments from the past as constituting a tradition of which contemporary 'Britpop' was seen as being the latest manifestation.

The result was a definition of both British cultural identity and popular music which excluded an extraordinary range of people, sounds and experiences. Black music evidently had nothing to do with British pop. Forms which had ever allowed women more than marginal roles – from feminist punk to sweet soul –

evidently had nothing to do with British pop. Traditionally gay-identified forms, like disco and hi-NRG had nothing to do with British pop. Most obviously, contemporary dance musics from house to jungle to trip-hop were implicitly defined as either not British, not pop, or both.

Britpop, as several commentators have suggested, was therefore a clearly reactionary response to a range of social and cultural changes which had dislodged the certainties of a previous generation of white men. Job insecurity, the multiple effects of the women's movement, the increasing hybridization of British culture, have contributed to the unsettling of a normative hegemony of white masculinity. As divergent and disparate as these phenomena are, it is the observation that they can all be seen as converging in a process of radical cultural differentiation that has led so many commentators to try to name them as a totality ('postmodernity', for instance). It is this overall process of differentiation, with all of its democratizing potential, that had undermined the cultural authority of that particular model of British identity and of cultural institutions which depend for their authority on an assumed cultural homogeneity. In the case of music culture, BBC Radio 1, *Top of the Pops*, *Smash Hits*, the indie press and the mainstream record industry had all suffered losses during the 1980s and early 1990s in terms of unit sales, audience figures, and cultural prestige, as dance culture and the digital revolution gave rise to a proliferation of smaller specialist outlets. It is perhaps not surprising, then, that these institutions should have given their enthusiastic support to a project which, in reasserting a very traditional notion of British identity, tried to re-imagine just that condition of cultural homogeneity which they so missed. Perhaps this is one reason for the fierce rivalry between Britpop's two star bands, Blur and Oasis; the need for a coherent sense of community, for a unified and univocal culture, could not tolerate competing visions of what that culture should look or sound like. And here we can see Britpop's close affinity to Tony Blair's New Labour. Rather than offer a radical solution to the collapse of their respective traditions, both projects sought at times to re-imagine a lost coherence, a moment when we all spoke with one voice, and one voice spoke for all of us.

The convergence between Britpop and Blairism did not begin with Oasis member Noel Gallagher's attendance at a No. 10 soirée, or with his rather confused endorsement of Tony Blair's 1997 conference speech, or with Alan McGee's (head of Creation, Oasis' record label) substantial donation to Labour Party funds. Indeed, it was apparent enough six months before the election; for the cover star of the Autumn 1996 edition of *New Labour New Britain*, 'The Magazine for Labour Party Members', was not the suited and smiling Shadow Cabinet spokesperson one might have expected, but an enigmatically be-shaded Noel Gallagher. Not only was Oasis' guitarist/songwriter on the cover, but the centre-fold of the magazine was a feature co-written by Martin Moriarty and the Labour Party's Press Secretary, Alastair Campbell, titled 'New Labour, New Britpop'. The article offered a brief account of Britpop which was remarkable at once for its precise and incisive analysis, and for its rather terrifying political implications.

Having dwelt on the previous year's much-hyped rivalry between indie bands Blur and Oasis, the piece concluded that:

> [if] the bands are very different, it might even be that it's what they share that so narks them. Neither of them could have happened without The Smiths in the 1980s (Damon inherited Morrissey's sense of theatre, Noel always wanted to play like guitarist Johnny Marr). And both of them are rooted in the 60's tradition of song-writing that includes the humma-bility of The Beatles, the alluringly rough edges of The Rolling Stones and the essentially English quirkiness of The Small Faces or The Kinks.

> And it's not just pop history that echoes down the decades. Thirty years ago the country was escaping from the stifling austerity of the Tory 1950s into the white heat of the technological revolution and Harold Wilson's 1960s Labour governments. After the first wave of Black American dance music (from Motown), it was British bands that provided the soundtrack for a generation as young people wanted an alternative to dancing away the blues, more rooted in their own experi-ence of pet-shops, bus stops and pie and mash.

> Thirty years on, after another wave of American-inspired dance music, (the house beats that dominated the charts from 1988 onwards) there's a demand for songs that couldn't have been written anywhere else but here, that Blur, Oasis and everybody else have shown themselves more than able to satisfy.

> Something has shifted, certainly. There's a new feeling on the streets. There's a desire for change. Britain is exporting pop music once again. Now all we need is a new government.[18]

Campbell and Moriarty were surely on to something. Oasis' love of the big chorus, a vague lyric and absolutely standard 'classic' rock sound offered some-thing not at all dissimilar to the vague inclusiveness of Blair's appeals to community, youth and virtue. But Blairism and Britpop shared terms more specific than a commitment to vague inclusiveness, as Campbell and Moriarty themselves explained. The historical elisions and inaccuracies in Campbell and Moriarty's article were less important than what it got right. The authors recog-nized that the single most striking characteristic of Britpop, looked at in the context of recent cultural history, was not its difference from the equally guitar-obsessed American rock which it sought to displace; but rather, it was Britpop's radical difference from the techno-futurism of dance culture and the multicult-uralism of the whole spectrum of black dance-derived pop musics, not to mention the multicultural pop feminism of the Spice Girls. It was this difference between Britpop and a more international and multicultural tradition stretching from Motown to house that Moriarty and Campbell so astutely identified, and their identification of Britpop with Blairism seemed to be of a piece with New

Labour's refusal to offer any opposition to the Criminal Justice Act, its absolute refusal to countenance reform of the drug and licensing laws, and its apparent lack of interest in projecting a multicultural image of British identity. It is hardly surprising that the most radical elements of British popular culture looked to musical and political forms which refused the terms shared by Britpop and the new communitarianism.

There were huge problems with the form that this refusal took, however. Earlier, we borrowed from Ernesto Laclau the term 'spatialization' to describe the tendency to eschew a politics of representation in favour of a politics of the moment, and his deployment of that term makes it quite clear that such a process is far from being progressive. Laclau writes that: 'The 'spatialization' of an event consists of eliminating its temporality'.[19] The failure to conceive of power and causality in temporal and historical terms is the overriding weakness of the emergent political culture which has so far had so little success in defending itself from the Criminal Justice Act. Its enacted deconstruction of the politics of representation and the culture of the voice has largely been conducted in terms which perpetuate an equally powerful metaphysics of presence, a metaphysics of the immediate and a metaphysics of the *deed*. A faith in representative politics is replaced not so much by a constructive critique of that politics but by a faith in the consoling virtues of 'direct action' as a *replacement for* engagement in forms of politics which – although failing to offer the unmediated experience of physically stopping someone from tearing down a house at just that moment – actually have any hope of achieving their stated goals.[20] It may have felt good up the tree, but it rarely stopped the road being built, and the refusal of crusties, greens and free party ravers to engage with the complexities of mainstream politics created a situation in which no political party had anything to gain by listening to them; if you're not going to vote for anyone, then no elected politician is going to care what you have to say. A real and effective materialist pragmatism was and remains a part of the discourse of the new direct action movements, but it is a part which was often rhetorically submerged by a disabling millenarianism and a literal metaphysics of presence (*being here now* was often given as the ultimate and only legitimate mode of political expression).

We can also see the dehistoricizing and reifying tendencies at work in rave culture when we consider that often the most powerful discourse operating within those strands of rave culture which were a part of this oppositional political movement understood their relation to existing modernity not in terms of a deconstructive critique of Enlightenment reason or phallogocentrism, but in terms of the teleological models of New Age philosophy. The belief in an 'evolutionary leap' as the source of our salvation, the belief that 'By changing ourselves we can change the world',[21] served to contain many of the radical possibilities that this culture could have had. New Age is, if nothing else, the ultimate politics of the *proper*. Individualizing all problems and all solutions, it offers a protection against the world, a picket-fence around your subjectivity, and (in its millenarian forms) a salvation without the difficulty of social action. Let us consider Jean-Luc Nancy's comment on ecstasy:

> Ecstasy ... defines the impossibility, both ontological and gnostological, of absolute immanence ... and consequently the impossibility either of an individuality, in the precise sense of the term, or of a pure collective totality.[22]

Immanence – in the form of a radically self-sufficient self-containment – was precisely what the discourses of New Age rave culture (and in certain ways the direct-action movement) sought to define as its central experiences. The ecstatic experience of raving was taken in all of its radical alterity and defined as on the one hand a cosy buffer against the presence of others, on the other as the point at which all identity collapses into an atemporal (therefore undifferentiated, therefore meaningless) unity. There was a strong convergence between psychiatric and New Age discourses around the idea of Ecstasy experiences as a form of therapy.[23] Therapy is always a very different matter from liberation, even if the one may at times masquerade as the other. The historicity and politicality of this experience were defined entirely in terms of an evolutionary (and technological determinist) teleology.[24] Drugs in themselves, outside of social relationships and situations, were thought of as sources of pleasure and enlightenment. Digital technology was thought of as liberating in itself.[25] 'The Earth' was thought of as an independent organism with an implacable and unitary will.

Even when not directly informed by New Age thinking, the radical strands of rave culture tended to be informed by a kind of vague anarchism which was just as purist, just as hostile to actual political engagement. One of the favourite slogans of groups like the Freedom Network, set up to fight the Criminal Justice Act, was 'In your face' (or, sometimes, 'In their face'). They were proud of their refusal to conform, of their unwillingness to compromise with the neat and tidy values of middle-class Middle England. Their disinterest in compromising – or even communicating – with Middle England, however, was similarly matched by Middle England's disinclination to compromise with them. The Criminal Justice Act was passed with almost no parliamentary opposition. Even the extra-parliamentary opposition to it has now almost entirely disappeared.

If the opportunities which rave culture has to engage in and articulate with democratic struggles are ever to be realized – and it has to be said that this seems increasingly unlikely – then it is as much the discourses of New Age and pseudo-anarchism as those of bourgeois Puritanism or rock culture which need to be deconstructed. The deconstruction of that metaphysics of presence which governs the thinking of many involved in the new direct-action movements (including those committed to the defence of rave culture) is a task imperative to the possible realization of their goals as much as anything else. Without some engagement with the politics of representation, with parliamentary politics, the Criminal Justice Act will never be repealed, and it still seems unlikely that a single road-building plan will be shelved. Without a politics of the future as well as of the present, the day after the 'E' wears off will always be a nightmare.

No jeans, no trainers: Glamour, distinction, class and the male gaze

It was suggested in Chapter 6 that 'rave' culture can be considered an anti-bourgeois phenomenon. Certainly in some manifestations this is true, and if we consider 'bourgeois discourse' simply to mean Puritanism then it is obviously so. But Puritanism is not the only form of bourgeois discourse. Asceticism and the valorization of the work ethic may have been important in the early development of capitalism, but they are not necessarily conducive to its later development. For as long as it has existed, and increasingly so ever since the moment of its emergence as a distinct mode of production, distribution and exchange, consumption has been central to the development of capitalism; without widespread and ever-intensifying demand for the commodities which it produces, there would be no such thing as capitalism. Marx himself began his study of capitalism with an analysis of the central status of the commodity to the capitalist economy.[26] Under these conditions, various ideologies of consumption have been elaborated throughout this period, with an ever-greater legitimacy granted to modes of conspicuous consumption. One idea which has been crucial to the elaboration of such ideologies has been that of glamour as a valorized term. In privileging certain modes of dress and deportment – particularly for women – the discourse of glamour serves to legitimize the culture of the ruling classes by making a lifestyle to which only the wealthy have access appear as the pinnacle of desirability. The fetishization of commodities (especially particular types of clothing) and of women as exchangeable commodities and as objects of consumption for the male gaze are the central terms of this discourse. We do not wish to appear to endorse a puritan position ourselves, here. There is nothing wrong with people wanting a luxurious lifestyle; it would be a much better world if we could all have one. But the discourse of glamour traditionally encourages individual aspirations which can never be realized without collective action effecting social change. Perhaps more importantly, it is a discourse which mobilizes the speculocentric terms of phallogocentrism; according to the discourse of glamour, the primary achievement for any woman is to be a pleasing visual prospect for a fetishizing bourgeois masculinity. It is the relative status of this discourse in contemporary dance culture that we want here to engage with.

Acid house may have arrived on a wave of anti-Thatcherite egalitarianism, but the club scene which developed in its wake was often quite different. Elitism and exclusivity quickly became defining characteristics of many strands of the culture, whether experienced in clubs, record shops, clothing boutiques, or through print and broadcast media. As Sarah Thornton has demonstrated, these are often the organizing terms of youth cultures. We can extend but also challenge Thornton's observation by considering the centrality to most dance cultures of particular discourses on glamour. It is worth noting that almost every British dance 'scene' since acid house has been characterized by a very specific attitude to glamour. Is it preferable to dress in expensive clothes, which look as different as possible from clothes one might wear for manual labour, clothes which at least in the case of women's wardrobes are conventionally 'sexy'? Or is it preferable to 'dress down', to 'dress to sweat', in loose clothes and trainers? Acid house was noted for its playful, childlike, sexless fashions. Since the passing of that moment there has been a consistent trend among clubs playing 'Balearic' house, garage, 'happy house' and more recently 'speed garage' to maintain door policies which insist that clubbers dress up,[27] eschewing workwear, sportswear, or, as Thornton points out, clothing which might indicate a cultural affiliation to hip hop.[28] On the other hand there have been a number of sets of fashion codes which explicitly reject that discourse: the childish playfulness of the 1991–92 hardcore scene, with its dummies, white gloves and bare-chests; the dreadlocks, psychedelic and 'ethnic' clothing that became associated with trance clubs in 1993; the combat trousers which became ubiquitous in clubs playing, first techno and then jungle, 'Big Beat' and post hip hop beats in the late 1990s.

Thornton's argument would tend to the observation that in either case, the discourses in circulation are equally exclusive, equally élitist. It is certainly true that 'anti-glamour' codes can create excluded others just as much as can 'pro-glamour' codes. It is also true that a strain of élitist purism runs through most of those areas of dance culture characterized by a hostile attitude towards glamour. But to see these processes as precisely equivalent is to ignore the cultural-political context within which they occur. Certainly the primary marker of 'hipness' in most of these cultures is conspicuous consumption – be it of obscure and highly-priced twelve-inch singles, clothes, or drugs. However, the way in which these markers are deployed is quite different, and, perhaps most importantly, the markers themselves are not of equivalent value. To take a recent example, the London speed garage scene was dominated in 1997 by clubs which refused entry to people wearing trainers or jeans (standard markers of working-class or poor black cultural affiliation), and its alleged drugs of choice were cocaine and cham-pagne.[29] The first qualification for entry into such a culture is a high amount of disposable cash; the poor are explicitly unwelcome. By the same token, clubs which do not insist on clubbers wearing expensive clothes are by definition less expensive to get into and therefore less exclusive. What's more, pro-glamour codes are clearly closer to the dominant codes of bourgeois fashion as they are circulated in the media. Perhaps most concretely, we know of very few recorded instances of anyone actually being excluded from a club for looking too rich (although clubs have been known to claim 'no suits' door policies). Clearly what is at stake in anti-glamour codes is an explicit and self-conscious rejection of those fashion discourses which circulate in society as a whole and which legiti-mate themselves precisely according to their exclusive accessibility to those with large disposable incomes. Such discourses are crucial in legitimating the culture of the wealthy as the dominant culture – while being very far from the terms of

Puritanism, they are none the less forms of specifically bourgeois discourse – and discourses which reject them have a specifically oppositional status in relation to them. It is no accident that the project of reglamorizing the dancefloor has received the most intense support from the largest and most profit-driven institutions of British club culture; the 'super clubs' like London's Ministry of Sound and Liverpool's Cream, and the commercial dance music press.

Furthermore, as we have already pointed out, the production of glamour is usually the production of women as objects. As Drew Hemment has suggested, 'the floors of many night clubs are filled with spectacular glamour ... this usually represents a recolonisation of the dancefloor by the male gaze'.[30] The glamorization of the dancefloor has been associated with its re-sexualization as 'club-wear' for women quickly came to designate a highly sexualized lycra wardrobe rather than T-shirts or sports clothes, and as the standard visual representation of club culture became increasingly informed by the conventions of glamour photography, the 'trippy' graphics of early acid house and rave media giving way to the emphasis on underdressed young women in the glossy Mixmag and DJ. This was the topic of a fascinating discussion organized by and printed in Mixmag in April 1997, in which a number of women took up very different positions on the relative status of glamour – as personified by the lycra-clad 'club babe' – in the dance club environment. Ultimately the discussion revealed little more than the incredible variability of the participants' experiences and perceptions – some thought that there was intense and oppressive pressure on young women to conform to sexualized, stereotypical notions of glamorous femininity, others thought that there was none at all – and collapsed into liberal waffle as the various positions became conflated into a general agreement about the importance of individual autonomy and self-determination. What the publication of the discussion made clear, however, is that this is an issue which participants in contemporary dance culture regard as controversial, and that there is considerable support for an account which regards the re-sexualization and re-glamorization of the dancefloor as a political setback for women.

Before entirely dismissing 'glamour' as a means by which dance culture can be rearticulated in terms of bourgeois, phallogocentric, speculocentric discourse, however, we should consider its very different status in gay cultures. Precisely *because* it is so central to the encoding of bourgeois femininity in twentieth-century western culture, the discourse of glamour has proved highly useful for queer strategies of parody and appropriation. The self-conscious appropriation of glamour is one of the central tropes of the discourse of camp, a discourse which many writers have identified as crucial to gay self-empowerment.[31] Glamour's inherent anti-Puritanism makes it easily appropriable by a group which have been so desperately marginalized by the hegemony of Puritan discourse. Furthermore, the self-consciously parodic use of signifiers of glamour (sequins, boas, and so on) is not a practice necessarily confined to gay male culture; ever since acid house, dancefloors have been sites for playful 'dressing up' in many forms. It is important to distinguish such practices from the unironic modes of designer clubbing, however. We would argue that camp irony is, in fact, far closer in spirit to the anti-glamour discourses which have manifested themselves in British dance culture than to the carefully policed codes of normalizing fashion, and that the promotion of the discourse of glamour on the British dancefloor has been one of the primary means by which dance culture's radical energies have been contained. The 'glamorization' of British dance culture has on the whole taken the form of an articulation of that culture's anti-Puritanism into a form which is in every other sense reactionary, sexist, élitist, and often (but by no means always) implicitly racist.

Boy's own: Happy Mondays and the birth of the new lad

A very different story of reactionary anti-Puritanism can be traced from the moment of 'Madchester' through to the 'New Lad' phenomenon of the mid- to late 1990s. During the period 1989–90, the indie music press and much of the British youth media became obsessed with the notion of Manchester as the epicentre of an Ecstasy-fuelled cultural renaissance. From a purely musical point of view, this was an extraordinary irony. On the one hand, almost all of the most important British indie bands had come from Manchester for almost a decade. The Buzzcocks, Joy Division/New Order, The Fall and The Smiths all hailed from the capital of the North, and the level of musical innovation offered by the new crop of Manchester bands was hardly comparable. On the other hand, Manchester had also produced the first two British house/techno artists of real importance: A Guy Called Gerald and 808 State. However, it was neither a decade of innovation nor the emergence of British electro-dance which excited the music press in 1989, but a trio of guitar bands, The Stone Roses, Inspiral Carpets and Happy Mondays. As Matthew Collin has pointed out, the former two were basically 1960s-obsessed retro outfits, lucky to be in the right place at the right time; to be able to mediate between a backward-looking, guitar-based indie press and a post-acid house drug culture with obvious affinities to the psychedelic 1960s. But it was the Happy Mondays who really defined the moment; self-publicizing musical bricoleurs from the council estates of Salford, their blend of rock, funk and other dance flavours always sounded more multicultural, more contemporary and more in tune with the working-class, post-Thatcherite 'E'-culture they came to represent than the music of their indie-boy counterparts.

The Mondays embodied other things, however. Their commercial success, their ubiquity in the media, their widespread popularity were all crucial to the dissemination of Ecstasy culture in Britain, and as such Happy Mondays became a discursive phenomenon with effects which far exceeded their music. The Mondays became the template for the first really widely circulated image of what it meant to be a 'raver' in Britain, and it was an image which had little to do with house music's roots in gay black America. Shaun Ryder, the band's lead singer, liked to tell interviewers that he voted Conservative (although he later claimed that he actually never voted at all), at a time when homophobia was still an explicit element of Conservative government policy. The Mondays' image was that of the 'E'-head as Thatcherite urchin; a streetwise and hedonistic entrepreneur who lived the rhetoric of the free market while refusing social authoritarianism. At least, that was the idea; those were the terms on which both house culture and the indie press gave the Mondays their initial approval. It became apparent soon enough, however, that the Monday's affinities to Thatcherism did not stop at selfishness and a belief in the free market. The macho, laddish image of the band and their hangers-on escalated into outright sexism (the band posed with topless models in *Penthouse*), and a homophobic outburst from celebrity hanger-on Bez, in what Collin rightly calls their 'watershed interview' with Steven Wells in the NME.[32]

That may have lost them the support of the indie press, but it only serves to confirm the Mondays' long-term significance. For the Happy Mondays, we suggest, were the first embodiment of that model of 1990s masculinity, the 'New Lad'. Anti-Puritan he may be, in his hedonism and resistance to work and authority, but the New Lad often seems to have been invented just to prove that such values can be successfully articulated with a wholly reactionary political agenda, an agenda which equates masculinity, in particular working-class masculinity, with anti-feminism, anti-intellectualism and homophobia. Not really coming centre-stage until the mid-1990s, the New Lad was consumer culture's latest offer of a self-conscious subject position for men. He liked beer, football, birds and bacon sarnies, and seemed to regard the four entities as pretty much of a piece, and most importantly he was prepared to pay for soft-porn consumer magazines like *Loaded*, *Stuff* and FHM to tell him about them (or at least show him pictures), guiding him through his world of objects in a style free from intellectual pretension or political correctness. His actual age was indeterminate, although his emotional age was militantly retarded. He may have been a media marketing construct, but if that was all he was, then he could hardly have revolutionized the magazines market as successfully as he did. The discourse which produced the New Lad delineated and popularized a hedonistic and anti-feminist sensibility which had its first strong manifestation in the Happy Mondays, and the fact that British dance culture had been disseminated via such an identity model had serious implications. For several years after the summer of 1989, many people associated Ecstasy culture with a hedonism which was reactionary in its articulation; white, straight, male, Tory. Although it represented quite a different process from the glamorization of the dancefloor, in both cases it was women and their bodies which became constituted as objects for male consumption, as is clearly still the case within New Lad culture. It seems that the rockist marginalization of Manchester's techno pioneers and the canonization of the proto-Lad Mondays was another mode according to which important elements of early British dance culture became articulated with entirely reactionary discourses. (It should be said that 808 State were just as bad, in their talking about rave records fronted by 'some wailing slag'.)

This isn't just another story of incorporation, however. With the Mondays' heroin-induced withdrawal from public life, the association between dance culture and Laddism weakened. By the mid-1990s and the launch of the New Lad bible, Loaded magazine, it had virtually disappeared, and it was the anti-dance, anti-'E' sound of Britpop which provided New Lads with their heroes and anthems. For the Mondays and their ilk rave had meant the rejection of politics, and so, implicitly, the enthusiastic acceptance of existing distributions of social power. The Conservative Government which Ryder had claimed to support soon put a stop to that; once they started trying to criminalize an entire culture, the notion of dance as depoliticized seemed ridiculous. Between 1990 and 1995 the visibility and success of the free party movement confirmed more strongly than ever the idea of rave culture's political radicalism. Even once the free party sound systems were driven back – underground into tiny enclaves, running parties for a few hundred friends at a time, holed up in resilient but isolated enclaves like the Exodus community in Luton or off around the world like the globe-trotting Spiral Tribe[33] – their ideological success, combined with that of the techno and trance scenes with which they had had strong connections, meant that dance culture could never again look a like a safe haven for Tory politics and sexual reaction. It remains part of the common-sense of contemporary culture – however inaccurate it may often be – that 'E'-culture is a site for the elaboration and celebration of less sexist forms of public interaction than any youth culture has known before. This should not be a cause for complacency, however. The important point to remember here is that the articulation of dance culture with feminism is by no means natural or inevitable, but something always to be defended if we want it to continue.

Weighing it up

We have spent some time in this book considering the ways in which dance music and culture transgress prohibitions laid down by powerful western discourses. In this chapter we have also considered some of the ways in which it has been articulated so as to minimize the impact of such transgression, posing little threat to the ideologies which constitute and legitimate class- and gender-based oppression. It may now be worth considering just what it is that 'dance culture' has achieved in its ten years at the heart of British music culture. What changes has it effected in British culture? How much of its radical potential has been realized? It is common today – and has been for some time – to hear or read that 'rave failed', that 'the dream died'.[34] It's not often clear exactly what people who make such comments actually expected 'rave' to achieve. Anyone who ever thought that some drugs and some dance records were going to dissolve existing social relationships was always likely to be disappointed. How disappointed should those of us with lesser expectations be, though? What exactly could we have expected 'rave' to deliver, and how much of it has come about?

The single most important point to consider here is that dance culture achieves a great deal simply by existing. As Georgiana Gore has put it, 'it represents a safe zone for dancing and drug taking',[35] and simply maintaining that safe zone in the face of western culture's extraordinary prohibitions on its very existence is a considerable achievement. Bethan Cole's lucid and realistic summing up of ten years of dance culture makes the point that making available that culture's central experiences to a wide public constitutes a some form of victory:

> The fact is, now any suburban 17 year-old can take Ecstasy, speed and smoke draw, go to house clubs and listen to dance music on Radio One. It's hardly even an act of rebellion any more ... Radio One now broadcasts a total of 27 hours of specialist dance music shows every week. In 1987 it had two.... And who'd have thought the 24 hour day of clubbers, DJs and promoters would incrementally become part of normal life, with inner-city supermarkets starting to open round-the-clock and many cities boasting relaxed, European-style all-night licensing legislation.[36]

These aren't small changes. In 1987, the 17 year old probably had little else to do but get drunk at his/her local pub; and (s)he couldn't do that after ten o'clock at night. Today, the communitarian, feminizing, ecstatic pleasures of dance culture are available to just about anyone who wants them. Underground élitists and acid house nostalgists may bemoan the fact that these things are 'hardly even an act of rebellion any more', but we would argue that this is precisely the measure of dance culture's cultural-political *success*. It isn't dance culture that has changed; 'mainstream' British culture has altered to accommodate it. The wild abandon, the polymorphous ecstasy, the fleeting sense of community to be found on many British dancefloors is not that different from that found in the earliest days of psychedelic gay disco.[37] It isn't dance culture which has been incorporated; it's the dominant culture which has been infiltrated and transformed.

This is not to say, however, that there have not been failures, unrealized potential, damaged dreams. Perhaps most notably, the free party movement has been largely curtailed by government legislation. The combined effects of the Criminal Justice Act and the growth of the legal club market have meant that the ideal of a non-commercial dance culture occupying open spaces and abandoned buildings, nomadic and participatory in its ethics, remains the preserve of a tiny handful of die-hard participants. Forty thousand ravers may have converged on Castlemorton Common in 1992, but attempts to organize an equivalent festival have consistently floundered.[38] At the time of writing (1999), free parties are no longer a significant strand of British dance culture for many people. They take place, and the London 'acid techno' party scene remains healthy and strong, as do various local party scenes in the provinces (in particular around Nottingham) but the ambition of creating new, ever-widening kinds of public space through the free parties and festivals seems to have given way to an 'underground' purism born of the ever-greater need for secrecy. Stories circulating early in 1999 tell of no great gatherings, of only occasional and sporadic successes for larger parties, of small events catering to a few hundred dancers at a time, successful but in secret.

This is not to imply that the free party movement failed, however. Arguably the reason it no longer attracts the support it once did is that it simply isn't needed; most of what it offered – cheap dancing, no dress codes, relaxed (i.e., no) security, less commercially oriented music, even New Age ideology, has been widely available to British clubbers since about the moment that the free party movement went into decline (the end of Summer 1992). The free party movement tends to see itself as an anarchist enclave, and in many ways this is true, but it might be as accurate to see it and its DIY ethos as the ultimate example of consumer protest. In the early 1990s dance clubs with all-night licenses were still few and far between, extortionately expensive and frequently implemented restrictive door policies. The rise in attendance at free parties was in many ways a response to this situation, and once the club market had expanded and changed so as to meet their demands, it was no longer needed. Many of the active participants in the free party movement themselves began to organize legal club nights. Indeed, today it's arguably often easier and cheaper to organize legal events than illegal ones, and it is certainly the case that legal, publicized events retain the open quality of democratic public spaces in a way that today's free parties – publicized by word of mouth, often featuring punishing gabber techno – do not. None of this is in any way to belittle the significance or the achievements of that movement. To have effected the changes they did is very important. At the same time, the *symbolic* success of the free party movement in the early 1990s was such that the idea of 'rave' as Thatcherite leisure activity was buried forever as a significant element of public discourse.

In terms of 'dance culture' in a wider sense, how far has it realized its radical potential? Bethan Cole suggests that individually and collectively passing through the ecstatic experience means that 'perhaps, just perhaps, we've got an emotional awareness, a spiritual and mental literacy that wasn't there before'.[39] In a broader sense, many commentators believe that dance culture has contributed to the 'feminization' of the culture and values of that generation which has passed through it. This process of 'feminization'[40] has been linked to changes in patterns of work and consumption, to large-scale changes in gender roles and social expectations. It is hard to see how dance culture could *not* have contributed to this process in a positive way. Even if all it has done is to give that 17 year old something to do at a weekend, it is still a huge step forward. In a world where young men can no longer expect the easy domination over women that there fathers 'enjoyed', where straightforward heterosexuality is no longer a strictly enforced cultural norm, where young women have to learn what it means to be women when that doesn't mean occupying a position of weakness, then having the deconstructive *jouissance* of the dancefloor – a place where the dissolution of certainty and identity is experienced as *pleasure*, where gender and sexuality can be suspended, looked at from different angles and possibly reworked – at the centre of youth culture is surely a step towards a more democratic culture. Especially in the case of those young white men who do still dominate British dancefloors, to experience the dissolution of their masculinity as pleasurable *jouissance* rather than as a source of terror must enable them to cope better with the erosion of masculine authority which, it is to be hoped, will continue throughout society. If Ecstasy and house music have even slightly displaced drunkenness and violence as the common culture of young men in Britain, then Britain can only be a better place for it.

There are ways in which dance culture's effects have been less positive, however. A phenomenon noted at least as much as the 'feminization' of the culture of young people in recent years is the de-politicization of that culture. 'De-politicization' is a problematic concept – it tends to imply a very narrow definition of what it means to be 'political' – but it is certainly true that participation of young people in elections has been in decline for years, and that young people's identification with 'politics' is at an all-time low.[41] As discussed in the previous chapter, there is a certain shared logic to dance music's eschewal of meaning and the eschewal of representative politics. Simon Reynolds has taken this point further, rightly pointing out that in certain senses the pursuit of genderless *jouissance* is a flight from culture itself.[42] If dance culture encourages a collective and individual withdrawal from 'mainstream' political society, then its participants are not likely to be able to effect any serious political or social change. It might have been hoped ten years ago that rave culture's refusal of the work ethic and the entire framework of puritan values would result in a clearly articulated set of basic political demands, such as for a shorter working week and higher wages (i.e., more money for less work), that its celebration of community would encourage a return to collectivist politics. Instead it seems to have encouraged an outlook which sees the realms of 'work' and 'leisure' as entirely separate and unrelated, the latter a site in which to invest all of our energies and interest, the former an unreformable region of wholly negative experience. Dance culture and its experiences have thus been articulated with a libertarianism which is so anti-political as to be self-defeating, to have no real sense of what it is that actually curtails most people's freedoms in a capitalist society. This would be a damaging and depressing outcome, but it would not take much to change it.

There is a whole range of concrete political issues with which dance culture and its 'values' could be easily articulated. Demands typical of the European labour movement, such as those just described, are among them. Dance culture's rejection of Puritanism might be thought to make it easily articulable with more radical demands, also, such as that for a universal right to a basic income, the right to which would not be dependent on compliance with the demands of the work ethic. In the UK, where elements of dance culture have affiliated themselves to political causes in their own defence, obvious issues such as the importance of the right to public assembly, to freedom of movement, and so forth, have been articulated with the defence of the right to party. It's a great pity that this has not led many participants in dance culture to involve themselves with campaigns against the anti-union legislation which had been slowly eroding those rights for over a decade before the passing of the 1994 Criminal Justice and Public Order Act. As Matthew Collin and Drew Hemment both point out, the British police learnt many of the techniques they used to break the free party movement meting out similar treatment to trade unionists in the 1980s.[43]

At the same time, such an articulation would probably require that the labour movement itself acknowledge the importance to many British people today of a range of issues in which it has traditionally taken no interest. The British left has its own very strong Puritan streak – Harold Wilson once said that the Labour Party and its philosophies owed 'more to Methodism than to Marxism' – so issues such as the reform of licensing legislation and the ending of drug prohibition have never been high on its agenda (the Labour Party's first election manifesto actually demanded the prohibition of alcohol). For members of the chemical generation, however, these are issues of central concern. This is not just a matter of ravers wanting drugs to be legalized. It might also be hoped that the historical affinity between dance culture and gay culture might lead its participants to widen their critique of the Puritan state into a critique of state interference in sexual activities between consenting adults, the usual targets of which have been gay men. Both of these issues are concerned with the right of the state to interfere with what people do with or put into their own bodies. This might be what a politics informed by the concerns of dance culture would retain from the discourse of possessive individualism; a belief in the right of individuals to bodily self-determination.

Finally, as we have discussed elsewhere, dance culture almost always manifests a particular politics of community. Whether it's only in the ecstatic collectivity of the dancefloor, or in the attempts to form new and temporary forms of autonomous community space that various groups have engaged in, or in the very real struggle to defend particular communities and their spaces, such as that exemplified by the struggles of the Exodus collective in Luton,[44] the construction of particular kinds of communitarian space is always part of what dance culture is about. The reconstruction of 'community', its protection and recovery from the destruction which capitalist modernity wreaks on most forms of social cohesion, is also a significant goal of political discourses which have been influential on governments in Europe and in America in recent years. Many commentators regard the chief goal of reforming western governments today to be the extension and maintenance of 'social inclusion', the building of societies which 'exclude' – by means of prejudice or poverty – as few people as possible.[45] Unfortunately, as many other commentators have noted, such 'communitarian' discourse tends to favour authoritarian solutions which tend towards the enforcement of normative values (for example, making everyone accept the centrality of work to human life). Projects for the maintenance of 'community' thus come to be construed in terms of the maintenance of social and cultural homogeneity. The values normally manifested within dance culture, on the other hand, could well be used to inform a very different politics of community. A politics which was more concerned with encouraging the development of new forms of community, which stressed the value of community as a means by which individuals come together in order to democratically empower themselves, rather than stressing the need for authoritarian and homogenizing government, would take a very different attitude than that which the British state has taken towards groups like Exodus, and indeed the whole of contemporary dance culture. Such a politics might want to see the state actually encourage groups who have the initiative and creative dynamism to take over unused land and buildings, to turn them into co-operative housing, to provide safe, free, and community-binding forms of entertainment. Whether it was in attempts such as Exodus's to contribute to solving the ongoing housing crisis which faces the UK, in the reclamation of places of beauty and co-operation from the dereliction of our cities' abandoned spaces, or simply in the enormous collective creativity of commercial club culture, it is easy to imagine a communitarian politics which would want to see the state help and facilitate such developments, rather than trying to trample them at every turn as the UK government has done to date. Whether or not such an attitude comes to inform the policies of the UK government, we would certainly continue to ally ourselves with such values, and would hope to see many participants in dance culture do so. At the same time, dance culture's *pluralistic* and libertarian communitarianism can inform forms of politics which are not as simplisitcally anti-statist as the anarchism which informs the rhetoric of groups like Exodus and Justice. The continued attempt to reform the British state, to devolve power back to the localities, to enshrine some civil rights in law, and to make our electoral systems more representative and more pluralistic, are all political projects informed by sentiments very close to those which inform much of contemporary dance culture.

Perhaps more than anything, what defines the political character of dance culture is that it is not afraid of the future. Its response to the dislocation of social structures is not simply despair, the celebration of atomization, or a reactionary attempt to recreate lost coherencies, but an attempt to make possible new forms of community and new networks of relation. New technologies have always been, for dance culture, neither means of disempowerment nor sites of inauthenticity, but tools to be manipulated and deployed as creatively as possible for the empowerment of individuals and communities, tools with which to challenge received notions of authorship and propriety. The break-up of patterns of work and leisure has provided the ground for a making of new patterns of social interaction. The dissolution of old identities has been not terrifying but liberating. It is this openness to the democratic possibilities of the future, this 'optimism of the will'[46] which is so sorely lacking in much of contemporary political culture, and which may remain dance culture's lasting legacy to a generation which had almost lost hope.

Notes

1 Irvine Welsh, *The Acid House* (London, Vintage, 1995), p. 240.
2 Raymond Williams, *Marxism and Literature* (Oxford, Oxford University Press, 1977).
3 Sarah Thornton, *Club Cultures* (Cambridge, Polity, 1995), pp. 87–115.
4 Ernesto Laclau and Chantal Mouffe, *Hegemony and Socialist Strategy* (London, Verso, 1985), p. 105.
5 For a useful discussion of the uses of this concept, see Morley and Chen (eds), *Stuart Hall; Critical Dialogues in Cultural Studies* (London, Routledge, 1996), pp. 141–5; Lawrence Grossberg, *We Gotta Get Out of this Place* (New York, Routledge, 1992), pp. 113–30.

6 See Matthew Collin, with contributions by John Godfrey, *Altered State: The Story of Ecstasy Culture and Acid House* (London, Serpent's Tail, 1997), p. 274.
7 We would like to thank students at the University of East London for having raised this issue in seminars for the course MED 313 *Popular Music*.
8 See Ernesto Laclau, *New Reflections on the Revolution of Our Time* (London, Verso, 1990), pp. 34–59.
9 E.P. Thompson, *Whigs and Hunters* (London, Allen Lane, 1975); and E.P. Thompson, *The Making of the English Working Class* (London, Penguin, 1980).
10 Jurgen Habermas, 'Modernity – An Incomplete Project', in Hal Foster (ed.), *Postmodern Culture* (London, Pluto, 1985).
11 Hakim Bey, *T.A.Z.* (New York, Autonomedia, 1985).
12 Laclau, *New Reflections*, p. 39.
13 It should be pointed out that this was not exactly new; the Beatles spawned look-a-likes and were supposed to represent the spirit of their age. However, what we should understand is that the Beatles and their contemporaries were different because, despite certain similarities, they legitimated themselves variously according to their ability to offer a good time or to the authority with which they claimed to lead their culture (being presented as in tune with rather than in opposition to the political culture of their day), representing the highest possible point of fulfilment of their audiences' aspirations (rather than representing the truth of their audiences' situations). Likewise, the David Bowie fans of the early 1970s who dressed up to look like Ziggy Stardust were self-consciously participating in a *critique* of authentic identity. The same phantasmatic processes may well have governed the behaviour of Smiths lads, as governed the behaviour of Bowie boys, but they certainly didn't recognize them as such. A proper consideration of these issues might lead us to Borch-Jacobsen's notion of mimetic identification on the one hand, to Judith Butler's model of phantasmatic identification on the other. See M. Borch-Jacobsen, *The Freudian Subject*, trans Catherine Porter (Stanford, Stanford University Press, 1988) and J. Butler, *Bodies That Matter*, (London, Routledge, 1993).
14 In Hanif Kureishi and Jon Savage (eds), *The Faber Book of Pop* (London, Faber & Faber, 1995), p. 653.
15 Laclau, *New Reflections*, p. xv.
16 See George McKay, *Senseless Acts of Beauty: Cultures of Resistance Since the Sixties* (London, Verso, 1996).
17 See NME, 15 April 1989.
18 Campbell and Moriarty, 'New Labour, New Britpop', in *New Labour New Britain*, Autumn 1996.
19 Laclau, *New Reflections*, p. 41.
20 For some interesting observations on these new and not so new political forms, see Doreen Massey's interview with Heather Hunt in *Soundings*, Autumn 1995 (London, Lawrence & Wishart).
21 This was the launch slogan of the New Age trance club, Megatripolis.
22 Jean-Luc Nancy *The Inoperative Community* (Minneapolis, University of Minnesota Press, 1991), p. 6.
2 See Nicholas Saunders, *Ecstasy and the Dance Culture* (London, Nicholas Saunders, 1995) and *Ecstasy Reconsidered* (London, Nicholas Saunders, 1997).
24 See, for instance, the writings of the 'rave guru' Terrence Mckenna, such as his *Food of the Gods* (London, Rider, 1992), in which he argues that the collective ingestion of pscilosybin is both the source and the key to the future of human evolution.
25 A view that is seemingly shared by cyber-utopians like Sadie Plant.
26 Karl Marx, *Capital* (London, Penguin, 1976).
27 See Collin, *Altered State*, p. 266.

28 Thornton, *Club Cultures*, p. 113.

29 See *Muzik* magazine, September 1997.

30 Drew Hemment, 'e is for Ekstasis', in *New Formations*, Spring/Summer 1997 (London, Lawrence & Wishart).

31 See Jonathan Dollimore, *Sexual Dissidence* (Oxford, OUP, 1991), pp. 311–13; Andrew Ross, *No Respect: Intellectuals and Popular Culture* (London, Routledge, 1989), pp. 135–70; Moe Meyer (ed.), *The Politics and Poetics of Camp* (London, Routledge, 1994).

32 Collin, *Altered State*, p. 175.

33 Ibid., pp. 184–239. See, also, Tash Lodge's website: http://ourworld.compuserve.com/homepages/tash_lodge/main.htm; and the *Squall* magazine site: http://www.users.dircon.co.uk/~squall/index.htm.

34 See Simon Reynolds, 'Rave Culture: Living Dream or Living Death', in Redhead, Wynne and O'Connor (eds), *The Clubcultures Reader* (Oxford, Blackwell, 1997).

35 Georgina Gore, 'The Beat Goes On; Trance, Dance and Tribalism in Rave Culture', in Helen Thomas (ed.), *Dance in the City* (London, Routledge, 1997), p. 65.

36 Bethan Cole, 'One Nation Under a Groove', *Muzik*, March 1998.

37 See Collin, *Altered State*, Chapter 1.

38 Ibid., p. 237.

39 Cole, 'One Nation Under a Groove'.

40 Helen Wilkinson, *No Turning Back: Generations and the Genderquake* (London, Demos, 1994).

41 Helen Wilkinson and Geoff Mulgan, *Freedom's Children: Work, Relationships and Politics for 18–34 Year Olds in Britain Today* (London, Demos, 1995), pp. 98–122.

42 Simon Reynolds, 'Rave Culture: Living Dream or Living Death'.

43 See Collin, *Altered State*, p. 65; and Drew Hemment, 'Dangerous Dancing and Disco Riots: The Northern Warehouse Parties', in George McKay (ed.), *DiY Culture: Party and Protest in Nineties Britain* (London, Verso, 1998), pp. 208–28.

44 See Saunders, *Ecstasy and the Dance Culture*; and Collin, *Altered State*, Chapter 6.

45 The British government has registered its commitment to such an agenda by granting responsibility for many of its key aims in social policy to its 'Social Exclusion Unit'.

46 Antonio Gramsci, *Selections from the Prison Notebooks*, trans. Quentin Hoare and Geoffrey Nowell Smith (London, Lawrence & Wishart, 1971), p. 175.

BIBLIOGRAPHY

Adorno, T. *Philosophy of Modern Music*, trans. A. Mitchell, New York, The Seabury Press, 1973.

Adorno, T. and Horkheimer, M. *The Dialectic of Enlightenment*, London, Verso, 1979.

Anthony, W. *Class of '88: The True Acid House Experience*, London, Virgin, 1998.

Attali, J. *Noise: The Politcal Economy of Music*, Manchester, MUP, 1985.

Austin, J. L. *How to do Things with Words*, Oxford, OUP, 1962.

Bangs, L. 'Kraftwerkfeature', in H. Kureishi and J. Savage (eds), *The Faber Book of Pop*, London, Faber & Faber, 1995.

Barthes, R. *Image Music Text*, trans. Stephen Heath, London, Fontana, 1977.

——*The Pleasure of the Text*, trans. Richard Howard, New York, Farrar, Strauss & Girouux, 1975.

Beadle, J. J. *Will Pop Eat Itself? Pop Music in the Soundbite Era*, London, Faber & Faber, 1993.

Bender, G. and Druckrey, T. *Culture on the Brink: Ideologies of Technology*, Seattle, Bay Press, 1994.

Benjamin, W. 'The Work of Art in the Age of Mechanical Reproduction', in H. Arendt (ed.) *Illuminations*, London, Fontana, 1992.

Bennington, G. and Derrida, J. *Jacques Derrida*, Chicago, UCP, 1993.

Bey, H. *T.A.Z.*, New York, Autonomedia, 1985.

Blackford, A. *Disco Dancing Tonight*, London, Octopus Press, 1979.

Blacking, J. (ed.) *The Anthropology of the Body*, London, Academic Press, 1977.

Born, G. *Rationalising Culture: IRCAM, Boulez and the Institutionalisation of the Musical Avant-Garde*, Berkeley, University of California Press, 1995.

Bowie, A. *Aesthetics and Subjectivity: From Kant to Nietzsche*, Manchester, MUP, 1990.

Bradby, B. 'Sampling Sexuality: Gender, Technology and the Body in Dance Music', *Popular Music*, Cambridge University Press, vol. 12, no. 2, 1993.

Brett, P., Thomas, G. and Woods, E. (eds) *Queering the Pitch: The New Gay and Lesbian Musicology*, London, Routledge, 1994.

Bussman, J. *Once in a Lifetime: The Crazy Days of Acid House and Afterwards*, London, Virgin, 1998.

Bussy, P. *Kraftwerk: Man, Machine and Music*, Wembley, SAF, 1993.

Butler, J. *Gender Trouble*, London, Routledge, 1990.

——*Bodies that Matter*, London, Routledge, 1993.

Buxton, D. 'Rock Music, the Star System and the Rise of Consumerism', in S. Frith and A. Goodwin (eds) *On Record: Rock, Pop and the Written Word*, London, Routledge, 1990.

Campbell, A. and Moriarty, M. 'New Labour, New Britpop', *New Labour New Britain*, Autumn 1996.

Chambers, I. *Urban Rhythms: Pop Music and Popular Culture*, London, Macmillan, 1985.

——*Migrancy, Culture, Identity*, London, Routledge, 1994.

187

Chanan, M. Musica Practica: The Social Practice of Western Music from Gregorian Chant to Postmodernism, London, Verso, 1994.

——Repeated Takes: A Short History of Recording and its Effects on Music, London, Verso, 1995.

Chapman, R. and Rutherford, J. (eds) Male Order, London, Lawrence & Wishart, 1988.

Coddington, A. and Perryman, M. (eds) The Moderniser's Dilemma, London, Lawrence & Wishart, 1998.

Cohn, N. Market, London, Secker and Warburg, 1965.

——Ball the Wall: Nik Cohn in the Age of Rock, London, Picador, 1989.

Cole, B. 'One Nation Under a Groove', Muzik, March 1998.

Collin, M., with Godfrey, J. Altered State: The Story of Ecstasy Culture and Acid House, London, Serpent's Tail, 1997.

Connor, S. Postmodernist Culture: An Introduction to Theories of the Contemporary, Oxford, Blackwell, 1989.

Corbett, J. Extended Play: Sounding Off from John Cage to Dr. Funkenstein, Durham, Duke University Press, 1994.

Cuisick, S. G. 'On a Lesbian Relationship with Music', in P. Brett, G. Thomas and E. Woods (eds) Queering the Pitch: The New Gay and Lesbian Musicology, London, Routledge, 1994.

Deleuze, G. and Guattari, F. A Thousand Plateaus, Capitalism and Schizophrenia, London, The Athlone Press, 1988.

Deleuze, G. and Foucault, M. 'Intellectuals and Power', in D. F. Bouchard (ed.) Language, Counter-Memory, Practice: Selected Interviews and Essays, Oxford, Blackwell, 1977.

Derrida, J. Between the Blinds (P. Kamuf, ed.), Hemel Hempstead, Harvester, 1991.

Dery, M. 'Black to the Future: Interviews with Samuel R. Delaney, Greg Tate and Tricia Rose', Flame Wars: The Discourse of Cyberculture, Durham, Duke University Press, 1994.

Docherty, T. After Theory, London, Routledge, 1990.

Docker, J. Postmodernism and Popular Culture: A Cultural History, Cambridge, CUP, 1994.

Dollimore, J. Sexual Dissidence, Oxford, OUP, 1991.

Durant, A. 'Improvisation in the Political Economy of Music', in C. Norris (ed.) Music and the Politics of Culture, London, Lawrence & Wishart, 1989.

——'A New Day for Music – Digital Technologies in Contemporary Music Making', Culture, Technology and Creativity in the Late Twentieth Century, London, John Libbey, 1994.

Dyer, R. 'In Defence of Disco', in S. Frith and A. Goodwin (eds) On Record: Rock, Pop and the Written Word, London, Routledge, 1990.

Elms, R. 'Hard Times', in H. Kureishi and J. Savage (eds) The Faber Book of Pop, London, Faber & Faber, 1995.

Eno, B. A Year with Swollen Appendices, London, Faber & Faber, 1996.

Eshun, K., 'Outing the In-crowd', in H. Kureishi and J. Savage (eds) The Faber Book of Pop, London, Faber & Faber, 1995.

——More Brilliant Than the Sun: Adventures in Sonic Fiction, London, Quartet Books, 1998.

Fornas, J. 'Listen to Your Voice!', New Formations, Winter 1994, London, Lawrence & Wishart, 1994.

Foucault, M. The History of Sexuality Volume One, trans. Robert Hurley, London, Penguin, 1978.

Freud, S. On Sexuality (Penguin Freud Library Volume 7), London, Penguin, 1977.

——On Metapsychology (Penguin Freud Library Volume 11), London, Penguin, 1984.

Frith, S. 'Art versus Technology: The Strange Case of Popular Music', in R. Collins (ed.) Media Culture and Society: A Critical Reader, London, Sage, 1986.

——Performing Rites, Oxford, OUP, 1996.

Frith, S. and McRobbie, A. 'Rock and Sexuality', in S. Frith and A. Goodwin (eds) *On Record: Rock, Pop and the Written Word*, London, Routledge, 1990.

Gelder, K. and Thornton, S. (eds) *The Subcultures Reader*, London, Routledge, 1997.

George, N. *The Death of Rhythm and Blues*, London, Omnibus, 1989.

Gilbert, J. 'Blurred Vision: Pop, Populism and Politics', in A. Coddington and M. Perryman (eds) *The Moderniser's Dilemma*, London, Lawrence & Wishart, 1998.

Gill, J. *Queer Noises: Male and Female Homosexuality in Twentieth Century Music*, London, Cassell, 1995.

Gilmour, H. B. *Saturday Night Fever*, New York, Bantam, 1977.

Gilroy, P. *The Black Atlantic: Modernity and Double Consciousness*, London, Verso, 1993.

——*Small Acts*, London, Serpent's Tail, 1993.

Goldman, A. *Disco*, New York, Hawthorn, 1978.

Goldman, L. *Towards a Sociology of the Novel*, London, Tavistock Publications, 1975.

Goodman, F. *The Mansion on the Hill: Dylan, Young and Springsteen and the Head-on Collision of Rock and Commerce*, London, Jonathan Cape, 1997.

Goodman, J., Lovejoy, P.E. and Sherratt, A. (eds), *Consuming Habits: Deconstructing Drugs in History and Anthropology*, London, Routledge, 1995.

Goodwin, A. 'Sample and Hold: Towards an Aesthetics of Digital Reproduction', *Critical Quarterly*, vol. 30, no. 3, Autumn 1988.

——'Drumming and Memory: Scholarship, Technology and Music-making', in T. Swiss, J. Sloop and A. Herman (eds) *Mapping the Beat: Popular Music and Contemporary Theory*, Oxford, Blackwell, 1998.

Gore, G. 'The Beat Goes On; Trance, Dance and Tribalism in Rave Culture', in H. Thomas (ed.) *Dance in the City*, London, Routledge, 1997.

Gramsci, A. *Selections from the Prison Notebooks*, trans. Q. Hoare and G. Nowell Smith, London, Lawrence & Wishart, 1971.

Grossberg, L. *We Gotta Get Out of this Place*, New York, Routledge, 1992.

Guattari, F. *Chaosmosis: An Ethico-Aesthetic Paradigm*, Sydney, Power Publications, 1995.

Habermas, J. 'Modernity – An Incomplete Project', in H. Foster (ed.) *Postmodern Culture*, London, Pluto, 1985.

Haden-Guest, A. *The Last Party*, New York, William Morrow, 1997.

Hall, S. *The Hard Road to Renewal*, London, Verso, 1988.

Hall, S. and Jefferson, T. (eds), *Resistance Through Rituals: Youth Subcultures in Post-war Britain*, London, Hutchinson, 1976.

Hanna, J. *Dance, Sex and Gender*, Chicago, UCP, 1988.

Hanson, K. *Disco Fever*, New York, Signet, 1978.

Haraway, D. J. 'A Manifesto for Cyborgs: Science, Technology and Socialist-feminism in the Late Twentieth Century', in D. J. Haraway (ed.) *Simians, Cyborgs and Women: The Reinvention of Nature*, New York, Routledge, 1991.

Hebdige, D. *Subculture: The Meaning of Style*, London, Routledge, 1979.

——'The Bottom Line on Planet One: Squaring Up to The Face', *Hiding in the Light*, London, Routledge, 1988.

Hemment, D. 'e is for Ekstasis', *New Formations*, Summer 1997, London, Lawrence & Wishart, 1997.

Hesmondhalgh, D. 'The Cultural Politics of Dance Music', *Soundings* 5, Spring 1997, London, Lawrence & Wishart.

Hill, C. *The Century of Revolution 1603–1714*, London, Routledge, 1980.

Holleran, A. *Dancer from the Dance*, London, Jonathan Cape, 1979.

Hughes, W. 'In the Empire of the Beat', in A. Ross and T. Rose (eds) *Microphone Fiends: Youth Music and Youth Culture*, London, Routledge, 1994.

Irigaray, L. *Speculum of the Other Woman*, trans. C. Porter, Ithaca, Cornell, 1985.

——*This Sex Which is Not One*, trans. C. Porter, Ithaca, Cornell, 1985.

Jenkins, H. ' "Strangers No More, We Sing": Filking and the Social Production of the Science Fiction Fan Community', in L. A. Lewis (ed.) *The Adoring Audience: Fan Culture and Popular Media*, London, Routledge, 1992.

Jensen, J. 'Fandom as Pathology: The Consequences of Characterisation', in L. A. Lewis (ed.) *The Adoring Audience: Fan Culture and Popular Media*, Routledge, 1992.

Kemptser, C. (ed.) *History of House*, London, Sanctuary, 1997.

Kohn, M. *Dope Girls*, London, Lawrence & Wishart, 1992.

Kristeva, J. *Revolution in Poetic Language*, trans. M. Waller, New York, Columbia, 1984.

Kruger, B. and Mariani, P. (eds), *Remaking History*, Seattle, Bay Press, 1989.

Laclau, E. *New Reflections on the Revolution of Our Time*, London, Verso, 1990.

Laclau, E. and Mouffe, C. *Hegemony and Socialist Strategy*, London, Verso, 1985.

Le Huray, P. and Day, J. (eds) *Music and Aesthetics in the Eighteenth and Early Nineteenth Centuries*, Cambridge, CUP, 1981.

Leppert, R. *The Sight of Sound: Musical Representation and the History of the Body*, Berkeley, University of California Press, 1993.

Lévi-Strauss, C. *The Raw and the Cooked*, London, Pimlico, 1994.

Lodge, T. website: http://ourworld.compuserve.com/homepages/tash_lodge/main.htm

Longhurst, B. *Popular Music and Society*, Cambridge, Polity Press, 1995.

Lovisone, C. *The Disco Hustle*, New York, Sterling, 1979.

McClary, S. *Feminine Endings*, Minneapolis, University of Minnesota Press, 1991.

McKay, G. *Senseless Acts of Beauty: Cultures of Resistance Since the Sixties*, London, Verso, 1996.

——(ed.) *DiY Culture: Party and Protest in Nineties Britain*, London, Verso, 1998.

Mckenna, T. *Food of the Gods*, London, Rider, 1992.

MacPherson, C. B. *The Political Theory of Possessive Individualism*, Oxford, Clarendon Press, 1964.

McRobbie, A. 'Settling Accounts with Subcultures', in S. Frith and A. Goodwin (eds) *On Record: Rock, Pop and the Written Word*, London, Routledge, 1990.

——*Feminism and Youth Culture*, London, Macmillan, 1990.

——*Postmodernism and Popular Culture*, London, Routledge, 1994.

McRobbie, A. and Nava, M. (eds) *Gender and Generation*, Basingstoke, Macmillan, 1982.

Marcus, G. 'Notes on the Life and Death and Incandescent Banality of Rock 'n' Roll', in H. Kureishi and J. Savage (eds) *The Faber Book of Pop*, London, Faber & Faber, 1995.

Marx, K. *Capital* , London, Penguin, 1976.

Massumi, B. *A User's Guide to Capitalism and Schizophrenia: Deviations from Deleuze and Guattari*, Cambridge, Mass., MIT Press, 1992.

Melechi, A. 'The Ecstasy of Disappearance', in S. Redhead (ed.) *Rave Off: Politics and Deviance in Contemporary Youth Culture*, Aldershot, Avebury, 1993.

Mellers, W. *The Sonata Principle*, London, Barrie & Rockliff, 1962.

Menser, M. and Aronowitz, S., 'On Cultural Studies, Science and Technology', in S. Aronowitz, B. Martisons and M. Menser (eds) *Technoscience and Cyberculture*, London, Routledge, 1996.

Meyer, M. (ed.) *The Politics and Poetics of Camp*, London, Routledge, 1994.

Middleton, R. *Studying Popular Music*, Buckingham, Open University Press, 1990.

——'Popular Music Analysis and Musicology: Bridging the Gap', Popular Music, vol. 12, no. 2, Cambridge University Press, 1993.

Mitchell, J. and Rose, J. (eds) Feminine Sexuality, London, Macmillan, 1982.

Morley, D. and Chen, K-H. (eds) Stuart Hall; Critical Dialogues in Cultural Studies, London, Routledge, 1996.

Nancy, J-L. The Inoperative Community, Minneapolis, University of Minnesota Press, 1991.

Parliamentary Office of Science and Technology, 'Common Illegal Drugs and their Effects' (HMSO, May 1996).

Patton, P. (ed.) Deleuze: A Critical Reader, Oxford, Blackwell, 1996.

Penley, C. and Ross, A. (eds) Technoculture, Minneapolis, University of Minnesota Press, 1991.

Pile, S. and Thrift, N. Mapping the Subject: Geographies of Social Transformation, London, Routledge, 1995.

Pini, M. 'Cyborgs, Nomads and the Raving Feminine', in H. Thomas (ed.) Dance in the City, London, Routledge, 1997.

——'Women and the Early British Rave Scene', in A. McRobbie (ed.) Back to Reality, Manchester, MUP, 1997.

Plato The Republic, trans. D. Lee, London, Penguin, 1974.

Plant, S. The Most Radical Gesture: The Situationist International in the Postmodern Age, London, Routledge, 1992.

——Zeroes and Ones: Digital Women and the New Technoculture, London, Fourth Estate, 1997.

Polhemus, T. 'Dance, Gender and Culture', in H. Thomas (ed.) Dance, Gender and Culture, London, Macmillan, 1993.

Redhead, S. The End of the Century Party: Youth and Pop Towards 2000, Manchester, MUP, 1990.

——(ed.) Rave Off: Politics and Deviance in Contemporary Youth Culture, Aldershot, Avebury, 1993.

——Unpopular Cultures: The Birth of Law and Popular Culture, Manchester, MUP, 1995.

Redhead, S. and Melechi, A. 'The Fall of the Acid Reign', New Statesman and Society, 23 December 1988.

Reynolds, S. Blissed Out, London, 1990.

——'Sounds of Blackness', The Wire, June 1995.

——'Rave Culture: Living Dream or Living Death?', in S. Redhead, D. Wynne and J. O'Connor (eds) The Clubcultures Reader, Oxford, Blackwell, 1997.

——Energy Flash: A Journey Through Rave Music and Dance Culture, London, Picador, 1998.

——Ardkore Archive and Gabber Archive on http://members.aol.com/blissout/index.htm.

Reynolds, S. and Press, J. The Sex Revolts: Gender, Rebellion and Rock and Roll, London, Serpent's Tail, 1995.

Rose, T. Black Noise, Rap Music and Black Culture in Contemporary America, Hanover, Wesleyan University Press, 1994.

Ross, A. No Respect: Intellectuals and Popular Culture, London, Routledge, 1989.

Rossolo, L. The Art of Noises, New York, Pendragon Press, 1986.

Saunders, N. E for Ecstasy, London, Nicholas Saunders, 1993.

——Ecstasy and the Dance Culture, London, Nicholas Saunders, 1995.

——Ecstasy Reconsidered, London, Nicholas Saunders, 1997.

Savage, J. England's Dreaming: Sex Pistols and Punk Rock, London, Faber & Faber, 1991.

——(ed.) The Haçienda Must Be Built, London, International Music Publications, 1992.

Schaffer, S. 'Babbage's Dancer and the Impresarios of Mechanism', in F. Spufford and J. Uglow (eds) Cultural Babbage: Time, Technology and Invention, London, Faber & Faber, 1996.

Serres, M. 'Mathematics and Philosophy: What Thales Saw...', in J. V. Harari and D. F. Bell (eds) *Hermes: Literature, Science, Philosophy*, Baltimore, John Hopkins University Press, 1982.

——*Genesis*, Michigan, University of Michigan Press, 1995.

Shepherd, J. *Music as Social Text*, Cambridge, Polity, 1992.

——'Music as Cultural Text', in J. Paynter, J. Howell, R. Orton and P. Seymour (eds) *The Routledge Companion to Contemporary Musical Thought*, London, Routledge, 1993

Shepherd, J. and Wicke, P. *Music and Cultural Theory*, Cambridge, Polity, 1997.

Silverstone, R. and Hirsch, E. *Consuming Technologies*, London, Routledge, 1992.

Solie, R. A. (ed.) *Musicology and Difference*, Berkley, University of California Press, 1993.

Spencer, P. (ed.) *Society and the Dance*, Cambridge, CUP, 1985.

Squall magazine site: http://www.users.dircon.co.uk/~squall/index.htm.

Stallybrass, P. and White, A. *The Politics and Poetics of Transgression*, London, Methuen, 1986.

Stone, C. J. *Fierce Dancing: Adventures in the Underground*, London, Faber & Faber, 1995.

Szwed, J. F. *Space is the Place: The Life and Times of Sun Ra*, Edinburgh, Payback Press, 1997.

Thomas, H. (ed.) *Dance in the City*, London, Routledge, 1997.

Thompson, E. P. *Whigs and Hunters*, London, Allen Lane, 1975.

——*The Making of the English Working Class*, London, Penguin, 1980.

Thornton, S. 'Club Class', *New Statesman and Society*, 16 November 1990.

——*Club Cultures: Music, Media and Subcultural Capital*, Cambridge, Polity Press, 1995.

Toop, D. *Rap Attack 2: African Rap to Global Hip Hop*, London, Serpent's Tail, 1991.

——*Ocean of Sound: Aether Talk, Ambient Sound and Imaginary Worlds*, London, Serpent's Tail, 1995.

Underdown, D. *Revel, Riot and Rebellion*, Oxford, OUP, 1985.

Venturi, R., Scott Brown, D. and Izenour, S. *Learning From Las Vegas*, Cambridge, Mass., MIT Press, 1977.

Villari, J. and Sims, K. *The Official Guide to Disco Dance Steps*, London, Hamlyn, 1979.

Volosinov, V. N. *Marxism and the Philosophy of Language*, trans. L. Matejka and I. R. Titunik, Cambridge, Harvard University Press, 1972.

Walser, R. *Running with the Devil: Power, Gender, and Madness in Heavy Metal Music*, Hanover, Wesleyan University Press, 1993.

Walsh, D. ' "Saturday Night Fever": An Ethnography of Disco Dancing', in H. Thomas (ed.) *Dance, Gender and Culture*, London, Macmillan, 1993.

Ward, A. 'Dancing in the Dark: Rationalism and the Neglect of Social Dance', in H. Thomas (ed.) *Dance, Gender and Culture*, London, Macmillan, 1993.

——'Dancing Around Meaning', in H. Thomas (ed.) *Dance in the City*, London, Routledge, 1997.

Warhol, A. *The Andy Warhol Diaries* (Pat Hackett, ed.), London, Simon and Schuster, 1989.

Weber, M. *The Protestant Ethic and the Spirit of Capitalism*, trans. T. Parsons, London, Unwin, 1930.

Welsh, I. *Ecstasy*, Vintage, London, 1997.

——*The Acid House*, London, Vintage, 1995.

Wilkinson, H. *No Turning Back: Generations and the Genderquake*, London, Demos, 1994.

Wilkinson, H. and Mulgan, G. *Freedom's Children: Work, Relationships and Politics for 18–34 year olds in Britain Today*, London, Demos, 1995.

Williams, R. *Marxism and Literature*, Oxford, OUP, 1977.

Willis, P. *Profane Culture*, London, Routledge, 1978.

INDEX